The European Convention on Human Rights

Nijhoff Law Specials

VOLUME 70

The titles published in this series are listed at the end of this volume.

The European Convention on Human Rights

Collected Essays

by

Loukis G. Loucaides

MARTINUS NIJHOFF PUBLISHERS

Leiden • Boston

2007

This book is printed on acid-free paper.

A C.I.P. record for this book is available from the Library of Congress.

ISBN: 978 90 04 15883 2

http://www.brill.nl

PRINTED AND BOUND IN THE NETHERLANDS.

To my grandchildren, Maro and Pavlos, and to all those who do not just speak or write about human rights, but who also defend them through their actions.

Table of Contents

Preface

This book is a collection of articles each of which was written to provide an exposition and analysis, *de lege lata* and *de lege ferenda,* of a specific topic of human rights. The topics are drawn mainly from the European Convention on Human Rights and many of them are either explored for the first time (for instance, "the Concept of 'Continuing Violations' of Human Rights", "the Right of Access to a Court and the Doctrine of Political Acts") or from a novel perspective (for instance, "Determining the Extra-territorial Effect of the European Convention: Facts, Jurisprudence and the *Banković* case" and "Freedom of Expression and the Right to Reputation").

Certain articles have already been published in legal periodicals of international standing. Their reproduction in book form will, I believe, make them more widely accessible. It is not possible here to give an outline of the various subjects covered, but the titles and sub-headings of the individual articles should offer sufficient guidance to the reader, as regards both content and the approach followed.

All the topics are examined and presented from a critical standpoint and some important judgments of the European Court of Human Rights are taken to task. I do not consider this to be incompatible with my status as a judge of that Court. On the contrary, I believe that expressing a different point of view, which in any event could – and in some instances did – take the form of a dissenting opinion, contributes to an effective consideration of the issues.

In this respect, I must state what I have always believed to be the correct approach: in modern democratic societies judges cannot claim to be entitled to special deference that stifles free discussion or strong criticism of their decisions. They are not infallible. They are entitled to the same respect as that due to any other organ of State and, indeed, to any human being. No more, no less. Judges are human and as such have the same shortcomings as everyone else. People should be free to point out what they believe to be mistakes in a judgment and to disagree with the effects, provided they do so in good faith and recognise the binding nature of judicial decisions.

Naturally those best placed to understand and criticise judicial decisions are jurists, including, of course, members of the judiciary themselves.

Those who specialise in human rights must express their views freely with the aim of improving and developing this field of law which affects every individual. But this alone is not enough. More important still is that everybody, especially those who understand the problems caused by violations of human rights, should defend them through their own acts.

L.G.L.
Strasbourg

Acknowledgement

I am particularly indebted to Viktoriya Maradudina for her valuable assistance in correcting the proofs and for the laborious task of preparing the index.

Chapter 1 The Rules of Interpretation of the European Convention on Human Rights

1. Introduction

Like any other legal instrument, the European Convention on Human Rights does not explicitly convey the fullness of its legal effect. Those entrusted with the application of its provisions are expected to interpret them so as to give them an effective meaning in accordance with the letter and spirit of the text of the Convention as a whole. The methods and principles of interpretation depend on various factors linked with the nature of the Convention and the field of its application.

The absence of a standing organ or method to effect quick amendments to the Convention to solve problems arising from ambiguous provisions makes the task of interpretation of the Convention and the responsibility of those entrusted with this particularly significant. An added difficulty is the fact that the provisions of the Convention are intended to apply in a uniform manner to States with different legal systems, customs and traditions. These provisions had to be construed authoritatively by the organs of the Convention (the European Commission and the European Court of Human Rights) composed of jurists with different legal training and experience. The process of interpretation of the Convention is further complicated by the fact that its provisions are expressed in English and in French, while both texts are equally authentic.

The Commission dealt at first instance with all applications for breaches of the provisions of the Convention.

The Commission was not a judicial body, but in practice it acted as a quasi-judicial organ, both with regard to examination of applications and in giving its opinion on these in terms of Article 31 of the Convention. Inevitably, in carrying out its duties, the Commission had to interpret the Convention whenever it was confronted with provisions or terms whose meaning or effect was unclear. Such interpretations were of particular importance considering that the Commission was the first organ; and until 1998, in the majority of cases, also the final one to pass judgment and to apply the Convention in those cases which were declared inadmissible by the Commission and in those cases which were not referred to the Court. This explains why the rules for interpreting the Convention have primarily been developed in the case-law of the Commission.

2. Consequences of Interpretation

The Convention consists of certain rules which, as its Preamble suggests, are based on "a common heritage of political traditions, ideals, freedom and the rule of law" of the High Contracting Parties. Nevertheless, such rules are autonomous, supra-national rules and set out standards and principles that may be found to be incompatible with the legal systems of particular States. In case of such incompatibility, the norms of the Convention must prevail, regardless of the importance of the municipal legislation at stake and of the ensuing consequences, legal, economic or political in the State concerned. This approach was first adopted by the Commission in the *Belgian Linguistic Case*[1] in which the Belgian Government argued:

> that any condemnation of Belgium would be a surprise for that country in that, at the time the Protocol was signed, the language legislation had been in force for 20 years, and no Belgian statesman had imagined that signature of the Protocol No. I (to the Convention) might expose Belgium to condemnation of (their relevant) legislation; that such a condemnation would upset the most important political and legal traditions of Belgian political life.

The Commission stated that it

> does not feel able to accept the principle that any interpretation of the Convention which would cause an unforeseen disturbance of the traditions governing important political and legal matters in one of the signatory States should be rejected. On several occasions the Commission of Human Rights has declared incompatible with the Convention laws which have been in force for many years. It has also found that in accordance with the general principles of international law, borne out by the spirit of the Convention as well as by the preliminary work, the Contracting Parties

1 Comm. Report, Eur Court HR, Series B no. 3, p. 275.

> have undertaken, without prejudice to the provisions of Article 64 of the Convention, to ensure that their domestic legislation is compatible with the Convention and, if need be, to make necessary adjustments to this end, since the Convention is binding on all the authorities of the Contracting Parties, including the legislative authority.
>
> In the Commission's opinion the fact that the legislation governs an important matter of political life in the State in question does not support the principle of interpretation suggested by the Belgian Government. This principle could only be applied if the legislation in question embodies a system which was traditional in all or most of the signatory States.

3. General Principles – The *Golder* Case

Certain general principles which should be applied in interpreting the provisions of the Convention were for the first time enunciated by the Commission in the *Golder* case,[2] which raised a difficult question of interpretation on whether the Convention guarantees the right of access to the courts. The importance of this case in relation to the topic under consideration necessitates a rather extensive quotation of the relevant passages of the Commission's Report. The Commission referred to the articles in the Vienna Convention on the Law of Treaties, invoked by both parties in the case, and then observed:

> the rather general provisions of the Vienna articles could be regarded as an expression of customary law and general principles recognised by nations, including the Contracting Parties to the European Convention. For the limited guidance one may find in these provisions, it is therefore not material whether the Vienna Convention is in force for the Contracting Parties, in particular the United Kingdom. The question of applying these and other commonly invoked principles to treaty interpretation to the Human Rights Convention should, however, be answered only after taking into account the special nature of this Convention.
>
> In the Commission's opinion the object of the international application of the Convention is to interpret its provisions objectively and not to interpret the Convention by reference to what may have been the un-

2 Comm. Report, Eur Court HR, Series B no. 16, p. 33 et. seq. The Court has basically followed the same approach as the Commission in its judgment in the same case: Eur Court HR, Judgment of 21 February 1975, Series A no. 18, pp. 13-18.

> derstanding of one Party at the time of its ratification. Furthermore, whatever may be the case as regards an ordinary international treaty, both the Commission ... have stated that the provisions of the Convention should not be interpreted restrictively so as to prevent its aims and objects being achieved.
>
> The Commission, in considering this question of interpretation, in accordance with the 'general rule' in Article 31 of the Vienna Convention, will first examine the ordinary meaning of the wording of Article 6(1) in its proper context, combined with the object and purpose of the Convention. It is only on the basis of its opinion in this respect that it will next take account of supplementary means of interpretation, namely the '*travaux préparatoires*' and other human rights instruments which have been invoked, with the object of assessing their effect on its preliminary opinion on the ordinary meaning of Article 6(1) ...

The Commission referred to the provisions of Article 32 of the Vienna Convention regarding the use of preparatory works and added:

> In considering whether ... the preparatory work should be relied upon in order to determine the meaning, the Commission apparently must decide whether the arguments drawn from the wording and context of Article 6 (1), in particular in relation to the Preamble and other provisions of the Convention such as Article 13, leave the result more or less ambiguous or obscure ...

As regards the importance of the context of a legal provision in the Convention the Commission stated:

> In law, as elsewhere, single words usually cannot be interpreted in isolation. Only the sentences in which they occur convey meaning, legal or otherwise, and one sentence must always, in order to be properly understood, be seen in its context. The sentence is only a fragment interacting with other sentences.
>
> The relevant context of a legal provision is not limited to the section or article in which it occurs. As regards treaties the Vienna Convention defines the context in more detail. By way of comparison it may be observed that for the interpretation of a provision in national legislation the whole existing body of legislation, and not only the particular act, is sometimes the relevant context. This is so at least as far as one may assume that the legislator was not unaware of the existing legislation other than that with

> which he was concerned. In defining the context of a treaty the Vienna Convention (Article 31) takes into account the special nature of inter-State relations where the subject, being the States, are only bound by written law to which they have given their consent.
>
> Besides the ordinary meaning of the terms in their *context* this general rule under Article 31 also refers to the *object* and *purpose* of the treaty. The Commission adopts the same approach. In examining the meaning of Article 6 (1), the text of wording, therefore, may only serve as a point of departure and the Commission is inevitably led to look beyond that point before drawing any conclusions.

The Commission then dealt with the literal meaning of the relevant text and stated:

> Indeed, the Commission considers that the reading into the Article of a right of access to courts probably cannot be arrived at on purely linguistic grounds to the exclusion of other possible interpretations ... But this situation is not unique. More often than not, what is read into legal texts as their 'natural' or 'ordinary' meaning goes beyond the purely linguistic appreciation which is based on the text itself and nothing else ... Both laymen and lawyers consciously or unconsciously are applying the pragmatism popularly called 'common sense'. This means a sense of purpose and consistency with the factual and legal background which, in the case of lawyers, are assisted by their professional skill. Therefore a pragmatic, as distinct from a merely linguistic, interpretation is always set in motion from the very outset.

Faced with a choice between an "extended" and a "restricted" meaning of the relevant text the Commission preferred the first and adopted the following approach:

> The decisive consideration here must be that the overriding function of this Convention is to protect the rights of the individual and not to lay down as between States mutual obligations which are to be restrictively interpreted having regard to the sovereignty of these States. On the contrary, the role of the Convention and the function of its interpretation is to make the protection of the individual effective. It is true that it represents only the 'first steps' for the enforcement of human rights as the Preamble says. But this fact cannot be relied upon to justify restrictive interpretations running contrary to its overall purpose.

4. Supplementary Means

In the process of interpreting Article 6 of the Convention in the *Golder* case, the Commission referred extensively to the principles embodied in the Vienna Convention. Furthermore, the Commission examined supplementary means of interpretation in order to see whether they contradicted the meaning adopted by the Commission. In particular, the Commission examined (a) the *travaux préparatoires* of the Convention,[3] (b) related provisions in the United Nations instruments, and (c) other treaties and practices. The Commission found that treaties and other international instruments were not relevant as a guide to interpretation in so far as they had a different purpose and needed to be construed in a different context.

However, the provisions of other international instruments in *pari materiae* were, on different occasions, used by the Convention Organs in order to resolve questions of interpretation of Articles of the Convention and to avoid according inconsistent meanings to similar guarantees by different international institutions. This was done, for example, in respect of Article 11 of the Convention by taking into account relevant United Nations Human Rights instruments and the ILO Convention Nos. 87 and 98. In respect of the latter Convention, the Commission stated:

> As they are a body of special rules binding also on European States, they should not be ignored in the interpretation Article 11, particularly if the European Convention is to keep pace with the rules of international labour law and if its concepts are to remain in harmony with the concepts used in international labour law and practice.

5. International Law

The Commission and the Court have been acting on the premise that the interpretation and application of the Convention is a matter of international law.[4] In the *Golder* case both the Commission and the Court

3 For the limited value of the *travaux préparatoires* see Jacobs, op. cit., p. 41 and Harris, O'Boyle and Warbrick, *Law of the European Convention on Human Rights*, p. 17.

4 For the relation between the Court and the general international law see Gerard Cohen-Jonathan et Jean-Francois Flauss, "Cour Européenne des

relied on the rules of interpretation set out in the Vienna Convention on the Law of Treaties. These were regarded "as an expression of customary law and general principles recognised by nations." In the case of *Ireland v. United Kingdom*,[5] the Commission applied the rule imputing the unauthorised acts of its agents to the State by express reference to what prevails "in connection with responsibility under international law generally." In the *De Becker* case,[6] the Commission referred to the obligation of the High Contracting Parties under the Convention to ensure that their domestic body of law is compatible with the Convention "in accordance with the general principles of international law, borne out by the spirit of the Convention as well as by the preparatory work."

In the *Golder* case[7] the Court had recourse to Article 31 of the Vienna Convention on the Law of Treaties in order to interpret Article 6 of the ECHR. The Court stated that the Vienna Convention had not yet entered into force and it specified, at Article 4, that it will not be retroactive, but its Articles 31 to 33 enunciate in essence generally accepted principles of international law to which the Court has already referred on occasion. In this respect, for the interpretation of the European Convention account is to be taken of those Articles subject, where appropriate, to "any relevant rules of the organization"– the Council of Europe – within which it has been adopted (Article 5 of the Vienna Convention). Furthermore, the Court referred in particular to paragraph 3(c) of the Vienna Convention which indicates that in interpreting a treaty account is to be taken; together with the context, of "any relevant rules of international law applicable in the relations between the parties". In this respect the Court also stated:

> Among those rules are 'general principles of law recognised by civilised nations' (Article 38(1) (c) of the Statue of the International Court of Justice). Incidentally the Legal Committee of the Consultative Assembly of the Council of Europe foresaw in August 1950 that 'the Commission and the Court must necessarily apply such principles' in the execution of their duties and thus considered it to be 'unnecessary' to insert a specific clause

Droits de L'Homme et Droit International Général", *Annuaire Français de Droit International*, XLIX-2003.

5 Comm. Report 25.1.76, Eur. Court HR, Series B no. 23, p. 512.

6 Application no. 214/56, Dec. 9.6.58, Yearbook 2, p. 234.

7 ECHR, Series A no. 28, para. 31 et seq. ... See also the case of *Johnston and Others v. Ireland*, appl. no. 9697/82, para. 51.

> to this effect in the Convention (Documents of the Consultative Assembly; Working papers of the 1950 session, Vol. III, no. 93, p. 982, para. 5).
>
> The principle whereby a civil claim must be capable of being submitted to a judge ranks as one of the universally 'recognised' fundamental principles of law; the same is true of the principle of international law which forbids the denial of justice. Article 6, para. 1 must be read in the light of these principles.

In the *Soéring* case[8] the Court sought to interpret the scope of Article 2 of the ECHR by reference to other international instruments of Human Rights and the international practice of State Parties to the Convention in respect of such instruments.

In the *Loizidou v. Turkey* case[9] the Court referred to its previous jurisprudence and pointed out that "it shall also take into account, together with the context, 'any subsequent practice in the application of the treaty which establishes the agreement of the parties regarding its interpretation'" (Article 31 para. 3(b) of the Vienna Convention).

In the case of *Al-Adsani v. the United Kingdom*[10] the Court stated that the Convention should so far as possible be interpreted in harmony with other rules of international law of which it forms part, including those relating to the grant of State immunity.

In the *Ribitsch* case,[11] the Commission stated:

> Responsibility under the Convention is based on its own provisions which are to be interpreted and applied on the basis of the objectives of the Convention and in the light of relevant principles of international law."

In this connection it should be noted that the Convention has a special nature. The Commission observed that:

> ... the obligations provided therein are essentially of an objective character, being designed rather to protect the fundamental rights of individual human beings from infringement by any of the High Contracting Parties

8 ECHR, Series A no. 161, para. 51.

9 ECHR, Series A no. 310, para. 7.

10 ECHR, appl. no.35763/97, para. 55.

11 Comm. Report 4.7.94, para. 110, Eur. Court HR, Series A no. 326, p. 37.

> than to create subjective and reciprocal rights for the High Contracting Parties themselves.[12]

The special character of the Convention affects the interpretation of its norms. The obligations under the Convention as between the High Contracting Parties remain obligations of international law but the Convention retains its autonomous character as regards those norms which guarantee directly the rights and freedoms provided therein as a result of the collective guarantee of the High Contracting Parties for the maintenance of the public order of Europe.[13]

As rightly observed by Cohen-Jonathan the European Court refers to the general principles of international law whenever that is useful for the proper functioning of the European system or even for its enrichment on condition that such reference should not be incompatible with the specificity and autonomy of this system.[14]

In interpreting the Convention regard must be had to its special character as a treaty for the collective enforcement of human rights and fundamental freedoms.[15]Thus, the object and purpose of the Convention as an instrument for the protection of individual human beings require that its provisions be interpreted and applied so as to make its safeguards practical and effective.[16] In addition, any interpretation of the rights and freedoms guaranteed has to be consistent with "the general spirit of the Convention, an instrument designed to maintain and promote the ideals and values of a democratic society".[17]

---

12 Application no. 788/60, Dec. 11.1.61, *Austria v. Italy*, Comm. Report, Yearbook 4, p. 140.

13 *Austria v. Italy*, op. cit., p. 140. See also Cohen-Jonathan, "Le rôle des principes généraux dans l'interprétation et l'application de la Convention Européenne de Droits de L'Homme" in *Mélanges en Hommage à Louis Edmond Pettiti*, at p. 167.

14 Ibid. p. 167.

15 See *Ireland v. the United Kingdom*, judgment of 18 January 1978, Series A no. 25, p. 90, § 239, Jacobs and White, The European Convention on Human Rights 4th ed. p. 40.

16 See, *inter alia*, the Artico judgment of 13 May 1980, Series A no. 37, p. 16, para. 33.

17 See the Kjeldsen, Busk Madsen and Pedersen judgment of 7 December 1976, Series A no. 23, p. 27, § 53; see Reid, op. cit., p. 44 where referring to the jurisprudence she points out, *inter alia*, "States are required to adopt

In view of the special nature and objectives of the Convention the Court on occasions departs from the general principles of international law including those set out in the Vienna Convention so as to satisfy the requirements of its substantive human rights guarantees. This has been proved for example in the cases of *Belilos* (1988) and *Loizidou* (1995) where the Court did not apply the rules of the Vienna Convention as regards the reservations to treaty provisions which were considered by the Court as inappropriate in respect of the Convention. In those two cases the Court has considered as invalid the reservations claimed by the respondent governments as being contrary to the objectives of the Convention.[18] One can usefully add here the fact that the Court interprets liberally the obligations of the States and in restrictive manner the limitations that the States may impose on the rights and liberties provided in the Convention. In contrast international law interprets the limitations to the sovereignty of States narrowly.[19]

The international Conventional law of human rights may be classified as part of the international legal order but it is substantively an autonomous branch which is not (or should not) be subject to the principles of international law except to the extent that (a) such principles relate to the interstate relations of the Parties to the Convention (b) the Convention expressly refers to these principles (e.g. Articles 7,15, 35 (1) and 1 of Protocol no I of the European Convention) and (c) there is no express provision in the Convention and the only relative guidance, which at the same time promotes the objects of the Convention, is found in international law.

Regarding the effect of international law on the Convention rights I reiterate here the view which I have expressed in my dissenting opinion in the *McElhinney* case.[20]

---

a certain pluralism and diversity. States must also afford protection to the media, which acts in democratic society as a 'watchdog' and governments must expect to bear more criticism than others and react with restraint."

18 Cohen-Jonathan, op. cit., p. 179.

19 In the Wemhoff case (27/6/1968) the Court stated that it was necessary "to seek the interpretation that is most appropriate in order to realise the aim and achieve the object of the treaty, not that which would restrict to the greatest possible degree the obligations undertaken by the parties".

20 ECHR 2001-XI.

> In a case like the one before the Court, the *lex specialis* is the European Convention on Human Rights. General principles of international law are not embodied in the Convention except insofar as reference is expressly made to them by the Convention (see, for example, Articles 15, 35 § 1 and 53 of the Convention and Article 1 of Protocol No. 1). Therefore, one should be reluctant to accept restrictions on Convention rights derived from principles of international law such as those establishing immunities which are not even part of the *jus cogens* norms.

The principles of international law regarding interpretation of treaties and other international law instruments do not preclude resort to general principles of law or rules and canons of interpretation developed in the context of private law insofar as these may help the interpretation to find the legal meaning and effect of the provisions of the Convention.[21]

After all, the rules for the interpretation of treaties have been elaborated mainly by borrowing from the private law of contract or other spheres of legal interpretation.[22] The Commission and the Court have expressly applied principles of interpretation of legal instruments in general, such as the one expressed in the Latin phrase *ut res magis valeat quam pereat*, often referred to as the rule of effectiveness,[23] the rule of law,[24] legal security,[25] the principle of proportionality and the "common sense" – construction rule referred to in the *Golder* case.

6. Municipal Laws and Practices

On the other hand, in view of the special history and foundations of the Convention which were closely linked with the common legal tradition of the Member States of the Council of Europe, the organs of

21 Cohen-Jonathan, op. cit., p. 181 et seq.

22 See A. McNair, Law of Treaties, p. 364 et seq.

23 See Application no. 15318/89, Dec. 4.3.91, *Loizidou v. Turkey*. In the *Belgian Linguistic Case*, the Commission adopted "the principle of effectiveness established by the case-law of the Permanent Court of International Justice and the International Court of Justice", Comm. Report 24.6.65, ECHR, Series B no. 3, p. 274 et seq.

24 See Loucaides, "The Rule of Law and Human Rights" in this volume pp. 35; Reid, *A Practitioner's Guide to the European Convention on Human Rights* 2nd Ed. pp. 42-44.

25 Ibid.

the Convention have often relied on comparative surveys on the laws of the Member States for the purpose of interpreting the scope of the rights guaranteed by the Convention[26]. For example, it has done so in respect of the laws relating to vagrancy,[27] the legislation on the right to respect for family life,[28] on aspects of criminal procedure,[29] on the age of criminal responsibility,[30] the legal status of transsexuals[31] and the regulation governing the duties of civil servants.[32] However, national law is not considered as decisive for the interpretation of the terms used in the Convention which are considered as embodying an autonomous Convention meaning.[33] This approach was the product of the necessity to achieve a uniform interpretation and application of the Convention in all States Parties. Furthermore, in assessing such matters as the "necessity" for a given measure in a "democratic society" account was taken of the practice of the Member States of the Council of Europe, as well as of the specific requirements of the situation facing the society in question.[34]

---

26 Cohen-Jonathan, op. cit., pp. 167-68.

27 See Eur. Court HR, Vagrancy cases, Judgment of 10 March 1972, Series A no. 14.

28 Application no. 3603/68, Collection 31, p. 48.

29 Application no. 2518/65, Dec. 14.12.65, Yearbook 8, p. 370.

30 *V v. the United Kingdom*, 16/12/1999.

31 *Goodwin v. the United Kingdom*, 11/7/2002 and *I v. the United Kingdom* (app. 26580/94).

32 See *Kosiek v. Federal Republic of Germany*, Comm. Report 11.5.84, para. 85, Eur. Court HR, Series A no. 105, p. 37.

33 See *Ringeisen v. Austria*, Comm. Report 19.3.70, Eur. Court HR, Series B no. 11, p. 69; see Letsas, "The Truth in Autonomous Concepts: How to Interpret the ECHR", *EJIL* (2004), Vol. 15, no. 2, 279-305 Cohen-Jonathan, op. cit. p. 181; Reid op. cit. p. 41; The following are examples of autonomous concepts recognised by the Convention organs: "civil rights and obligations", "criminal charge", "witness", "independent and impartial tribunal", "law".

34 *McVeigh and Others v. the United Kingdom*, Comm. Report 18.3.81, D.R. 25, p. 34, para. 157; Cohen-Jonathan op. cit., pp. 185-187; *Marckx* judgment, 14 /6/1979.

7. Dynamic Approach

In interpreting the Convention, the organs of the Convention followed a dynamic approach in the sense that they extended and applied the Convention, in the light of political and social developments and changes of conditions of life, beyond the original conceptions of the period when the Convention was drafted or entered into force. In the *Tyrer* case the Court expressly accepted the position of the Commission that the Convention is a "living instrument" which must be interpreted in the light of the "present day conditions."[35] As the delegate of the Commission pointed out in that case:

> This conclusion of the Commission is also to be seen in the context of a dynamic interpretation of an international instrument drawn up over twenty-five years ago after the horrors of the Second World War. The Commission could well have reached a different conclusion in such a case twenty-five years ago. But much has changed since then and meaning must be given to notions of fundamental rights in present-day circumstances.

Because of this approach the Commission and the Court have interpreted many provisions of the Convention in a progressive manner so as to keep pace with changing conditions of life and current human and social values, thereby permitting their application to many important emerging threats to the rights safeguarded by the Convention.[36] An impressive example is the development of the case-law in respect of the concept of private life. The result of this was to extend such concepts with a clearly personalised approach, so as to cover a wide range of elements and manifestations of the individual's personality and in order to take account of new technological developments.[37] Other examples refer to changes in the concept of the family, education, "inhuman and

35 *Tyrer v. the United Kingdom*, Comm. Report 14 .12.76, Eur. Court HR, Series B no. 24, p. 15.

36 This method of interpretation precludes the establishment of a doctrine of binding precedent in the sense that the Commission is bound by its previous interpretations of the Convention.

37 See L. G. Loucaides, *Essays on the Developing Law of Human Rights*, p. 83 et seq.

degrading treatment" and torture,[38] "civil rights and obligations," freedom of speech, freedom of religion, trade union freedom, the right to property, children born out of wedlock,[39] equality of sexes[40] etc. Many of these changes might not have entered the minds of the drafters of the Convention.

Referring to the dynamic interpretation of the Convention Jacobs rightly observes:[41]

> It cannot be objected that this approach to interpretation extends the obligations of the Contracting States beyond their intended undertakings. On the contrary, this approach is necessary if effect is to be given to their intention, in a general sense. They did not intend solely to protect the individual against the threats to human rights which were then prevalent, with the result that, as the nature of the threats changed, the protection gradually fell away. Their intention was to protect the individual against the threat of the future, as well as the threats of the past.

8. Court Followed the Commission

As already pointed out, the rules of interpreting the Convention have developed primarily through the case-law of the Commission. The Court has generally followed the Commission by adopting and applying the innovation enunciated in the Commission's reports in those cases brought before the Court. Such innovation related to the development of the scope of the rights by way of clarification, elaboration and adap-

38 *Selmouni v. France*, July 28, 1999 where the Court stated: "The Court has previously examined cases in which it concluded that there had been treatment which could only be described as torture. However, having regard to the fact that the Convention is a 'living instrument which must be interpreted in the light of present-day conditions', the Court considers that certain acts which were classified in the past as 'inhuman and degrading treatment' as opposed to 'torture' could be classified differently in future. It takes the view that the increasingly high standard being required in the area of the protection of human rights and fundamental liberties correspondingly and inevitably requires greater firmness in assessing breaches of the fundamental values of democratic societies" (para. 101).

39 *lnze v. Austria*, 28/10/1987.

40 *Schuler-Zgraggen v. Switzerland*, 24/6/1993.

41 *The European Convention on Human Rights*, 1975, p. 18.

tation of concepts to new circumstances. Such innovations also arose from drawing implications regarding the extent and effect to the obligations under the Convention, e.g., (i) that the obligation to secure the rights guaranteed by the Convention implies not only a duty to abstain from actions that amount to interference with these rights, but also a duty to take positive action to protect the rights in question by removing obstacles;[42](ii) that the clause "prescribed by law" presupposes the existence of substantive law the effects of which are foreseeable[43]; (iii) that rights may be implied (access to court) subject to limitations also permitted by implication (*Golder* case); and (iv) that the Convention implies a just balance between the protection of the general interest of the Community and the respect due to fundamental human rights, while attaching particular importance to the latter.[44]

9. Main Considerations

By way of conclusion, it may be useful to sum up the main considerations, which, according to the established case-law of the Commission, should be taken into account in interpreting the Convention. These considerations are:

(a) The general context of the Convention, including its Preamble, as well as its object and purpose. The text or wording of an article serves as a point of departure.[45]

(b) The general rules of international law, particularly those expressed in the Vienna Convention on the Law of Treaties.

(c) The special features of the European Convention, especially the fact that the obligations undertaken thereby are of an objective character.

(d) The pragmatic, as distinct from a merely linguistic, interpretation should be applied in determining the natural or ordinary meaning of the text.

---

42 See *Airey v. Ireland*, Comm. Report 15.12.76 Eur. Court HR. Series B no. 30, p. 33.

43 See *Sunday Times v. the United Kingdom*, Comm. Report 1.3.78, Eur. Court HR, Series B no. 28, p. 65.

44 See the *Belgian Linguistic Case*, Comm. Report, loc. cit.

45 If the French and the English text are not equally clear, it is justified to rely primarily on the text which is clearer: see *Ringeisen v. Austria*, Comm. Report, loc. cit., p. 70.

(e) In case of ambiguity, the extended meaning of the relevant obligations should be preferred to that which would restrict such obligations.
(f) The *travaux préparatoires* can be taken into account as supplementary means of interpretation as a guide to the general intentions of the parties, but with due regard to the principle that the Convention must be interpreted objectively with the aim of making the protection of the individual effective.
(g) International instruments with similar provisions to those of the Convention may be taken into account.
(h) The national law practice may be taken into account, but this is not decisive for the interpretation of the terms used in the Convention, which embody autonomous notions.
(i) The Convention must be interpreted in the light of present day conditions.

Chapter 2 The Concept of "Continuing" Violations of Human Rights

1. Their Significance

The topic of this article will basically be examined in the context of the European Convention on Human Rights ("the Convention"). If a violation occurred at a time when the Convention was not yet in force, or before the respondent State had accepted the competence of the European Commission of Human Rights ("the Commission") to deal with individual petitions, the Commission has no competence *ratione temporis* to deal with such a violation.

Again, the Commission is prevented from dealing with an application alleging a violation which took place more than six months earlier. Likewise, where final decision of the domestic remedies was taken more than six months before the making of the application, it is inadmissible. Furthermore, in accordance with Article 27 of the Convention, the Commission shall not deal with any individual petition which is "substantially the same as a matter which has already been examined by the Commission".

The European Court of Human Rights ("the Court") has no competence to deal with breaches of the Convention which occurred before its competence was accepted by the State against which the complaint is made.

None of these hurdles apply in respect of "continuing" violations: these fall within the time when the Commission and the Court have competence *ratione temporis.*

Furthermore, the continuing nature of violations of human rights is considered to be an *aggravating factor*[1] and may qualify as "systematic", "constant", "gross" or "flagrant" or as a "consistent pattern" of violations of human rights for the purposes of those international instruments or resolutions of international organisations where these terms are used,

1 See the Report of the Commission in the case of *Cyprus v. Turkey*, appl. no. 8007/77, DR 72, pp. 7-17 at p. 6.

e.g. International Law Commission's Draft Code of Crimes against the Peace and Security of Mankind, the Resolutions of the Commission on Human Rights of the Economic and Social Council of the United Nations and the Resolutions adopted by the General Assembly or Security Council of the UN.[2]

2. Instantaneous Acts and Continuing Violations

But what are continuing violations?

The Court has, in its case-law, accepted the concept of continuing violations of human rights, but has not as yet elaborated on its meaning and scope.[3] Nor has the Court laid down relevant criteria.

The jurisprudence of the Commission speaks of "continuing violations", as opposed to violations constituted by "instantaneous acts". This

2 E.g. General Assembly Resolutions 2144 (XXI) of 26 October 1966 and 254 7 B (XXI V) of 15 December 1969; See Joost Pauwelyn, "The Concept of a 'Continuing Violation' of an International Obligation: Selected Problems", *British Yearbook of International Law*, 1995, LXVI, p. 415.

3 *Papamichalopoulos and Others v. Greece*, Series A no. 260-B, pp. 20-21; *Agrotexim and Others v Greece*, Series A no. 330, p. 22; *Titina Loizidou v. Turkey*, Judgment of 18.12.1996. The Court in the inter-state case of *Cyprus v. Turkey* has found Turkey responsible for massive and continuing violations of a number of human rights most of which have commenced in July 1974 and affected thousands of Greek Cypriots. Some of these findings are the following: continuing violations of Article 2 of the Convention on account of the failure of the Turkish authorities to conduct an effective investigation into the whereabouts and fate of Greek-Cypriot missing persons who disappeared in life-threatening circumstances; continuing violation of Article 3 of the Convention in respect of the relatives of the Greek-Cypriot missing persons; continuing violation of Article 8 of the Convention by reason of the refusal to allow the return of any Greek-Cypriot displaced persons – again exceeding 200,000 – to their homes in northern Cyprus; continuing violation of Article 1 of Protocol No. 1 by virtue of the fact the Greek-Cypriot owners of property in the occupied part of Cyprus – again exceeding 200,000 – are being denied access to and control, use and enjoyment of their property as well as any compensation for the interference with their property rights.

This is the first time in the history of the European Convention that the Court has found a High Contracting Party responsible for continuing violations of so many rights affecting such a great number of persons for such a long period of time.

distinction is comparable to a similar distinction in the field of criminal law, according to which there are instantaneous offences, whose constitutive legal elements are executed at a stroke, and continuing offences, which are prolonged in time, both in terms of *actus reus* and *mens rea*. Thus, in Belgium, Italy, France and Greece, the concept of continuing offence is defined, in a general manner, as being constituted by an action or an omission which is prolonged in time by the constant reiteration of the guilty will of the offender after the initial act.[4] Examples of continuing offences are illegal possession of weapons, etc., illegal detention, receipt of stolen goods, criminal trespass to immovable property, etc.

The distinction between continuing violations and instantaneous violations is also found in the general principles of public international law. The International Law Commission of the United Nations ("I.L.C.") in its Commentary on the Draft Articles on the Origin of State Responsibility described a "continuing act" as "one which is a single act extending over a period of time and of a lasting nature".[5] Also, the I.L.C. has defined a "continuing act" as one "which proceeds unchanged over a given period of time: in other words an act which, after it occurs continues to exist as such and not merely in its effects and consequences".[6] Again according to the I.L.C an instantaneous act is "an act that does not extend in time, i.e. an act that ends as soon as committed; where the breach having occurred also automatically ceases to exist".[7]

Examples of continuing violations in international law are: maintenance in effect of legislation incompatible with a State's international obligations, unlawful detention of a foreign official, unlawful occupa-

4 See the bibliography set out in footnote 4 of the article of Joost Pauwelyn, op. cit.; see also Cohen-Jonathan, *La Convention Européenne Des Droits De L'Homme*, p. 99. The following exposition of the concept of "a continuing injury" in English law provides useful guidance: "If the act complained of creates a continuing source of injury, and it is of such a nature as to render the doer of it responsible for the continuance, then in cases in which damage not of the essence of the action, as in trespass, a fresh cause of action arises *de die in diem*, and in cases in which damage is of the essence of the action, as in nuisance, a fresh cause of action arises as often as fresh damage accrues" (Clerk and Lindsell on Torts, 17 Ed, para. 30.21).

5 Report of the I.L.C., 1976, p. 220.

6 I.L.C Report on its 30th Session, p. 90.

7 Ibid; see also the Judgment of the International Court of Justice in the case concerning Military and Paramilitary Activities in and against Nicaragua (I.C.J. Report, 1986, p. 14).

tion of part of the territory of another State, etc.[8] An example of instantaneous act in international law is the sinking by one State of a ship of another State lawfully exercising the right of innocent passage in the former's territorial waters.

3. Composite and Complex Acts

According to the I.L.C's Draft Articles on State Responsibility (18 & 25), acts which constitute continuing violations of international law, distinguishable from instantaneous acts, are not only "acts which continue in time" but also composite acts which consist of a sequence of separate courses of conduct, actions or omissions adopted in separate cases, but all contributing to the commission of the aggregate act in question.[9]

Also, there may be continuing violations through complex acts of the State, i.e. where there are a series of actions or omissions by the State which all relate to the same case and taken as a whole represent the position taken by the State in that particular case.[10] In the *Agrotexim* case, the Court accepted that a series of events may constitute a continuing breach of the Convention. The Court noted that: "A preliminary study of the case leads the Court to conclude that it may be possible to regard the successive actions of Athens Municipal Council as a series of steps amounting to a continuing violation and indicating the existence of a plan by the Municipal Council to purchase the two sites at the lowest possible price".[11]

Similarly, in the *Phocas v. France* case (op. cit.), the Commission considered the applicant's complaint regarding unjustified interference with his property – in the form of a threat of expropriation of his land, a refusal to grant him permits to build thereon and other events which affected the applicant's possibility for a normal use of his property during a period of about 15 years – to be a factual situation of a continuing

8 See Pauwelyn, op. cit., at p. 417; see also the case of U.S. Diplomatic and Consular Staff in Teheran, I.C.J. Report, 1980, p:3; the case of Military and Paramilitary activities in and against Nicaragua, op. cit., p. 14; the case of the Rainbow Warrior (Arbitral Awards of 30.4.1990), 82 I.L.R 499.

9 Yearbook of the I.L.C., 1978, p. 226.

10 Ibid., p. 230, cf. the Decision of the Commission in the case of *Phocas v. France*, appl. no. 17869/91; *Mc Feeley v. the United Kingdom*, 20 DR 44; and *Agrotexim and Others v. Greece*, Series A no. 330, p. 22, op. cit.

11 Op. cit., at para. 58.

nature. Also, in *McFeeley v. the United Kingdom*, [12] repeated disciplinary punishments for persistent refusal to obey the prison rules were considered to amount to a continuing situation.

4. Instantaneous Acts with Continuing Injurious Effects

There is no difficulty in understanding the concept of continuing violations of human rights in respect of all those cases where the cause of the violations is clearly a continuing act or omission, e.g. the continuing illegal physical prevention of persons from possessing and enjoying their properties or their homes or joining their families,[13] the non-enforcement of specific legal rights contrary to the Convention – such as a person's right of access to his child,[14] or to the execution of a judgment in his favour[15] – of legislation compatible with the obligations under the Convention of the State concerned or the failure to pass a law which such State is obliged by the Convention to enact, etc.

Also, there is no problem in understanding the concept of instantaneous acts and in distinguishing them, as a separate category of violations, in cases where the acts constituting the violation are executed at a stroke and are not accompanied with lasting effects, e.g. the destruction of moveable property, killing. In other words, when the violation is completed once and for all at a given point in time without any continuing injurious effects. But there is a problem in respect of those cases where acts have continuing, negative consequences.[16] If such consequences by themselves, without reference to the act which caused them, do not qualify as breaches of the Convention (e.g. pain resulting from a single act of assault) then there should be no question of them being "continuing violations". But the real problem arises in respect of all those cases where the lasting consequences or effects of an instantaneous act are

12 Op. cit.

13 See the inter-State Applications of *Cyprus v. Turkey*, (nos 6780/74, 6950/75, and 8007/77).

14 *Hokkanen v. Greece*, 19 March 1997.

15 *Hornsby v. Greece*, 19 March 1997.

16 See Pauwelyn, op. cit., p. 419, Sorensen, "Le probléme intertemporel dans l'application de la Convention", *Mélanges Modinos*, Paris 1968, pp. 304-319 at pp. 312-316 and Higgins, "Time and the Law: International Perspectives on an Old Problem", *International and Comparative Law Quarterly*; Vol. 46, p. 501 et seq. at pp. 504-507.

themselves contrary to the Convention, e.g. unlawful detention (resulting from unlawful arrest), unlawful possession of property (resulting from unlawful expropriation or confiscation), etc.

5. The Case-law Distinction

The case-law of the Commission[17] distinguishes between (a) instantaneous acts occurring at a given point in time with enduring effects – which are not considered as continuing violations, and (b) violations which continue, or which amount to a continuing situation.

It is submitted that this distinction does not provide a clear and practical test for determining the concept of "continuing violations"; and it was rightly criticised as not stating precisely the criteria used by the Commission for making such distinction.[18] In answer to that criticism, Max Sorensen attempted to explain the distinction by adopting the following approach which, in his opinion, emerged from the relevant case-law:

> ... la distinction est fonction des allégations du requérant par rapport à la disposition de la Convention invoquée. Si la disposition garantit la jouissance d'une certaine situation et si le requérant allègue qu'il a été privé de ce bénéfice pendant une période qui se prolonge après l'entrée en vigueur de la Convention, la Commission est compétente *ratione temporis* pour examiner la requête. Si, d'autre part, le requérant allègue qu'il se trouve, après l'entrée en vigueur de la Convention, dans une situation défavorable, mais contre laquelle la Convention ne le protège pas, en vertu d'une décision prise avant l'entrée en vigueur, cette décision est un 'acte instantané à effets durables', et la question de savoir s'il a été pris conformément à la Convention ou non ne se pose pas, ou – en d'autres termes – échappe à la compétence de la Commission *ratione temporis*.[19]

17 See e.g. *De Becker v. Belgium*, Yearbook 2, pp. 215, 242, 244, and *X. v. the United Kingdom*, 7379/76, DR 8, p. 111.

18 Monconduit, *La Commission Européenne Des Droits De L'Homme*, p. 212, Antonopoulos, *La Jurisprudence des Organes de la Convention Européenne des Droits de l'Homme*, Leyden 1967, pp. 35-36, cf. Pauwelyn, op. cit., p. 419.

19 Sorensen, op. cit., at p. 315.

This approach again seems unsatisfactory. Especially in so far as it refers to "a situation" which the Convention does or does not protect. The Convention safeguards rights not situations. Breaches of rights may of course amount to situations and in that sense a situation may be taken into account in deciding whether it is a case of continuing violations or not. But it should be borne in mind that every lasting situation normally commences with an initial instantaneous act. The question is what is the test, in such situations, for determining whether there is a prolongation of the original act giving rise to a continuing violation. Sorensen does not give us the answer to that. On the contrary his approach is begging the question in so far as he assumes a distinction between "situations" in respect of which the Convention extends its protection and "situations" for which no protection is given by the Convention. For the purposes of the issue under consideration, the question whether a "situation" enjoys the protection of the Convention depends on whether such "situation" amounts to a continuing violation. The test proposed by Mr Sorensen appears then to be a circular argument.

6. The *De Becker* Case

The Commission dealt for the first time with the concept of continuing violations in the *De Becker* case.[20] The applicant in that case had been sentenced to death in 1946 for treason during the War. This sentence was later convened into imprisonment and in 1961 the applicant was released subject to conditions. Under Belgian criminal law, such a sentence resulted in the limitation of certain rights – including the right to freedom of expression – and these situations continued to apply after the release. The Commission held that this was a continuing situation and found the complaint admissible *ratione temporis*.

According to the Commission, the judgment which imposed the sentence in question

> ... merely initiated the automatic application of a legal provision giving rise to a permanent situation and that, therefore, the Commission is being asked to examine not the compatibility of the above decisions with the Convention, but that of the said legal provision.

20 Op. cit.

The Commission added:

> Whereas, moreover, the Applicant does not complain of an act occurring at a given point in time nor even of the enduring effects of such an act, but … of *a legal provision giving rise to a constant and even perpetual state of affairs, against which no domestic remedy is available to him*; … whereas this legitimate concern for order, stability and peace cannot be allowed to stand in the way of the consideration, by the Commission, of the permanent state of which De Becker complains, insofar as this state of affairs is not a thing of the past, but still continues … *whereas, in the circumstances, it is exactly as though the alleged violation was being repeated daily thus preventing the running of the six months period*." (emphasis added)

The Commission took into account the nature of the complaint of the applicant, i.e. the legal regime which applied to him continually, and its effects on the applicant's rights, and found that this regime amounted to a continuing violation.

It is submitted that in the *De Becker* case the Commission did not attach the proper importance to the fact that it was the judicial decision which was the real cause of the continuing interference with the applicant's rights. Furthermore, the decision in that case failed to clarify the distinction between the "enduring effects of an act occurring at a given point in time" and the "permanent state of affairs … (which) is not a thing of the past but still continues". The result was a series of subsequent contradictory decisions of the Commission and the creation of certain confusion.

7. Contradictory Solutions

It has already been stated above that the distinction between enduring effects of an instantaneous act and violations which are continuing is not a clear and practical test for determining whether any alleged violations are of a continuing nature. The ensuing confusion and problems arising from the application of this distinction are demonstrated by the following case-law of the Commission.

After the *De Becker* case the Commission in another Belgian case, that of *X v. Belgium* (appl. no. 1028/61), found that the forfeitures of civil and political rights pronounced by the Court by virtue of the Belgian Criminal Code were not the result of the automatic application of law, but of the exercise of the Court's discretionary power and, for that reason, it was distinguishable from the *De Becker* case. In this respect the Commission stated that

> The complaint in question would not appear to relate solely to a legal provision that has created a permanent situation; whereas the complaint also, and perhaps primarily, concerns a judicial sentence, i.e. a specific act which did not bring this provision automatically into play for an indefinite period, but maintained it for a limited time only and could have terminated its application.

The reasoning of the Commission in distinguishing this case from the *De Becker* case is not convincing. In so far as the Commission found that in *X v. Belgium* the complaint concerned a judicial sentence and not the operation of a legal provision, one may also recall that in the *De Becker* case the real cause of the legal regime complained of by the applicant was again a judicial sentence and therefore in effect the complaint concerned a judicial sentence as much as it did in *X v. Belgium*. It is, therefore, submitted that the distinction has no substance.

It may be added that in so far as the case-law considers judicial or administrative acts as being incapable of causing continuing violations, apparently on the assumption that they are pronounced at a clearly defined moment and that the resulting consequences are of a temporary nature, the approach appears to be wrong.[21] The consequences of such acts may certainly not be of a temporary nature, e.g. detention and the element of momentary occurrence cannot reasonably be decisive for (as also pointed out above) every continuing violation normally commences with an initial instantaneous act; it becomes continuing through the prolongation of the operation of such act. Legislative measures are also taken at a specific moment and yet they were (rightly) found in the *De Becker* and other cases to be capable of creating a continuing violation.

In Application no. 369/58 (Yearbook 2, p. 376) the applicant's complaint was directed against his imprisonment, which was imposed as a result of a commutation of a death sentence pronounced in a judgment which, according to Belgian law, became final six months after its publication even though it was given by default. The Commission, while accepting that in the circumstances of the case a serious problem arose regarding the fairness of the relevant judicial proceedings,

21 See also van Dijk and van Hoof, *Theory and Practice of the European Convention on Human Rights*, pp. 103-104, and Pauwelyn, op. cit., p. 423.

found that the case did not concern a continuing violation because the detention complained of, although it was prolonged in time, was the result of a judgment before the coming into force of the Convention. According to the Commission, this judgment and the judicial decisions which rejected the applicant's complaints in the domestic legal order were instantaneous acts, which could not, for that reason, be examined by the Commission, given that they were delivered before the Convention came into force.

It is submitted that in this case the approach of the Commission was wrong. The direct complaint of the applicant was against his continuing detention. The examination of the compatibility of the detention in question with the Convention had to be carried out by reference to the legality of the original instantaneous judicial decision in so far as that was the continuing cause of such detention. But this did not justify treating the violation complained of as being an instantaneous violation. A continuing illegal detention appears to be a typical case of a continuing violation initiated by an instantaneous act; and it is submitted that this is the approach that should have been adopted by the Commission. In fact one can discern such an approach in the case of *Lynas v. Switzerland*[22] where the Commission decided to examine a complaint regarding illegal detention in Switzerland pending extradition in so far as it related to a period after the entry into force of the Convention with respect to Switzerland, the original act of arrest having taken place a few years before the introduction of the application. Here again the detention was the result of an instantaneous act. But the detention was rightly considered as being a constant state of affairs, i.e. a continuing deprivation of the liberty of the applicant which could qualify as a breach of the Convention.

In the case of *X v. Switzerland*[23] the applicant complained about the Swiss authorities' refusal to allow him to visit his spouse residing in Switzerland, following his expulsion therefrom a few years before he filed his application with the Commission. The Commission accepted that his inability to enter Switzerland to visit his wife fell into the category of a continuing violation and could be examined by the Commission in spite of the fact that the expulsion took place before the date on which the Convention entered into force with respect to Switzerland. Here we notice again that, although there was an initial act at a given

22 DR 6, p. 141.

23 DR 6, p. 124.

point of time, i.e. the expulsion, this did not complete the violation complained of once and for all, but it gave rise to a constant situation, i.e. the inability of the applicant to visit his wife in Switzerland.

There are other cases where the Commission found the violations complained of to be of a continuing nature even though they originated from instantaneous judicial decisions (e.g. appl. no. 8701/79: deprivation of the right to vote in national and local elections since a decision taken in 1944; *Cinar v. Turkey*, DR 79-B, p. 5: exposure to the death row phenomenon as a result of a sentence of death imposed some years before the filing of the application). It is submitted that in these cases, the approach of considering the alleged violations as continuing, in spite of the fact that they originated from instantaneous acts, was correct.

8. Interference with Property

The jurisprudence of the Strasbourg organs makes a distinction between formal or *de jure* expropriation and *de facto* expropriation. In the first case the violation is considered as instantaneous and the ensuing deprivation as an "enduring effect" regardless of whether the lawfulness of the original act of expropriation or its compatibility with the Convention is in issue.[24] The case of *de facto* expropriation is considered as a continuing violation.[25]

24 There are many examples of such cases, e.g. *X. v. the United Kingdom*, DR 8, p. 211; Appl. no. 7742/76, DR 14, p.146; Appl. no. 347/58, Yearbook 2, p. 407 and a group of recent decisions of the Commission rejecting the admissibility of certain complaints regarding deprivations of properties which were originally effected through expropriations in connection with land reform carried out between 1945-1949 in the former soviet-occupied zone of Germany: Appl. nos. 19048/91, 19049/91, 19342/92, 19549/92 and 1890/91 of 4 March 1996.

25 See the *Papamichalopoulos* case, op. cit., and the *Loizidou* case, op. cit. It should be noted that where the property which was the object of the *de facto* deprivation was movable the jurisprudence has consistently considered the deprivation as amounting only to an instantaneous and not a continuing violation, e.g. Application no. 220/56 (theft of objects of art during the German occupation of France considered to refer to facts which could not be examined *ratione temporis*). But this position seems to have been reversed by the approach adopted more recently both by the Commission and the Court in the case of *Vasilescu v. Romania* (judgment of 22 May 1998, *Reports of Judgments and Decisions*

The idea behind this distinction is that formal or *de jure* expropriation is taken as amounting to immediate abolition of an applicant's right to property and therefore as a violation which is completed instantaneously. What follows is simply the effects of such an instantaneous act. This distinction is open to criticism.[26]

It is submitted that, in so far as the act of formal or de jure deprivation of possessions, e.g. expropriation or confiscation, may be incompatible with the Convention, and therefore unlawful, the deprivation which follows cannot be considered as a simple "enduring effect" of the original act, but as a continuing breach of the right of peaceful enjoyment of one's possessions. This should be so as a matter of legal reasoning; if, the original act of "deprivation" of a possession has been illegal the keeping of the property by the State by virtue of such an act cannot but amount to a continuing interference with such property.[27] This, of course, presupposes a continuing involvement of the government in respect of the unlawful keeping of the property. In such circumstances the government should be accountable during all the period which has elapsed since the original act of "deprivation". It is not fair and it is not compatible with the spirit of the Convention for the State to escape liability under its provisions on the ground of lack of competence of the Commission to examine the complaint *ratione temporis*, so long as the enjoyment of the right to possession has been in reality continuously prevented by the conduct of the State; and it would certainly be wrong for the State to benefit through unlawful enrichment, invoking the fact that the property has been held by it as a result of a formal act of expropriation or confiscation even though that act was illegal.

1998-III): retention of gold coins unlawfully seized by the militia in 1966 found to be a continuing situation amounting to a violation of Article 1 of Protocol No. 1 (Recognition of the jurisdiction of the Court by Romania on 20.6 .94).

26 See also Pauwelyn, op. cit., p. 424.

27 It seems that in all cases of *de facto* expropriations considered by the Strasbourg case-law as amounting to continuing situations, the illegality of the expropriations was not really in issue either because such illegality was not disputed or it was manifest. This however cannot be a valid ground for refusing to take into account the illegality of a deprivation of property, in order to decide whether it is a case of a continuing situation or not; in all other cases in which such legality can clearly be established (cf. *Brumărescu v. Romania*, 28342/95, Comm. Report 15.4.98; contra *Portugalia S .A. v. Portugal*, 20272/92 Comm. Dec. 7.4.95).

One may argue that this approach may lead to absurd results, e.g. examination by the Strasbourg organs of alleged violations of the right to property whose origin (illegality) must be traced 50 or 100 years earlier. It is submitted that the time element should not change the nature of the violation. It did not in the cases of *Papamichalopoulos, Loizidou* and *Vasilescu,* and it should not in any other case. This must be so if the principle that the fruits of illegality must not be recognised (*ex injuria jus non oritur*) is to have any meaning. This, of course, is always subject to the principle of *nemo tenetur ad impossibilia.* In any event the applications brought before the Strasbourg organs in respect of alleged interference with property rights with a long history behind them will in practice be very rare.

It is true that in other fields of public international law there is support for the view that the act of confiscation of property by legislation is not considered as a continuing violation. Thus, the I.L.C.'s Special Rapporteur Mr Robeno Ago and the I.L.C. itself consider any act of confiscation by law as an instantaneous act with lasting effects since "the act of the State as such ends as soon as the confiscation has taken place even if its consequences are lasting".[28] However, the contrary view is not without support. According to the Report of the subsequent Special Rapporteur Arangio Ruiz, confiscation by legislation constitutes a continuing act, not terminated with the legislation but lasting as long as the measure stands.[29] One could also mention here the dissenting opinion of Judge Cheng Tien-Hsi in the *Phosphates in Morocco* case (*Italy v. France*).[30] In that case the Permanent Court found that the monopolisation in the exploitation of phosphates mines, established as a result of depriving an Italian citizen of his vested property rights, was not a continuing violation of a relevant international obligation. Judge Cheng said:

> The monopoly, though instituted by the legislation of 1920, is still existing today. If it is wrongful, it is wrongful not merely in its creation but in its continuance ... this prejudice does not merely continue from an old exist-

28 I.L.C . Report on its 28th Session, para. 21 (Yearbook of the I.L.C., 1976, Vol. 2, Part 2, pp. 87-122; Pauwelyn, op. cit., p. 420). See also the judgment of the Permanent Court in the *Phosphates in Morocco* case (*Italy v. France*), P.C.I.J., Series A-B no. 74.

29 Preliminary Report of Arangio Ruiz, 18 May 1988, p. 14 (U.N. Doc. A/CN.-416 and Addenda).

30 Op. cit., p. 36.

> ence but assumes a new existence every day, so long as the legislation that first created it remains in force.

9. The Involvement of the State

This brings us back to the test of continuing violations according to the *De Becker* case and the missing clarification regarding the distinction between the "enduring effects of an act occurring at a given point in time" and the "permanent state of affairs ... (which) is not a thing of the past but still continues". It is submitted that what is lacking can be deduced from a passage of the decision in that case and can be understood in the light of the relevant obligations of the State. The passage is the following:

> ... whereas, in the circumstances, it is exactly as though the alleged violation was being repeated daily thus preventing the running of the six months period.[31]

It is submitted that this passage implies as a requirement of continuing violations – as opposed to "enduring effects" of a past act – the maintenance of the adverse effects of the initial act by intentional conduct or involvement of the State.

In other words, the basic idea of the concept of a continuing violation of any human right is similar (*mutatis mutandis*) to that of the concept of a continuing criminal offence, i.e. a continued interference with a specific human right resulting from continued conduct or involvement of the State. Consequently, for a violation to be considered as continuing, in all those cases where the alleged interference with a specific right originates from an instantaneous act, it is necessary that such interference subsists as a result of a continuing operation of the initial act or the maintenance of its effects through relevant involvement or conduct of the State ("as though the alleged violation was being repeated daily"; cf. the prolongation in time of *actus reus* and *mens rea* in continuing criminal offences). This was in reality the situation in the *De Becker* case. The restrictions on Mr De Becker's exercise of his profession continued because of the maintenance in force by the State of these restrictions by virtue of the relevant judgment and legislative provisions. This was also the situation in respect of the continuing detention of the applicant in the above quoted case of *Lynas v. Switzerland* which was maintained by

31 Op. cit., p. 244.

the State by virtue of the original judgment. These and other cases can be explained on the basis of the above clarification.

10. The Test

In the light of the above, it is submitted that the test of whether violations are continuing in all those cases where the interference complained of originates from an initial instantaneous act should be composed of the following factors:

a) the nature of the complaint, i.e. the particular act or conduct alleged to be a violation;
b) the effects of the act or conduct complained of on the rights of the applicant;
c) the duration of such effects, and
d) the prolongation of the operation of the relevant act or conduct or the maintenance of the effects in question through the involvement or conduct of the State.

The answer will be given as a result of the combination of these factors and their application to the facts of each particular case. As the Commission pointed out in its decision in Application no. 369/58(Yearbook 2, pp. 376-381):

> The existence of a continuing situation susceptible to constitute a violation of the Convention cannot be appreciated in the light of a general principle, but it is an issue that the Commission must decide, if need be *ex officio*, on the basis of the particular circumstances of each case.

Nevertheless, one may venture to formulate the following principle in respect of the cases where the violation is triggered by an instantaneous act: there is a "continuing" violation if the complaint is directed against a constant interference with a right safeguarded by the Convention, which is an extension[32] of an interference caused by an initial instantaneous act whose effects still subsist as a result of a prolongation of the operation of the act or its effects through an involvement or conduct of the State. In this context the "involvement" of the State may even simply

32 *Cf. Yagci and Sargin v. Turkey*, Series A no. 319-A, where the Court said that it mattered not if the acts were "merely extensions of an already existing situation".

be an acceptance or adoption of a violation. This view is reinforced by the definition of a continuing violation by the UN Committee of Human Rights in the case of *Simunek v. the Czech Republic*[33] where the Committee stated that:

> A continuing violation is to be interpreted as an affirmation, after the entry into force of the Optional Protocol, by act or by clear implication, of the previous violations of the State party. (para. 6.4.)

11. Concluding Remarks

The concept of a "continuing" violation of a human right is important in particular as regard the *ratione temporis* competence of the human rights tribunals.

In most cases there is a clear distinction, both in theory and in practice, between instantaneous and continuing violations. However there are difficulties as regards the distinction between a continuing violation and an instantaneous violation with lasting effects. The difficulties concern the test of distinction and its actual application in specific cases. An attempt has been made in this article to illustrate this, in the context of the European Convention on Human Rights, and at the same time to suggest the factors that have to be taken into consideration in order to determine whether violations are continuing in cases where the interference complained of originates from an initial instantaneous act.

The legal theory on this topic is not particularly helpful and the relevant jurisprudence is incomplete and to a certain extent unclear and inconsistent.

It may be noted that there is a reluctance to accept that a violation is continuing in respect of all those cases where the alleged illegality has an old history. This is due to reasons of expediency: firstly, because such cases have usually a political aspect with which tribunals are, in principle, hesitant to deal and, secondly, because of the fear that the examination of such cases will increase considerably the workload of the organs with competence to deal with complaints for violations of human rights

In the domain of general international law abstract definitions of the concept of continuing acts may readily be found. But actual applications of the concept are rarer than in the field of human rights. Moreover, it

33 No. 516/1992, 54th Session of the Human Rights Committee.

appears that the European Court of Human Rights and the UN Committee on Human Rights have been more liberal than the International Court of Justice in assuming that acts occurring prior to the jurisdictional starting date may sometimes have a continuing life of their own after that date, sufficient to found a cause of action.[34] I might add that a liberal application of the concept of continuing violations of human rights is consonant with the present-day primary importance of these rights and the need for their effective protection on a universal basis.

34 Higgins, op. cit., pp. 506-507.

Chapter 3 The Rule of Law and Human Rights with Special Reference to the Jurisprudence of the European Court of Human Rights (ECHR)

1. Introduction

The Rule of Law or its equivalent French principle of *pre-eminence de droit* has been established in its original form as a principle aiming primarily at the protection of individuals from an arbitrary exercise of power by the State. The principle dictated that no state power could be exercised without authority of the Law.

Since the days of Greek philosophers there has been recourse to the notion of "law" as a primary means of subjecting governmental power to control. Aristotle emphatically maintained that "government by laws was superior to any government by men".[1] According to him justice exists only as between men whose relations to one another are governed by a system of law: "... he who commands that law should rule" he said "may thus be regarded as commanding that God and reason alone should rule; he who commands that a man should rule adds the character of the beast".[2] In the same context, Aristotle also pointed out that "laws when good should be supreme" and "personal rule, whether it be exercised by a single person or a body of persons, should be sovereign only in those matters on which law is unable, owing to the difficulty of framing general rules for all contingencies, to make an exact pronouncement".[3]

Regarding the question of what a good law is Aristotle stated that "laws must be constituted in accordance with constitutions; and if this is the case it follows that laws which are in accordance with right constitutions must necessarily be just, and laws which are in accordance with wrong or perverted constitutions must be unjust".[4] The great phi-

1 *The Politics of Aristotle*, edited and translated by Ernest Barker, pp. 145-146.

2 Ibid., p. 146.

3 Ibid., p. 127.

4 Ibid., p. 127.

losopher spoke also about equality and "justice", the latter consisting, according to him, in what tends to promote the common interest.[5]

Solon provided Athens with laws so that they would have "the certainty of being governed legally in accordance with known rules". His laws were equal laws for the noble and the base.

The necessity that the State should be based on the law was further developed by Roman lawyers. The roots of the modern concept of the rule of law can be found in the British Legal System. Magna Carta in 1215 expressed the principle that justice must be administered according to law and that it should neither be denied nor delayed. The English Petition of Grievances of 1610 emphasised the basic notion of a government subordinate to law and the Bill of Rights in 1689 affirmed that the monarchy was subject to the law.

2. Dicey's Views

The concept of the rule of law was given particular prominence by the British jurist Dicey in his work "Introduction to the Study of the Law of the Constitution" first published in 1885. Dicey gave the rule of law three meanings:[6]

a) absolute supremacy or predominance of regular law as opposed to the influence of arbitrary power, excluding the existence of arbitrariness, of prerogative, or even of wide discretionary authority on the part of the government ...;
b) equality before the law, or the equal subjection of all classes to the ordinary law of the land administered by the ordinary law courts; and
c) individual rights and freedoms should be formulated and safeguarded by the common law which according to him is the pre-eminent means of creating the rule of law rather than by abstract constitutional declarations.

However Dicey's views regarding the principle of the Rule of Law have, with the passage of time, been qualified and adjusted in the light of legal developments. Today the principle of Rule of Law in the British legal

5 Ibid., p. 129.

6 Dicey, Introduction, op. cit., 107-122; Bradley and Ewin, *Constitutional and Administrative Law* 12th ed, pp. 102-103.

system expresses[7]: a) a preference for law and order within a community rather than anarchy, warfare and constant strife. In this sense, it is linked with basic democratic notions; b) a legal doctrine of fundamental importance namely that Government must be conducted according to law and in disputed cases what the law required is declared by judicial decision; and c) a body of political opinion about what the detailed rules of law should provide in matters both of substance and procedure. The basic ideas in today's British constitutional expression of the rule of law were in the second half of 19th century, in one way or another, developed in the German system through the doctrine of "Rechtsstaat" and later on in the French legal system through the doctrine of *"pre-eminence du droit"* and its variant *"Etat de Droit"*.[8] Later on we find the American principle requiring "due process" covering part of the domain of justice served by the Rule of Law. The principle has gradually been adopted in various national legal systems and in different terms embracing in the process a number of concepts essential in a free society. It is now established that the principle of the rule of law implies at least five separate values: a) government bound by law; b) equality before the law; c) law and order; d) efficient and predictable justice, and e) human rights.[9]These values were incorporated in the concept of the rule of law in response to different needs emerging from the requirements of justice.

3. Human Rights

Since 1945 the rule of law was linked with the effort to promote international protection of human rights. It was transferred in the domain of international law and gradually through the human rights jurisprudence it has acquired an autonomous meaning and effect in the context of in-

7 Ibid., pp. 105-109.

8 See Morin, "La Préeminence du Droit dans l'ordre juridique Européen", in *Theory of International Law at threshold of the 21st century, Essays in honour of Krzysztof Skubiszewski*, page 642, at pp. 650-666.

9 See Rachel Kleinfeld Belton, "Competing Definitions of the Rule of Law", Carnegie Papers, Number 55, January 2005, which also provides an excellent exposition on the subject; see also Grote, "Rule of Law, *Rechtstaat* and *Etat de Droit*", who concludes, with good reason, that the idea of the Rule of Law "belongs to the category of open-ended concepts which are subject to permanent debate".

ternational law of human rights.[10] Nowadays, it covers a wide and open ended spectrum of requirements of justice and fairness procedural and substantive necessary for the effective protection of human rights.[11] In the Universal Declaration of Human Rights adopted in 1948 we find an express reference to the Rule of Law as follows:

> Whereas it is essential, if man is not to be compelled to have recourse, as a last resort, to rebellion against tyranny and oppression, that human rights should be protected by the rule of law.

There followed the European Convention on Human Rights signed in 1950. In the Preamble to the Convention the High Contracting Parties expressed the determination, as the Governments of European countries which have "a common heritage of political traditions, ideals, freedom and the Rule of Law to take the first steps for the collective enforcement of certain human rights".

The European Court of Human Rights through its jurisprudence has dealt with the concept of Rule of Law. The Court has never given any definition of this concept and has acted on the premise that its meaning is self-evident. This allowed a broad application of this principle in order to interpret, supplement and enhance the human rights set out in the European Convention on Human Rights with the object of safeguarding the individual against the dangers of arbitrariness and making the protection of human rights more effective on the basis of fairness and justice. The following are cases where the Court has expressly invoked the principle of the Rule of Law.

4. The Case-law of the ECHR

4.1 Principle of Interpretation

The first case in which this principle served as basis for the judgment of the Court was the case of *Golder v. the United Kingdom.*[12] In that case the applicant complained that he was deprived of the possibility to

10 Morin, op. cit., p. 666 et seq.

11 Summers, "The Principles of the Rule of Law", *Notre Dame Law Review*, June 1999; Freigang, "Is Responsive Regulation Compatible with the Rule of Law?", *European Public Law*, Vol. 8, issue 4, December 2002.

12 Series A no. 18.

consult a lawyer with a view to bringing a civil action for libel against a prison officer. The question was whether Article 6 § 1 of the Convention, which expressly provides for certain procedural guarantees in respect of the "determination" of one's "civil rights and obligations", could be interpreted as guaranteeing at the same time a right of access to the Court in spite of the fact that such right is not stated in the Article in express terms. The Court, basing itself on the concept of the Rule of Law, referred both in the Preamble to the Convention, and in Article 3 of the Statute of the Council of Europe, found that Article 6 of the Convention does by implication include the right of access to the Court. The following passages from the judgment are of particular importance:

> One reason why the signatory Governments decided to 'take the first steps for the collective enforcement of certain of the Rights stated in the Universal Declaration' was their profound belief in the Rule of Law. It seems both natural and in conformity with the principle of good faith ... to bear in mind this widely proclaimed consideration when interpreting the terms of Article 6 § 1 ... according to their context and in the light of the object and purpose of the Convention ... And in civil matters one can scarcely conceive of the Rule of Law without there being a possibility of having access to the courts ... It would be inconceivable, in the opinion of the Court, that Article 6 § 1 ... should describe in detail the procedural guarantees afforded to parties in a pending lawsuit and should not first protect that which alone makes it in fact possible to benefit from such guarantees, that is, access to a court. The fair, public and expeditious characteristics of judicial proceedings are of no value at all if there are no judicial proceedings ... Taking all the preceding considerations together, it follows that the right of access constitutes an element which is inherent in the right stated by Article 6 ... This is not an extensive interpretation forcing new obligations on the Contracting States: it is based on the very terms of the first sentence of Article 6 ... read in its context and having regard to the object and purpose of the Convention, a lawmaking treaty ..., and to general principles of law.

The concept of the Rule of Law has therefore permitted in the *Golder* case[13] an interpretation leading to the widest possible meaning of the relevant human right thus effectively protecting the individual against the omnipotence of the State. As rightly pointed out by the Court:

13 op. cit.

> ... were Article 6 § 1 to be understood as concerning exclusively the conduct of an action which had already been initiated before a court, a Contracting State could, without acting in breach of that text, do away with its courts, or take away their jurisdiction to determine certain classes of civil actions and entrust it to organs dependent on the Government. Such assumptions, indissociable from a danger of arbitrary power, would have serious consequences which are repugnant to the aforementioned principles and which the Court cannot overlook.

Following this judgment the Court continued to refer to the Rule of Law as a principle which is "inherent in every Article of the Convention" (*Amuur v. France*[14]) and which provided guidance for its interpretation. In the case of *Engel v. the Netherlands*[15] the Court refused to give an extensive meaning to the provisions of Article 5 of the Convention which allows the deprivation of liberty "in order to secure the fulfilment of any obligation prescribed by law" so as to justify the detention of the applicant for having been absent during his military service. The Court observed that the wide interpretation supported by the Government "would entail consequences incompatible with the notion of the Rule of Law from which the whole Convention draws its whole inspiration". In the same case the Court proceeded to state that

> in a society subscribing to the Rule of Law, there belong to the 'criminal' sphere deprivations of liberty liable to be imposed as a punishment, except those which by their nature, duration or manner of execution cannot be appreciably detrimental.

4.2 Judicial Control and Quality of Law

The Court in its case-law proceeded to declare that "judicial control of interferences by the executive with the individual's right to liberty is implied by the Rule of Law" and that any other interferences should be subject to an effective control. The latter should normally be assured by the judiciary; at least in the last resort, judicial control offering the best guarantees of independence, impartiality and a proper procedure (*Klass*

14 *Reports of Judgments and Decisions (Reports)* 1996-III.

15 Series A no. 22.

and Others v. Germany,[16] *Van de Huck v. the Netherlands,*[17] *Brannigan v. the United Kingdom,*[18] *Brogan and Others v. the United Kingdom*[19]). The Court also stressed the special role of the judiciary in the application of the Rule of Law. According to the judgment in the case of *Prager v Austria*[20] the "judiciary ... as the guarantor of justice, a fundamental value in a law-governed State, it must enjoy public confidence if it is to be successful in carrying out its duties." In his dissenting opinion in the case of *Ahmet Sadik v. Greece*[21] Judge Martens stressed what appears to be an indisputable fact, namely that under the principle of Rule of Law the domestic courts are, to the extent of their powers, bound to see to it that the obligation to safeguard human rights is honoured. Another important finding of the Court was that the terms "law" or "lawful" in the Convention "[do] not merely refer back to domestic law but also [relate] to the quality of the law, requiring it to be compatible with the Rule of Law". This was explained in the case of *Olsson v. Sweden*[22] to mean that there must be a measure of protection in domestic law against arbitrary interference by public authorities with the rights safeguarded by, *inter alia*, Article 8 of the Convention. In the same case the Court stated that "a law which confers a discretion is not in itself inconsistent with the requirement of foreseeability, provided that the scope of the discretion and the manner of its exercise are indicated with sufficient clarity, having regard to the legitimate aim of the measure in question, to give the individual adequate protection against arbitrary interference". Explaining the term "in accordance with the law" the Court repeated that the expression also relates to the quality of the law requiring it to be compatible with the Rule of Law. In this respect the Court stressed: "the need for the law to be accessible to the person concerned, who must, moreover, be able to foresee its consequences for him" (*Valenzuela v. Spain*[23]).

16 Series A no. 28.

17 Series A no. 288.

18 Series A no. 258-B.

19 Series A no. 145-B.

20 Series A no. 313.

21 *Reports* 1996-V.

22 Series A no. 130.

23 *Reports* 1998-V.

4.3 Democracy and Legal Security

The principle of the Rule of Law in modern times presupposes a democratic regime. In fact the concept of the Rule of Law is, according to the jurisprudence of the Court, linked to that of democratic society ("the Rule of Law, one of the fundamental principles of a democratic society": *Iatrides v. Greece,*[24] *Colacrai v. Italy;*[25] *Hirst v. the United Kingdom*[26]). The principle demands the institution of democracy (c.f. *Poitrimol v. France*[27] and the document referred in the concluding remarks). Therefore a necessary corollary of the requirement referring to the quality of law in the context of the Rule of Law should be understood to refer to a law which is enacted by a competent democratic institution of the State. It cannot include laws or decrees emanating from dictatorial regimes or other undemocratic or illegal institutions unless such law or decrees were later adopted by the competent democratic authorities in order to preserve legal continuity.[28]

Legal security and confidence in law are also contained in the wider Rule of Law principle. The Court stated that:

> The right to a fair hearing before a tribunal as guaranteed by Article 6 § 1 of the Convention must be interpreted in the light of the Preamble to the Convention, which declares, among other things, the Rule of Law to be part of the common heritage of the Contracting States. One of the fundamental aspects of the Rule of Law is the principle of legal certainty, which requires, *inter alia,* that where the courts have final-

24 *Reports* 1999-II.

25 15/07/2005, § 58.

26 30/03/2004.

27 Series A no. 277-A; see also *Refah Partisi v. Turkey,* 31 July 2001, § 43:

> There is a very close link between the Rule of Law and democracy. As it is the function of written law to establish distinctions on the basis of relevant differences, the Rule of Law cannot be sustained over a long period if persons governed by the same laws do not have the last word on the subject of their content and implementation.

28 Loucaides, *Essays on the Developing Law of Human Rights,* p. 188. As rightly pointed out by Belton, "states such as Nazi Germany or apartheid South Africa (which were run by law but used that law as an instrument to deprive some citizens of peace and safety) were not governed by the Rule of Law at all" (op. cit., pp. 14-15).

ly determined an issue, their ruling should not be called into question. (*Brumarescu v. Romania*[29])

In the case just referred to the issue was whether the procedure which allowed the Procurator General to apply for a final judgment to be quashed without there even being any time-limit for the exercise of such power was compatible with Article 6 § 1 of the Convention. The Court found that this procedure infringed the principle of legal certainty and breached the applicant's right to a fair hearing under the Article in question.

In this respect, reference should also be made to the finding of the Court according to which an important element of the Rule of Law is that the verdicts of a tribunal should be final and binding unless set aside by a superior court on the basis of irregularity or unfairness and that this principle must apply equally to all forms of tribunal, including juries (*Pullar v. the United Kingdom*[30]). Moreover, according to the jurisprudence of the Court the Rule of Law does not permit the non-execution of judicial decisions. This was first decided in the case of *Hornsby v. Greece*[31] where the Court pointed out that the right of access to the Court would be illusory if a Contracting State's domestic legal system allowed a final, binding judicial decision to remain inoperative to the detriment of one party. Such a situation would be incompatible with the principle of the Rule of Law which the Contracting States undertook to respect when they ratified the Convention. In another case, the Court accepted that procedural rules concerning formalities and time-limits in court proceedings were intended to ensure the Rule of Law and legal certainty. In particular, time-limits governing the filing of appeals by the prosecution had to be scrupulously complied with in order to avoid any imbalance between it and the defence to the detriment of the latter.

4.4 Discretionary Powers

In the case of *Malone v. the United Kingdom*,[32] which concerned a complaint for telephone tapping, it has been stressed that the necessary le-

29 *Reports* 1999-VII, § 61; see also *Salov v. Ukraine*, judgment, Section II, dated 6 September 2005.

30 *Reports* 1996-III.

31 *Reports* 1997-II; see also *Iatrides v. Greece*, op. cit.

32 Series A no. 82.

gal protection against arbitrary interferences by public authorities in line with the Rule of Law is particularly important where a power of the executive is exercised in secret, which is the case of the measures of secret surveillance of communications. In such a case the Court stated that

> it would be contrary to the Rule of Law for the legal discretion granted to the executive to be expressed in terms of an unfettered power. Consequently, the law must indicate the scope of any such discretion conferred on the competent authorities and the manner of its exercise with sufficient clarity, having regard to the legitimate aim of the measure in question, to give the individual adequate protection against arbitrary interference.

The risks of arbitrariness in respect of secret measures being evident it would be according to the Court contrary to the Rule of Law for the legal discretion granted even to the judge to be expressed in terms of an unfettered power (case of *Huvig v. France*[33]). The Court repeatedly pointed out that the principle of the Rule of Law implies an effective control of the interferences by the authorities with the individual's rights especially where the law bestows on the executive wide discretionary powers the application of which is a matter of practice susceptible to modification (case of *Silver and Others v. the United Kingdom*[34]). In the same context the Court found that in the absence of any detail at all as to the kind of restrictions permitted or their purpose, duration and extent or the arrangements for their review, "the [relevant] provisions [permitting the exercise of discretionary power leading to restrictions of the rights under the Convention] do not offer the minimum degree of protection against arbitrariness required by the Rule of Law in a democratic society".[35]

4.5 Onerous and Retrospective Legislation

Dealing with the right to property the Court found that extended prohibitions on properties resulting in adverse effects on the property owners is a situation irreconcilable with the position that should obtain in a

33 Series A no. 176-B.

34 Series A no. 176-B.

35 *Herczegfalvy* case, Series A no. 244.

State governed by the Rule of Law. In the case of *Stran Greek Refineries and Stratis Andreadis v. Greece*[36] the Court held that the determination through legislative action by the State of a property case pending before the Court in which the State was a Party was repugnant to the notion of the Rule of Law. Interpreting the right of access to a court established in the *Golder* case[37] the Court found that:

> The fact of having access to domestic remedies, only to be told that one's actions are barred by operation of law does not always satisfy the requirements of Article 6 § 1. The degree of access afforded by the national legislation must also be sufficient to secure the individual's 'right to a court', having regard to the principle of the Rule of Law in a democratic society. For the right of access to be effective, an individual must have a clear, practical opportunity to challenge an act that is an interference with his rights.

Relying on this case the Court held in another case that:

> The Court should be especially mindful of the dangers inherent in the use of retrospective legislation which has the effect of influencing the judicial determination of a dispute to which the State is a party. Respect for the Rule of Law and the notion of a fair trial require that any reasons adduced to justify such measures be treated with the greatest possible degree of circumspection.[38]

The guarantee *nullum crimen nulla poena sine lege* embodied in Article 7 of the Convention was expressly declared by the Court to be an essential element of the Rule of Law and "it should be construed and applied, as follows from its object and purpose, in such a way as to provide effective safeguards against arbitrary prosecution, conviction and punishment" (*C.R. v. the United Kingdom*[39]).

36 Series A no. 301-B.

37 Op. cit.

38 *Pravednaya v. Russia*, application no. 69529/01, § 26.

39 Series A no. 335-C.

4.6 Deprivation of Liberty

In the *Engels* case, already referred to above, the Court, guided by the principle of the Rule of Law, leaned in favour of a restrictive interpretation of the provisions of Article 5 (1) b of the Convention which permit deprivation of a person's liberty "in order to secure the fulfilment of any obligation prescribed by the law". Mr Engel was arrested for two days "in order to secure his obligation of maintaining military discipline" as a consequence of the fact that he failed to do so by not abiding to a previously imposed disciplinary punishment. The Court in finding that the arrest in question was not permitted under the aforesaid provisions invoked by the respondent Government stated

> ... that the words 'secure the fulfilment of any obligation prescribed by law' concern only cases where the law permits the detention of a person to compel him to fulfil a specific and concrete obligation which he has until then failed to satisfy. A wide interpretation would entail consequences incompatible with the notion of the Rule of Law ... It would justify, for example, administrative internment meant to compel a citizen to discharge, in relation to any point whatever, his general duty of obedience to the law.

In the *Winterwerp* case[40] the Court stated that

> ... the importance of the aim underlying Article 5 § 1(art. 5-1): in a democratic society subscribing to the Rule of Law ... no detention that is arbitrary can ever be regarded as 'lawful'.

And in the *Brogan* case[41] the Court reiterated the object of Article 5 of the Convention as being the protection of the individual against arbitrary interferences by a State with his right to liberty and the necessity of judicial control in order to minimise the risk of arbitrariness. "Judicial control", said the Court, "is implied by the Rule of Law one of the fundamental principles of a democratic society ... which is expressly referred to in the Preamble to the Convention."

40 Series A no. 33.

41 Series A no. 145-B.

4.7 Freedom of Speech

In the case of *Castells v. Spain,*[42] in which freedom of expression was in issue, the Court declared that the pre-eminent role of the press in a State governed by the Rule of Law must not be forgotten.

In another case concerning again freedom of expression the Court found that the seizure of printed matter and its withdrawal from circulation only conformed to the fundamental principle of the Rule of Law contained in the concept "prescribed by law" if they were ordered in the context of criminal proceedings. The Court added that "given the importance of the right to freedom of expression only such proceedings afforded sufficient safeguards". However, in the same case the Court recognised that the proper functioning of a democratic society, based on the Rule of Law, may call for security services, which "in order to be effective, must operate in secret and be afforded the necessary protection. In this way a State may protect itself against the activities of individuals and groups attempting to undermine the basic values of a democratic society" (case of *Vereniging Weekblad Bluf! v. the Netherlands*[43]).

In the case of *Sidiropoulos v. Greece,*[44] which was another freedom of speech case, the Court pointed out that "the irresponsible publications of a newspaper could not be used as evidence by a court, or indeed by the government of a State which respected the Rule of Law".

4.8 Presumption of Innocence

In a series of cases the Court pointed out that the principle of the presumption of innocence is not only provided in Article 6 of the Convention but is also derived from the principle of the Rule of Law (see, *inter alia*, the case of *Englert v. Germany*[45]).

Dismissal of an appeal on points of law on the ground that the appellant has absconded was found by the Court to amount to a disproportionate sanction, having regard to the special importance of the rights of the defence "and of the principle of the Rule of Law in a democratic

42 Series A no. 236.

43 Series A no. 306-A.

44 *Reports* 1998-IV.

45 Series A no. 123.

society" (*Poitrimol v. France*[46]). Having adopted the same approach in another case the Court explained that "such inadmissibility was not prescribed by law but had been introduced by case-law and was contrary to the 'presumption of innocence, since it was based on the idea that the accused had deliberately sought to evade justice". (*Guerin v. France*[47]) In a Swiss case which concerned the imposition of fines on the heirs of a deceased person who was responsible for tax evasion the Court found that such action is contrary to the presumption of innocence and the Rule of Law. The Court stated that "inheritance of the guilt of the dead is not compatible with the standards of criminal justice in a society governed by the Rule of Law" (*A. P., M.P. and T.P. v. Switzerland*[48]).

4.9 Torture or Inhuman Treatment

In the famous case of *Soering v. the United Kingdom*[49] which concerned a request by the USA for extradition of a fugitive in order to be tried for the offence of murder entailing in case of conviction the sentence of death preceded by the so-called "death row", namely a long period of awaiting the execution of the sentence, the Court found that because of this "death row" such extradition would lead to a situation of torture or inhuman treatment. In this respect the Court invoked the principle of Rule of Law as follows:

> It would hardly be compatible with the underlying values of the Convention, that "common heritage of political traditions, ideals, freedom and the Rule of Law" to which the Preamble refers, were a Contracting State knowingly to surrender a fugitive to another State where there were substantial grounds for believing that he would be in danger of being subjected to torture, however heinous the crime allegedly committed.

46 Op. cit.

47 *Reports* 1998-IV.

48 *Reports* 1997-V.

49 Series A no. 161.

4.10 Fair Trial

The Court also pointed out that the principle of the Rule of Law implies the need for a proper administration of justice and a fair trial.[50] According to the Court the administrative authorities form one element of a State subject to the Rule of Law and their interests accordingly coincide with the need for the proper administration of justice.[51] In the *Salabiaku* case the Court stated:

> the object and purpose of Article 6 (art. 6), which, by protecting the right to a fair trial and in particular the right to be presumed innocent, is intended to enshrine the fundamental principle of the Rule of Law.

In the case of *Pini and Bertani and Manera and Atripaldi v. Romania*,[52] the Court pointed out that

> ... [the] bailiffs, who work to ensure the proper administration of justice and thus represent a vital component of the Rule of Law, is incompatible with their position as law enforcement officers and that action should be taken against those responsible.

The Court on several occasions linked the Rule of Law with the principles of fair trial enshrined in Article 6 of the Convention as follows:

> Account must be taken of the central position occupied ... by Article 6 which reflects the fundamental principle of the Rule of Law
>
> (see, *inter alia, The Sunday Times v. the United Kingdom (no. 1)*, judgment of 26 April 1979, Series A no. 30, p.34, § 55, and *Worm v. Austria, Reports of Judgments and Decisions*, 1997-V p.1537, § 40).

As regards the degree of access to court for the purposes of a fair trial under Article 6 of the Convention the Court accepted that although limitations may be imposed, "It must ... be established that the degree of access afforded under the national legislation was sufficient to secure

50 *Antonetto v Italy* , *Salabiaku v. France*, Series A no.141-A: *Sovtransavto Holding v. Ukraine, Reports* 2002-VII; *Surugiu v. Romania*, 20/04/2004.

51 Ibid.

52 22/06/2004.

the individual's 'right to a court', having regard to the Rule of Law in a democratic society ... the limitations applied must not restrict or reduce the access left to the individual in such a way or to such an extent that the very essence of the right is impaired ... Furthermore, a limitation will not be compatible with Article 6 § 1 (art. 6-1) if it does not pursue a legitimate aim and if there is not a reasonable relationship of proportionality between the means employed and the aim sought to be achieved."[53] As rightly observed by Morin,[54] here again, as in the *Golder* case, the Court guided by the notion of the Rule of Law spelled out a principle of interpretation which is not written in the Convention.

The Court also pointed out that a special vigilance should be exhibited in making sure that the right to a court is not barred in civil or criminal proceedings unless there are good reasons. "Absence of constraint is at all events one of the conditions to be satisfied; this much is dictated by an international instrument founded on freedom and the Rule of Law".[55]

4.11 Equality

The principle of equality of individuals before the law was also found to be corollary of the Rule of Law. Thus in the case of *Prosperity Party v. Turkey*[56] the Court stated:

> The Rule of Law means that all human beings are equal before the law, in their rights as in their duties. However, legislation must take account of differences, provided that distinctions between people and situations have an objective and reasonable justification, pursue a legitimate aim and are proportionate and consistent with the principles normally upheld by democratic societies. But the Rule of Law cannot be said to govern a secular society when groups of persons are discriminated against solely on the ground that they are of a different sex or have different political or religious beliefs. Nor is the Rule of Law upheld where entirely different legal systems are created for such groups.

53 *Ashingdane* case, Series A no. 93.

54 Op cit., p. 674.

55 *Deweer* case, Series A no. 35.

56 Op. cit., § 43.

4.12 The Dominant Role of the Rule of Law

The Court did not hesitate to rely on the principle of the Rule of Law in disregarding the norms of the non-democratic regime of East Germany that were incompatible with the requirements of that principle and in finding that the conviction by the succeeding democratic regime of a soldier for killing a person who tried to cross the border to West Germany was in line with the European Convention on Human Rights regardless of the fact that the soldier was executing orders of his superiors under those norms. The Court noted that the killing in question was in breach of the right to life and the laws of the latter regime and pointed out the following:

> The Court considers that it is legitimate for a State governed by the Rule of Law to bring criminal proceedings against persons who have committed crimes under a former regime; similarly, the courts of such a State, having taken the place of those which existed previously, cannot be criticised for applying and interpreting the legal provisions in force at the material time in the light of the principles governing a State subject to the Rule of Law.

4.13 Unsatisfactory Jurisprudence

Although the jurisprudence of the ECHR has established the application of the Rule of Law in concrete situations in the context of human rights and has contributed to the employment of the concept of the rule of law in enhancing and better protecting human rights, there are several situations in respect of which, judging on the basis of this jurisprudence, one is justified to criticise the solutions given as being contradictory and unsatisfactory. A striking example of such a solution is the narrow interpretation of the term "civil rights and obligations" in Article 6 § 1 of the Convention in respect of which the right to a fair trial applies. The Court consistently held that this term could not cover all legal rights and obligations but only those that are considered "civil". No clear guidance was given as to the notion of "civil"[57]. I consider this approach incompatible with the requirements of the principle of Rule of Law. As I explained in a dissenting opinion on this subject:

57 Loucaides, "Questions of Fair Trial under the European Convention on Human Rights", *Human Rights Law Review*, Vol. 3, no. I, 2003, pp. 28-29.

> It is, I believe, evident that the object and purpose of Article 6 was to ensure, through judicial guarantees, a fair administration of justice to any person in the assertion or determination of his legal rights or obligations. It would be absurd to accept that the judicial safeguards were intended only for certain rights, particularly those between individuals, and not to any legal rights and obligations including all those *vis-à-vis* the administration where an independent judicial control is especially required for the protection of the individuals against the powerful authorities of the State. (*Maaouia v France*[58])

Other examples of solutions which are difficult to reconcile with the requirements of the Rule of Law are the cases where the Court found that diplomatic and parliamentary immunity can block access to the Court regardless of the merits of the case of a complainant (see the cases of *Al-Adsani v. the United Kingdom,*[59] *Fogarty v. the United Kingdom,*[60] *McElhinney v. Ireland*[61] and *A. v. the United Kingdom*[62] – civil actions for acts amounting to torture, sex discrimination, assault and defamation respectively). It is submitted that blocking access to the Court through automatic application of immunities which are legal institutions outside the structure of the Convention is difficult to reconcile with the concept of the Rule of Law in a democratic society. The same applies to the jurisprudence according to which a conviction in a criminal case can be based on illegally obtained evidence (*Khan v. the United Kingdom*). Similar criticism can be adopted in respect of the judgment of the Court in the *Cyprus v. Turkey* case[63] decided in 2001 where the Court adopted the position that the requirement to exhaust domestic remedies applied to judicial remedies of the judicial system established in the Turkish occupied part of Cyprus by the subordinate illegal administration of the occupying country on the basis of an illegal constitution contrary to the will of the majority of the people, the relevant treaties concerning

58 *Reports* 2000-X.

59 *Reports* 2001-XI.

60 *Reports* 2001-XI.

61 *Reports* 2001-XI.

62 *Reports* 1998-VI.

63 *Reports* 2001-IV.

the establishment of the Republic of Cyprus, the UN Security Council's Resolutions and relevant principles of international law.[64]

5. Concluding Remarks

In actual fact in spite of some contradictions the overall effect of the jurisprudence of the European Court of Human Rights supports the conclusion that the concept of the Rule of Law has gradually been extended to embrace various requirements of justice and fairness. In his dissenting opinion in the *Borgers v. Belgium*[65] case, Judge Martens rightly points out that the German Federal Constitutional Court habitually refers to "the requirement of maintaining an administration of justice which is able to function effectively", and that this requirement is derived from the Rule of Law and the idea of justice implied therein. Of particular interest is the document of the Copenhagen meeting of the Conference on the Human Dimension of the Conference on Security and Cooperation in Europe (CSCE) adopted in July 1990 where the participating States (34 western countries) declared, *inter alia*, that "the Rule of Law does not mean merely a formal legality which assures regularity and consistency in the achievement and enforcement of democratic order, but justice based on the recognition and full acceptance of the supreme value of the human personality and guaranteed by institutions providing a framework for its fullest expression", that "democracy is an inherent element of the Rule of Law" (para. 3), and that "international instruments in the field of human rights" are "an important contribution to the Rule of Law at a national level" (para. 5.20).

---

64 Loucaides, *Human Rights Review*, op. cit., pp. 43-44 and "The judgment of the European Court of Human Rights in the case of *Cyprus v . Turkey*", *Leiden Journal of International Law* 225 at p. 235 (2002).

65 Series A no. 214-B.

Chapter 4 The Prohibition of Discrimination under Protocol 12 of the European Convention on Human Rights

1. Introduction

Equality as a basic social value has had a long history. Although different meanings have been attached to the notion, the basic idea that all men are created equal and are therefore entitled to equal rights and treatment has remained the core and the aim of the relevant legal safeguards.[1] As was rightly pointed out by Judge Cardozo, "from the moment of birth onward, humankind, as the law views it, is a society of equals".[2] The first definitions of equality are based on the principle of Aristotle that equality consists in treating equals equally and unequals unequally.[3] The principle of equality and its corollary rule of non-discrimination have received universal recognition "as the most important

1 For an elaborate and excellent exposition of the principle of equality and its applications see the book of Polyvios G. Polyviou, *The Equal Protection of the Laws*, a Duckwoth publication (1980). The literature on equality is vast. Some of the most prominent are set out in footnote 14 of the work of Mr Polyviou. The following, which are more specifically relevant to the topic of the present article, should be added; Morawa, "The Evolving Human Right to Equality", *European Yearbook of Minority Issues*, Vol. 1, 2001/2, pp. 157-205 and the articles referred to in footnote 1 therein; Hendriks, "Disabled Persons and their Right to Equal Treatment: Allowing Differentiation while ending Discrimination", *Health and Human Rights*, Vol. 1, no. 1, pp. 153-173; Lord Lester of Herne Hill, "Equality and United Kingdom Law: Past, Present and Future", *Public Law* 2001, pp. 77-96; Reid, *A Practitioner's Guide to the European Convention on Human Rights*, 2nd ed., 2004, pp. 259-268; Harris, O' Boyle, Warbrick, *Law of the European Convention on Human Rights*, pp. 462- 488; Van Dijk and Van Hoof, *Theory and Practice of the European Convention on Human Rights*, 3rd ed., pp. 710-730.

2 Cardozo, *Law and Literature* (1931), 110.

3 Aristotle, *The Nicomachean Ethics*, bk. 5, Chs. 2-4, Oxford University.

single principle that any nation can take as its ideal".[4] Judge Douglas stated that "wherever equality is the theme, men live together in peace. Wherever inequality is the practice, grievances and complaints fester".[5] Equality is also aptly described as "the complement of democracy".[6]

The majority of modem constitutions contain clauses directed against arbitrary discrimination and aiming at ensuring equal rights. Constitutional guarantees of equality take a great number of forms. Certain provisions make use of the concepts of equality before the law, equal protection and equal treatment, while others refer to the concept of discrimination. A great number of international instruments also include guarantees of equal treatment and protection from discrimination.

Naturally one would have expected that in a major human-rights instrument like the European Convention on Human Rights (hereinafter referred to as "the Convention"), equality in the sense of the right to equal treatment or the prohibition of discrimination between individuals standing in the same or an analogous position would have been included as one of the basic rights. Yet ever since its adoption in 1950 the Convention has not guaranteed such an autonomous right. It was only on 26 June 2000 that the Committee of Ministers of the Council of Europe approved Protocol No. 12, which introduced for the first time a general clause prohibiting discrimination.[7] The Protocol was opened for signature on 4 November 2000 and came into force on 1 April 2005 when the requirement of ratification by ten States was satisfied.

---

4 Douglas, *We the Judges*, (1956), 426.

5 Ibid., no. 11, ad. 425.

6 Mason, Brandeis, *A Free Man's Life* (1946), 439.

7 Mc Cafferty, "General Prohibition of Discrimination: The New Protocol to the Human Rights Convention", *Human Rights*, March 2002, pp.20-25; Gonzalez, "Le Protocole additionnel no. 12 à la Convention européenne des droits de l'homme portant interdiction général de discriminer", *Revue française de droit administratif*, 18e année; no.1; Frederic, "Le Protocole no. 12 à la Convention Européenne des Droits de l'Homme", *l'Europe des Libertés*, 2eme année, no. 4, pp. 11-16; Buonomo, "Protocol 12 to the European Convention on Human Rights ", *European Yearbook of Minority Issues*, Vol. 1, 2001/2, pp. 425-433; Khaliq, "Protocol 12 to the European Convention on Human Rights: a step forward or a step too far?", *Public Law*, 2001, pp. 457-464.

There was great reluctance to accept such a right as part of the Convention. This was due to the fear of adopting a clause of general protection of equality, the concept of which could possibly give rise to multiple interpretations and whose implementation would be effectively supervised through the judicial machinery of the Convention.

2. Article 14

It is true that Article 14 of the Convention provides for the prohibition of discrimination, but this applies only in respect of the enjoyment of the specific rights and freedoms set forth in the Convention. In other words, Article 14 does not have an independent existence. It can only come into play in respect of and in conjunction with the rights guaranteed by the Convention. For example, Article 14 can be invoked if there is an interference with or a restriction of a discriminatory nature in respect of a right provided in the Convention, such as freedom of speech or the right to respect for one's private life, but it cannot be invoked in respect of discriminatory treatment of an individual by a public authority in connection with any matter which does not concern a right under the Convention. The case-law has extended the application of Article 14 even in cases where no right under the Convention regarded in isolation is violated provided that the discrimination complained of must affect the enjoyment of such right.[8] Such a situation can arise when a limitation or restriction, otherwise allowed, is applied in a discriminatory manner.

The lacuna resulting from the lack of a general safeguard against discrimination in the Convention was particularly striking in view of the evident importance of such a safeguard and in view of its inclusion in many international and constitutional legal instruments. Guarantees of equal treatment and protection from discrimination figure prominently both in the Universal Declaration of Human Rights and in the 1966 United Nations Covenants on Economic, Social and Cultural Rights and on Civil and Political Rights. Also, a great number of international instruments and resolutions of the UN General Assembly have condemned and dealt with particular forms and types of discrimination.

8 *Thlimmenos v. Greece*, ECHR 2000-IV.

3. A New Protocol

There were various attempts from the 1960s to the 1980s to include the right to equality and non-discrimination in the Convention but it was only after 1990 that the efforts to incorporate the right into the Convention began to have prospects of success. This was due to a great extent to developments in combating discrimination against women and racial discrimination. In 1998 the Committee of Ministers entrusted the Council of Europe's steering Committee for Human Rights to draft a Protocol extending in a general way the guarantee of non-discrimination.[9]

In the preparatory stages there was a difference of opinion as to whether or not the Protocol should adopt the wording of Article 26 of the UN Covenant on Civil and Political Rights, according to which "all persons are equal before the law and are entitled without any discrimination to the equal protection of the law". Without going into the arguments of the different sides on this question, I would simply point out that the problem related to whether or not the concept of equality should be included and to the fear that that concept might entail unlimited positive obligations on the part of States. The result was a compromise; the Protocol refers to equality in its Preamble but adopts the concept of discrimination in its operative provisions.

The Preamble to the Protocol refers to "the fundamental principle according to which all persons are equal before the law and are entitled to the equal protection of the law" and to the resolution of the signatory States "to take further steps to promote the equality of all persons through the collective enforcement of a general prohibition of discrimination by means of the Convention for the Protection of Human Rights".

The operative part reads as follows:

> 1. The enjoyment of any right set forth by law shall be secured without discrimination on any ground such as sex, race, colour, language, religion, political or other opinion, national or social origin, association with a national minority, property, birth or other status.
> 2. No one shall be discriminated against by any public authority on any ground such as those mentioned in paragraph 1.

9 Moon, "The Draft Discrimination Protocol to the European Convention on Human Rights: A Progress Report", E.H.R.L.R. Issue 1., 2000, 49-53.

As pointed out in the Explanatory Report on the Protocol, while the equality principle is not expressly stated in the operative part of Article 1 of the Protocol "the non-discrimination and equality principles are closely intertwined". It is true that failure to observe the principle of equality (equal treatment of equal situations and different treatment of unequal situations) results in discrimination. But the concept of equality is wider than the prohibition of discrimination. It may encompass positive duties in order to achieve the objectives of the principle and generally it may be interpreted as offering more extensive protection than the prohibition of discrimination. Rights guaranteed in positive terms under prescriptive provisions do in principle offer a wider scope of protection than those guaranteed under proscriptive provisions. As rightly pointed out by Harris, O'Boyle and Warbrick in their treatise on the Convention, the concept of "discrimination" affords protection against discrimination rather than promoting equality.[10] In any event when there are already deeply rooted *de facto* inequalities resulting from general sources non-discrimination alone cannot ensure equal opportunities for all.[11]

As André Hauriou rightly pointed out: "[I]l est bien évident que l'égalité de droit reste, dans un large mesure, théorique, lorsqu'elle est contradite par l'inégalité de fait ... l'égalité de droit est largement conditionnée par l'égalité de fait".[12]

4. Reverse Discrimination

In any event, the scope of the protection guaranteed by the operative part of Article 1 of the Protocol is sufficiently broad to provide a remedy in a wide spectrum of situations which are incompatible with the concept of equal treatment, and the provision is capable of being interpreted to entail positive obligations,[13] even though the drafters of the

10 Harris, O' Boyle, Warbrick, op. cit., p. 463.

11 Cf. Lester, op. cit., pp. 83-84.

12 André Hariou, *Droit constitutionnel et Institutions publiques*, 4e édition, 1970, p. 186. In support of this statement, the author refers to the case of admission to public posts, pointing out that those who do not possess the financial means necessary for the acquisition of the required qualifications are put in a disadvantageous position as compared to those who do, in spite of the application of the principle of equality.

13 Mc Cafferty, op. cit., p. 24; Buonomo, op. cit., p. 429.

Protocol sought to avoid such an eventuality as far as possible. It may even be argued that under the provisions of the new Protocol a legal obligation may arise on the part of States to engage in a policy of reverse discrimination, that is to say differential treatment designed to correct factual inequalities.[14] Such obligations already exist in European law in the form of various kinds of assistance for the poor. In any event, the scope of the protection guaranteed by the Protocol may extend to economic and social rights the implementation of which aim at preventing unacceptable levels of material inequality and gives rise to some of the most broad discrimination questions. In this respect, one thinks of the challenge relating to impoverishment resulting from economic developments combined with the problems in maintaining or improving the welfare society.[15]

In the commentary on the provisions of the Protocol contained in the Explanatory Report, which is an aid to the intended interpretation of the Protocol, we read the following:

> The wording of Article 1 reflects a balanced approach to possible positive obligations of the Parties under this provision. This concerns the question to what extent Article 14 obliges the Parties to take measures to prevent discrimination, even where discrimination occurs in relations between private persons (so-called indirect horizontal effects). The same question arises as regards measures to remedy instances of discrimination. While such positive obligations cannot be excluded altogether, the prime objective of Article 1 is to embody a negative obligation for the Parties: the obli-

14 According to the case-law in respect of Article 14 a State may engage in reverse discrimination without being in breach of Article 14. See *Belgian Linguistic case*, Series A no. 6, para 10 (1968). Cf. *DG and DW Lindsay v. the United Kingdom*, no. 11089/84, 49 *Decisions and Reports* (DR) 181 at pp. 190-191 (1986) (a tax advantage for married women, which fell within the ambit of the right to property, Article 1, First Protocol, had "an objective and reasonable justification in the aim of providing positive discrimination" to encourage married women back to work). On the subject of reverse discrimination see also Polyviou, op. cit., p. 348 et seq. and Jean-François Flauss, "Discrimination positive et Convention européenne des droits de l'homme", in: *Pourvoir et liberté – Études offertes à Jaques Morgeon*, Bruxelles, Bruylant, 1998, pp. 415-437.

15 Cf. Sudre, *La Protection Des Droits Sociaux Par La Cour Européenne Des Droits De L'Homme: Un Exercice de Jurisprudence Fiction?*, p. 774; see also Lord Lester, op. cit., pp. 83, 85, and Flauss, op. cit. pp. 419; 426; 436-37.

gations not to discriminate against individuals ... On the other hand ... the duty to "secure" under the first paragraph of Article 1 might entail positive obligations. For example, this question could arise if there is a clear lacuna in domestic law protection from discrimination. Regarding more specifically relations between private persons, a failure to provide protection from discrimination in such relations might be so clear-cut and grave that it might engage clearly the responsibility of the State and then Article 1 of the Protocol could come into play.

5. The Scope of the Protection

As regards the scope of protection under Article 1 of the Protocol the Explanatory Report gives the following information:

> The additional scope of protection under Article 1 concerns cases where a person is discriminated against:
> i. in the enjoyment of any right specifically granted to an individual under national law;
> ii. in the enjoyment of a right which may be inferred from a clear obligation of a public authority under national law, that is, where a public authority is under an obligation under national law to behave in a particular manner;
> iii. by a public authority in the exercise of discretionary power (for example, granting certain subsidies);
> iv. by any other act or omission by a public authority (for example, the behaviour of law enforcement officers when controlling a riot).

It is evident that the Protocol provides protection against direct and indirect discrimination[16]and prohibits both *de jure* discrimination – that is to say, unjustified distinctions established by law – and *de facto* discrimination – that is to say, equal treatment of persons and things which are (in the relevant respects) different and should therefore have been treated differently. This latter aspect of discrimination has already been dealt with by the European Court of Human Rights under Article 14 of the Convention with regard to the prohibition of discrimination in the enjoyment of the rights guaranteed by the Convention in the case of *Thlimmenos v. Greece,* (judgment of 6 April 2000). In that case the Court found that the provision of the Civil Servants Code according to

16 Harris, O' Boyle, Warbrick, op. cit., pp. 477-478.

which no person convicted of a felony could be appointed to the civil service were discriminatory in so far as no exceptions were provided to cover cases such as that of the applicant, who had only been convicted for his refusal to wear military uniform because he had considered that his religious beliefs, as a member of the Jehovah's Witnesses, prevented him from doing so. In essence, the applicant's argument amounted to saying that he was discriminated against in the exercise of his freedom of religion, as guaranteed by Article 9 of the Convention, in that he was treated like any other person convicted of a serious crime although his own conviction resulted from the very exercise of this freedom. Seen in this perspective, the Court accepted that the "set of facts" complained of by the applicant – his being treated as a person convicted of a serious crime for the purposes of an appointment to a chartered accountant's post despite the fact that the offence for which he had been convicted was prompted by his religious beliefs – "falls within the ambit of a Convention provision", namely Article 9. The Court pointed out that "unlike other convictions for serious criminal offences, a conviction for refusing on religious or philosophical grounds to wear the military uniform cannot imply any dishonesty or moral turpitude".[17] Therefore, according to the Court, the treatment of the applicant's conviction on the same footing as other criminal convictions for the purposes of the law in question was not justified and for this reason the State was responsible for violating the prohibition on discrimination. In the words of the Court:

> the right not to be discriminated against in the enjoyment of the rights guaranteed under the Convention is also violated when States without an objective and reasonable justification fail to treat differently persons whose situations are significantly different. (paragraph 44)

6. Jurisprudence in Respect of Article 14

It is reasonable to expect that the Court will continue to abide by its case-law regarding the prohibition of discrimination under Article 14 of the Convention, the provisions of which will be overlapping to a substantial extent with those of the new Protocol. Reference to the Court's consistent case-law on the notion of discrimination is made in the Explanatory Report on Protocol 12. In interpreting and applying Article 14, the Court may also be guided by the case-law of the Constitutional Courts

17 Op. cit.

of the member States and other States whose Constitutions guarantee the principle of equality or non-discrimination, such as the USA, which has a long history of applying this principle and has developed an extensive body of jurisprudence on the matter.[18]

Judgments of the Court concerning the prohibition of discrimination under Article 14 of the Convention may well be valid and applicable in relation to equivalent or similar questions arising under the new Protocol. For example, the meaning of the notion of discrimination, which is used both in Article 14 and in the new Protocol, has been the subject of consistent interpretation by the Court. According to Court's interpretation, not every distinction or difference of treatment amounts to discrimination.[19] A problem of discrimination may only arise if the applicant is seeking to compare himself to others in a comparable or analogous position or in a "relevantly similar" situation to those others.[20] Distinctions for which an objective and reasonable justification exists or which are based on some difference which bears a just and proper relation to the intended difference in treatment do not constitute discrimination, depending in each case on the objective and effects of the law or measure in issue and taking into account the principles prevailing in democratic societies.[21] There must be a legitimate aim and the means employed must be proportionate to the aim sought to be realised. A certain margin of appreciation is afforded to national authorities in assessing whether and to what extent differences in otherwise similar situations justify different treatment.

IRA Category A prisoners were found by the Court not to be in an analogous position to prisoners presenting no security risk; accordingly, their complaint alleging discriminatory treatment as regards the secu-

18 "The Constitution of the United States of America, Analysis and Interpretation", prepared by the Congressional Research Service, Library of Congress; Antieau, *Modern Constitutional Law*, 2nd Ed., p. 265 et seq.

19 Reid, op. cit., p. 260 et seq.; Harris, O' Boyle, Warbrick, op. cit., p. 470 et seq.

20 Reid, op. cit., pp. 260-261; *Marckx v. Belgium*, June 13, 1979, Series A no. 31, 2 *EHRR* 330; *Van der Mussele v. Belgium*, November 23, 1983, Series A no. 94, *EHRR* 471; *Larkos v . Cyprus*, February 18, 1999, ECHR 1999-I, 30 *EHRR* 597, para 30; *Stubbings v. the United Kingdom*, October 22, 1996, RJD 1996-IV, 23 *EHRR* 213.

21 Reid, op. cit., p. 262.

rity conditions attached to their detention was not justified.[22] On the other hand, the Court found that a judicial decision refusing a woman a disability pension purely on the basis of the assumption that women gave up work for having children was a difference in treatment based on sex and had no objective and reasonable justification.[23] Likewise, the fact that a man could not place his surname before that of his wife while the law allowed a woman to add her surname to that of her husband amounted to a difference in treatment based on sex and had no convincing justification.[24] Accordingly, the Court rejected the Swiss Government's arguments that family unity required a single joint surname, and found that no genuine tradition was at stake. The Court also found in the case of *Canea Catholic Church v. Greece*[25] that there was no objective and reasonable justification for the situation whereby the applicant church could not take legal proceedings to protect its property rights since it had no legal personality, whereas the Orthodox Church and the Jewish Community could do so without complying with any formalities or procedural requirements.

22 19085/91 (dec.), December 9, 1992.

23 *Schuler-Zgraggen v. Switzerland*, June 24, 1993, Series A no. 263, 16 *EHRR* 405; In view of this case and the principle of non-discrimination as developed by the case-law of the Court it is difficult to follow the approach of the Court in the *Stec and Others v. the United Kingdom* case, (12/04/2006) where the Court found that there had been no violation of Article 14 taken in conjunction with Article 1 of Protocol No. 1 as regards the different treatment between men and women concerning State pensionable age which was at the root of a scheme for the payment of a disability benefit. In my dissenting opinion I pointed out that the reasoning of the majority that a reform was planned to take place and that the far-reaching and serious implication for the economy in general in consequence of an immediate equal treatment claimed by the applicants were matters falling within the State's margin of appreciation did not justify the finding for a difference of treatment which was clearly lacking reasonable and objective justification.

24 *Burghartz v. Switzerland*, February 22 1994, Series A no. 280.

25 December 16 1997, *Reports of Judgments and Decisions*, 1997-VIII 60.

7. Discrimination and Degrading Treatment

In the *East African Asians* case[26] the European Commission of Human Rights held that discrimination based on race constituted special form of affront to human dignity. In aggravating circumstances, it could constitute degrading treatment. This was found in respect of the exclusion from the United Kingdom of Asians from East Africa who were British citizens of varying categories, but who had nowhere else to go since their residence was rendered difficult or illegal in their African state of origin and who were at risk of being "shuttlecocked" from one place to another. The position that a complaint alleging discriminatory treatment could give rise to a separate issue of degrading treatment was also accepted by the Court. In the inter-state case of *Cyprus v. Turkey* (judgment of 10 May 2001) the Court found that the Greek Cypriots living in an area of the Turkish-occupied part of Cyprus had been subjected to discrimination amounting to degrading treatment. In that connection, the Court stated that:

> the interferences at issue were directed at the Karpas Greek-Cypriot community for the very reason that they belonged to this class of persons. The treatment to which they were subjected during the period under consideration can only be explained in terms of the features which distinguish them from the Turkish-Cypriot population, namely their ethnic origin, race and religion ... The conditions under which that population is condemned to live are debasing and violate the very notion of respect for the human dignity of its members.

It should be noted that the grounds of prohibited discrimination set out in the new Protocol, namely sex, race, colour, religion etc, are identical to those set out in the existing provisions against discrimination under Article 14 of the Convention. It was decided not to include explicitly certain additional non-discrimination grounds (e.g. disability, sexual orientation and age). According to paragraph 20 of the Explanatory Report this solution was preferred "not because of a lack of awareness that such grounds have become particularly important in today's societies as compared to the time of drafting of Article 14 of the Convention, but because such an inclusion was considered unnecessary from a legal point of view since the list of non-discrimination grounds is not exhaustive,

26 December 14, 1973, DR 5.

and because inclusion of any particular additional ground might give rise to unwarranted *a contrario* interpretations as regards discrimination based on grounds not so included. It is recalled that the European Court of Human Rights has already applied Article 14 in relation to discrimination grounds not explicitly mentioned in that provision".[27]

8. Positive Obligations

Reverting to the scope of protection under the new Protocol, attention should be drawn to the fact that the general prohibition clause prohibiting discrimination specifically refers to the "enjoyment of any right set forth by law" and to discrimination "by any public authority". According to the Explanatory Report, this wording supports the view that any positive obligation in the area of relations between private persons would concern, at the most, relations in the public sphere normally regulated by law, for which the State has a certain responsibility (for example, arbitrary denial of access to work, access to restaurants, or to services which private persons may make available to the public). Further on, the Report states that "it is understood that purely private matters would not be affected". According to the Report "regulation of such matters would also be likely to interfere with the individual's right to respect for his private and family life, his home and his correspondence, as guaranteed by Article 8 of the Convention".

In my view it is not clear what the report means by "private matters". In any case, the term "law" includes international law. Therefore, rights which derive their existence from international law (including, in this respect, the Convention), such as the right not to be discriminated against, may be entitled to protection through appropriate restrictions of other individual rights in such a way that a balance is maintained between conflicting situations. On the basis of this approach, I believe that it is legitimate to regulate individual rights, such as the right to respect for one's private life, by imposing restrictions on their enforcement with a view to prohibiting discrimination in the activities of private persons. In this connection, it may be argued that a law prohibiting individuals from expressing attitudes in their relations with other individuals which amount, for example, to substantial racial or other discrimination may be justified under the new Protocol. An instance of such a law

27 See e.g. *Salgueiro de Silva Mouta v. Portugal*, December 21, 1999, ECHR 1999 (homosexuality).

is the English legislation against racial discrimination (Race Relations Act 1976). One possible example of a positive obligation is to impose and enforce a duty on private individuals not to discriminate between parties in respect of broadcasting facilities by private stations.[28]

9. By any Public Authority on any Ground

The second paragraph of Article I of the new Protocol, which provides that "no one shall be discriminated against by any public authority on any ground ..." is of particular legal interest. Firstly, in so far as it extends the scope of protection beyond the exercise of strictly legal rights, it amounts to a novel formula of legal protection in comparison to those found in other important international or constitutional instruments (e.g. Article 26 of the UN Covenant on Civil and Political Rights and 14th Amendment to the American Constitution). Secondly and more importantly it commands respect of the principle of non-discrimination in connection with any act, omission, conduct or behaviour, regardless of whether it relates to a right enshrined in law, and that, I believe, is a great improvement on the principle of non-discrimination. This interpretation is strengthened by the wording of the second paragraph and by the Explanatory Report. As has already been pointed out, the Report gives the following explanation as to the scope of the protection provided by Article 1 of the new Protocol which explanation, in my opinion, relates in particular to the paragraph under consideration:

> ... the additional scope of protection under Article 1 concerns cases where a person is discriminated against: ... iv ... by any other act or omission by a public authority (for example, the behaviour of law enforcement officers when controlling a riot).

10. Selective Justice

One is encouraged to believe that this extended protection of a kind of *de facto* discrimination may prevent what I would call "selective justice", expressed in various ways such as selective and arbitrary police reporting and investigation, prosecution of offenders in respect of the same offence, and generally selective enforcement or application of laws in a discriminatory manner. The following may be given as examples of this

28 See Harris, O' Boyle, Warbrick, op. cit., p. 485, no. 18.

unfair conduct: hundreds of cars exceeding the speed limit may be seen by the law-enforcement officers but they may choose to report arbitrarily only one or two cases. Similar conduct may be exhibited in respect of illegal parking, illegal constructions, illegal trading, non-compliance with town-planning rules, etc. In such situations, the enforcement of the prohibition on non-discrimination is confronted with the application of a principle according to which there can be no right to equal treatment in respect of illegality. This principle may be supported by valid arguments when it is invoked against persons who claim exemption from the enforcement of the law because other persons in the same position were given that benefit. The soundness of the principle is, however, shaken when it is resorted to not in respect of such claims but with regard to complaints by individuals that the law has not been applied in cases other than their own accompanied by demands for equal enforcement of the law. In such cases it is not a question of a demand for equal illegality but of a demand for equal application of the law. It may be argued that the authorities have a duty to apply the law equally to all similar cases and that any *de facto* omission to do so through the adoption of double standards should bring the case within the reach of the prohibition clause embodied in Article 1 of the new Protocol, which should provide a corresponding remedy to those affected by such conduct. This may entail a duty to take positive measures in order to eliminate the discriminatory effects of the failure to enforce the law in respect of all similar cases. Failure to take such measures should, in the absence of a satisfactory explanation, amount to a breach of Protocol No. 12. The other possible solution would simply be a finding by the Court that there has been a violation of the prohibition of discrimination, and an award of compensation.

In *Renate Saszmann v. Austria* the applicant complained about discrimination prohibited by Article 14 of the Convention in that only she was convicted by the Austrian courts while criminal proceedings against the persons who signed the leaflet in respect of which she was herself prosecuted, were discontinued. The Commission examined the complaint under Article 10 in conjunction with Article 14 of the Convention. The Commission found that the applicant was not placed in an analogous situation as others against whom criminal proceedings have been discontinued because the proceedings did not concern the same factual circumstances and dismissed the application. However, the Commission also took into account that charges against those who signed the leaflet in question were still pending.

In a case before the UN Human Rights Committee referred to by Morawa[29] the complaint was that the applicant who was a demonstrator who, after violent disturbances during a gathering, was convicted for acts of violence by throwing stones, considered himself to be treated in a discriminatory fashion "because no police officers were prosecuted after the disturbances, although independent reports had established that the police had used unreasonable violence". The Committee dismissed the complaint on the ground that "the prosecution of one person and the failure to prosecute another as such does not raise an issue of equality before the law, since each case has to be judged on its own merits". Morawa criticises this decision as not being correct. I agree with his statement that "while of course the failure to prosecute others will not *per se* serve as a cause for having a case against someone thrown out, a practice of non-prosecution may indeed amount to discrimination".

The selective discriminatory enforcement of laws through such practices as selective prosecution has been the subject of considerable judicial examination by the United States Supreme Court in connection with the application of the constitutional provision for equal protection by the law. The result has been the development of a significant body of case-law accepting, under certain conditions, that selectivity in law enforcement amounts to the denial of equal protection by the law. As long ago as 1886 the US Supreme Court went so far as to invalidate an ordinance that prohibited the operation of laundries in wooden buildings because it was applied against Chinese nationals but not against other laundry owners. The authorities had denied the applications of 200 Chinese subjects for permits to operate shops in wooden buildings but granted the applications of 80 individuals who were not Chinese subjects to operate laundries in wooden buildings under similar conditions. The Court found that the law in question was not unconstitutional on its face and was not discriminatory in tendency, but was made so by the manner of its administration.[30]

According to the American case-law,[31] for the selective enforcement of a law to be found to be incompatible with the principle of equality there must be evidence of conscious discriminatory intention and effect. To establish a discriminatory effect, the claimant must show that similarly

29 Op. cit., pp. 166-167; *Hoelen v. the Netherlands* (03/11/1999).

30 *Yick Wo v. Hopkins*, 118 U.S. at 356, 30 L. Ed. 220.

31 See, *inter alia*: *United States Petitioner v. Christopher Lee Armstrong et al.* 134 L.Ed. 2d 687 1996.

situated individuals did not receive the treatment complained of. A selective prosecution is not a defence on the merits of the criminal charge itself, but an independent assertion that the prosecution has brought the charge for reasons forbidden by the Constitution. It is recognised that there is broad discretion in the enforcement of criminal law, but the prosecutor's discretion is subject to constitutional constraints, one of them being imposed by the equal-protection principle – namely that the decision whether to prosecute may not be based on unjustified standards or arbitrary classifications.

The Supreme Court of Cyprus has through a constant case-law applied the principle that equality of treatment entails the obligation to prosecute and punish all offenders for the same crime without any exception. However, the non-prosecution of any of these offenders does not mean that those prosecuted escape liability. In other words the non-compliance with the principle of equal treatment of the offenders in respect of one or more of them does not justify the discharge of the rest. The courts still have a duty to punish those prosecuted for their crime. However the non-prosecution or the decision to discontinue the prosecution of any of those responsible for the same offence is a factor for mitigating the sentence of those brought before the court so as to reduce the imbalance resulting from the unequal treatment of the offenders and consequently to lessen the feeling of injustice which is inevitably caused by such treatment. So long as the courts cannot control the decision not to prosecute offenders for any crime the omission to prosecute any of them must be taken into consideration by the courts in imposing sentence on those prosecuted.[32]

11. Concluding Remarks

The European Court on Human Rights has not had the opportunity to deal with many aspects of the principle of equality or non-discrimination in view of its restricted competence to deal with the subject under Article 14 of the Convention. The independent general prohibition of discrimination under the new Protocol will provide an opportunity for

32 See, *inter alia*, *Georghiou and other v. Republic* (1986) 2 C .L.R. 109; *Dimitriou v. Republic*, criminal appeal no. 6493, 6/4/99; *Attorney General of the Republic v. Loizou*, criminal appeals nos 6789-6798, 4/7/2000; *Chrysantos Antoniou Cattou and another v. The Police*, criminal appeals nos 5460, 5461, 22/10/1991.

the Court to develop its case-law and, to extend the relevant protection to a plethora of situations. In carrying out its task, the Court will be helped by the broad terms of the new Protocol.

Three caveats must be entered here.

Firstly, the Court can only condemn a discriminatory act or omission and award compensation. It cannot remedy the resulting situation through the adoption of any measures or the introduction of a new regime in the place of the one that was found to be incompatible with Protocol No. 12. The burden of providing such a remedy rests with the State concerned, acting in this respect under the supervision of the Committee of Ministers. To fulfil their obligations in this field the States may be required to be more active than some may possibly find politically acceptable.

Secondly, the judges should bear in mind that the concept of non-discrimination is an evolving one that should be left flexible enough to adapt to changing social needs. Specific conceptions of equality change from one generation to the next. Many classifications have been held in the past to be acceptable but are no longer so. An illustration concerns women in the armed forces. In 1989 the Human Rights Tribunal in Ottawa held that it would constitute sex discrimination to bar them from positions involving combat.[33] It would not have been so some years before that decision. The judicial approach should not, therefore, aim at codifying in a rigid manner any particular set of ethical opinions, and the personal views of judges should not be translated into constitutional limitations. Too much formalism amounts to an urge to limit progress and to bind future courts to current values.

Thirdly, the efforts to find a solution to the already quite serious problem of the Court's workload should be accelerated. Over 70,000 cases are now pending before the Court. Evidently, as a consequence of Protocol No. 12 it is expected that the Court will be flooded with applications. Therefore, if we want the protection of human rights under the Convention to be meaningful, we should find a way to deal with complaints expeditiously. My proposal has always been to amend the Convention so as to give the Court power to deal only with cases that present substantial problems in terms of human rights. One could then argue that such a method of judicial examination would accord with the principle of equality: the distinction between the cases examined

33 *Isabelle Gauthier and others v. Canadian Armed Forces*, decision of 20/2/1989

by the Court and those that were not so examined would be justified by the difference between the two categories, based on the nature and severity of the relevant applications. Unfortunately this approach has not been adopted until now by those whose task has been the study of the workload problem of the Court. The argument that if the proposal in question is rejected the Court system is bound to collapse in a few years' time has not been taken seriously.[34]

34 See Interim Report of the Group of Wise Persons to the Committee of Ministers CM (2006) 88, para. 33.

Chapter 5 Determining the Extra-territorial Effect of the European Convention: Facts, Jurisprudence and the *Banković* Case

1. The *Banković* Case

The case of *Banković v. Belgium and 16 other countries*,[1] concerned the question of whether the bombing by States Parties to the European Convention on Human Rights ("ECHR") of a territory which was not party to the Convention entailed responsibility under the Convention. The facts of the case were simple:

On January 30, 1999, and following a decision of its North Atlantic Council ("NAC"), the North Atlantic Treaty Organisation ("NATO") announced air strikes on the territory of the Federal Republic of Yugoslavia ("FRY") in the case of non-compliance with the demands of the international community. Negotiations consequently took place between the parties to the conflict from February 6-23, 1999 and from March 15-18, 1999. The resulting proposed peace agreement was signed by the Kosovar Albanian delegation, but not by the Serbian delegation.

Considering that all efforts to achieve a negotiated, political solution to the Kosovo crisis had failed, the NAC decided on, and on March 23, 1999 the Secretary General of NATO announced, the beginning of air strikes (Operation Allied Force) against the FRY. The air strikes lasted from March 24 to June 8, 1999.

On April 23, 1999, just after 2.00 am approximately, one of the RTS buildings at Takovska Street was hit by a missile launched from a NATO forces' aircraft. Two of the four floors of the building collapsed and the master control room was destroyed. Sixteen people were killed and another sixteen were seriously injured in the bombing of the RTS building. Five relatives of the deceased and a survivor of the bombing brought a complaint before the Strasbourg Court against the NATO Member States, in so far as they were bound by the ECHR. The applicants argued that the television station had not been a legitimate target; they alleged

1 (2001) 11 B.H.R.C. 435, (App. no.52207/99), decision of December 12, 2001.

breaches of notably Article 2 (the right to life) and Article 10; (the freedom to impart information).

The key question in that case was whether the victims of these bombings fell within the "jurisdiction" of the respondent States. The Court's answer was negative. Despite the fact that NATO subjected the victims to their bombing operations and caused their deaths, the Court found that the victims were within the jurisdiction of Serbia and not within the jurisdiction of the NATO countries. The decision of the Court was strongly criticised by a number of jurists.[2] Professor Jean-Francois Flauss believes that the Court, which was already suffering from a heavy

---

2 See, *inter alia*, R. Lawson, "Life after Bankovic: on the Extraterritorial Application of the European Convention on Human Rights" in F. Coomans and M. Kamminga, eds, *Extraterritorial Application of Human Rights Treaties* (Intersentia, 2004), pp. 83 et seq.; M. Scheinin, "Extraterritorial Effect of the International Covenant on Civil and Political Rights", ibid., pp. 73 et seq.; M. Gondek, "Extraterritorial Application of the European Convention on Human Rights: Territorial Focus in the Age of Globalization?" (2005) 52 *Netherlands International Law Review* 349; G. Cohen-Jonathan, "La territorialisation de la juridiction de la Cour européenne de droits de l'homme" (2002) 52 *Revue trimestrielle des droits de l'homme* 1070; N. Riou, "Commentaire de l'arrêt Bankovic" (2002) 7 *L'Europe des Libertés* 17; Pacifico, (fn. 25), pp. 78 et seq.; J.-F. Flauss, "Actualité de la Convention européenne des droits de l'homme" [2002] AJDA 500; A. Laursen, "NATO, the War over Kosovo, and the ICTY Investigation" (2002) 17 *American University International Law Review* 765, pp. 799 et seq. See also the following comments: T.L.W Scheirs, "European Court of Human Rights Declares Application against NATO Members States Inadmissible" (2002) 18 *International Enforcement Law Reporter* 154; C.M. Cerna, "Extraterritorial Application of the Human Rights Instruments of the Inter-American System" in Coomans and Kamminga, ibid., p. 141 at pp. 157-159; T. van Boven, "Case note on Bankovic" (2003) 4 *Militair Rechtelijk Tijdschrift* 151-158; S. Karagiannis, "Le Territoire d'Application de la Convention Européenne des Droits de l'Homme Vaetera et Nova" (2005) 61 *Révue Triméstrielle des Droits de l'Homme* 33; K. Altiparmak, "Bankovic: An obstacle to the application of the European Convention on Human Rights in Iraq?" (2004) 9 *Journal of Conflict & Security Law* 213; A. Orakhelashvili, "Restrictive Interpretation of Human Rights Treaties in the Recent Jurisprudence of the European Court of Human Rights" (2003) 14 E.J.I.L. 529; F. Benoit-Rohmer, "Pour la construction d'un espace juridique européen de protection des droits de l'homme" (2004) 15 *Revue d'actualite juridique* 000; Weckel, "Chronique de Jurisprudence Internationale" (2002) 106 *Revue Générale de Droit International Public* 437; Alexandra Rüth and Mirja Trilsch, "In-

case-load, did not want to get involved in "remote conflicts that are politically sensitive",[3] and he adds that "the fact remains that the solution given has created a feeling of frustration and even lack of understanding on the part of the victims".[4] This statement has been adopted by Professor Cohen-Jonathan.[5] Professor Lawson states that:

> a possible explanation for the outcome may be found in a speech of the Court's President, Mr Wildhaber, on the occasion of the opening of the judicial year 2002 of the European Court of Human Rights where he points out the effects of terrorism after the events of 11 September and states that:
>
> > 'it must therefore be possible for democratic States governed by the Rule of Law to protect themselves effectively against terrorism; human rights law must be able to accommodate this need. The European Convention should not be applied in such a way as to prevent States from taking reasonable and proportionate actions to defend democracy and the Rule of Law ... We do have to realise that the Convention was never intended to cure all the planet's ills and indeed cannot effectively do so.'[6]

2. Criticism of the Decision

The grounds given by the Court have been the object of criticism by those who disagreed with the decision. I share this criticism. I also expressed my disagreement with the decision in a concurring opinion in the *Assanidze v. Georgia* case[7] and in a partly dissenting opinion in the *Ilaşcu v. Moldova and Russia* case.[8] The full text of these opinions is set out below. But I will first explain why I think that the grounds relied on by the Court make it an example of bad law influenced by the considerations relating to the factual situation.

---

ternational decisions" (2003) 97 *American Journal of International Law* 168, p. 172.

3 Flauss, ibid., no. 61, 1082.

4 Ibid., p. 501.

5 Cohen-Jonathan, fn. 2 above, p. 1082.

6 Lawson, fn. 2 above.

7 (2004) 39 E.H.R.R. 32.

8 (2005) 40 E.H.R.R. 46.

3. The Rules of Interpretation – Object and Purpose

The Court relied first on the rules of interpretation of the Vienna Convention on the Law of Treaties 1969 and in particular Art. 31 according to which "a treaty shall be interpreted in good faith in accordance with the ordinary meaning to be given to the terms of the treaty in their context and in the light of its object and purpose" including "any subsequent practice in the application of a treaty which establishes the agreement of the parties regarding its interpretation". It also took into account "any relevant rules of international law ... mindful of the Convention's special character as a human rights treaty".[9] In applying these provisions the Court found that as regards the "ordinary meaning" of the words "within their jurisdiction",[10] the Court was satisfied that, from the standpoint of public international law, the jurisdictional competence of the State is primarily territorial, without excluding extraterritorial jurisdiction in exceptional cases requiring special justification in the particular circumstances of each case.

The "ordinary meaning" of the word "jurisdiction" is "power or authority in general".[11] That meaning in the context of a human rights treaty is not incompatible with public international law or the object and purposes of the Convention. Pausing here for a moment, I must recall the background which led to the Convention and which explains its object and purposes. The Convention was "a reaction to the serious human rights violations that Europe had witnessed during the Second World War".[12] These violations were not confined within the territory of one particular country, but they covered practically all countries of Europe. Therefore, one can wonder whether the object and purpose of the Convention was to confine the obligations provided therein within the limits of each and every territory of the High Contracting Parties and not beyond that. On the contrary I believe that the logical conclusion is that the Convention intended to impose a code of conduct on the High Contracting Parties in respect of all their activities within or outside their territories in order to prevent repetition of the widespread violations such as those caused by the Nazi regime in and outside Germany.

---

9 (2001) 11 B.H.R.C 435 at [57].

10 Ibid., at [59].

11 *New Shorter Oxford Dictionary*; J.I. Rodale, *The Synonym Finder.*

12 D.J. Harris, M. O'Boyle and C. Warbrick, *Law of the European Convention on Human Rights* (Butterworths, 1995), p. 2.

In this respect, the following words of Churchill when talking about the German question at the 1948 Hague Congress of Europe which prepared the ground for the Convention, in other words the "preparatory work", or the "circumstances of the conclusion of the Treaty",[13] are particularly pertinent:

> To revive the ancient fame of the German race *without exposing their neighbours and others to a rebuilding or reassertion of their military power.*[14] (emphasis added).

In interpreting terms in the Convention "in their context and in the light of its objects and purpose", the provisions in its Preamble should also be taken into account, one of them being the reaffirmation of the High Contracting Parties of their profound belief

> in those fundamental freedoms which are the foundation of justice and peace in the world and are best maintained on the one hand by an effective political democracy and on the other by a common understanding and observance of the human rights upon which they depend.

Extra-territorial conduct of the States Parties contrary to the observance of human rights enshrined in the Convention is hardly compatible with such reaffirmation.[15]

On the other hand it is absolutely normal that a State's "jurisdiction" is generally and primarily exercised within the territory of a State. In that sense "jurisdiction" is "primarily territorial". But that does not mean that

13 Vienna Convention on the Law of Treaties, Art. 32.

14 *Europe Unites* (Hollis & Carter, 1949), p. 16.

15 Mr Rozakis, one of the judges who took part in the *Banković* decision, admits in his article "How Far Can We Go? Recent Developments of Strasbourg Case-Law on the Concept of Jurisdiction", in *El Derecho Internacional: Normas, Hecbos y Valores. Liber Amicorum Jose Antonio Pastor Ridruejo* (2005), p. 219 at p. 212, that the concept of "jurisdiction" as interpreted and applied by the Commission in the *Cyprus v. Turkey* cases, i.e. "actual authority and responsibility [of the High Contracting Parties] whether that authority is exercised within their territory or abroad *relied mainly on the Convention's purpose as a human rights treaty* and produced a test of extraterritorial jurisdiction, which has had lasting effects on the Strasbourg case-law" (emphasis added).

it cannot also be exercised in one form or another outside a State's territory. What is equally problematic, vague and legally unworkable is the statement of the Court that extra-territorial jurisdiction is exceptional, requiring special justification in the particular circumstances of each case. What are the criteria of that "special justification" and in "what circumstances" such jurisdiction may be acceptable cannot be envisaged even through the method of speculation, and such an approach is incompatible with any legal rule or method. There can be only one acceptable meaning of the term "jurisdiction". There cannot be several meanings of the same term adjustable in the circumstances of exceptional cases on the basis of "special justifications".

4. Subsequent Practice

As regards subsequent "State practice in the application of the Convention" as an indication of the meaning of the term "jurisdiction", I fail to follow the argument of the Court that:

> Although there have been a number of military missions involving Contracting States acting extra-territorially since their ratification of the Convention (*inter alia*, in the Gulf, in Bosnia and Herzegovina and in the FRY), no State has indicated a belief that its extra-territorial actions involved an exercise of jurisdiction within the meaning of Article 1 of the Convention by making a derogation pursuant to Article 15 of the Convention.[16]

In my view a practice in respect of a multilateral treaty means a constant pattern of acts accepted without any exception by all concerned parties. I do not think that such a practice has ever existed as regards the subject under consideration. An acceptance by other parties entails an express or implied acquiescence which in its turn presupposes the raising of a relevant issue. By way of support I would draw attention to the finding by the Court in the case of *Cyprus v. Turkey* that Turkey had jurisdiction outside its territory, i.e. in the occupied part of Cyprus, and to the objections of several countries to the territorial reservations asserted by Turkey in respect of her acceptance of the competence of the European Commission of Human Rights to receive individual petitions and the compulsory jurisdiction of the Court. That happened years before the *Banković* case. In any event, no practice can frustrate the meaning

16 (2001) 11 B.H.R.C. 435 at [62].

of any term in a legal instrument as expressed by the wording and the object and purpose of the relevant text.

Moreover there are additional flaws in the reasoning of the Court set out below:

> ... no State has indicated a belief that its extra-territorial actions involved an exercise of jurisdiction within the meaning of Article 1 of the Convention by making a derogation pursuant to Article 15 of the Convention ... and the Court does not find any basis upon which to accept the applicants' suggestion that Article 15 covers all 'war' and 'public emergency' situations generally, whether obtaining inside or outside the territory of the Contracting State. Indeed, Article 15 itself is to be read subject to the 'jurisdiction' limitation enumerated in Article I of the Convention.[17]

This reasoning is defective in two respects:

(1) The lack of any derogation does not mean that no derogation was required and therefore it does not support in any way the view that the relevant extraterritorial military operations or activities did not as a matter of practice involve an exercise of jurisdiction within the meaning of Article 1 ECHR. The State engaging in military operations outside its territory may for various reasons (for example, disputing the exercise of jurisdiction to escape any obligations under the Convention, misconception of the legal situation, political reasons or expedience) avoid making a derogation under Article 15 ECHR even where it might be expected that the competent party *ratione loci* should make such a derogation in order to benefit from the provisions of that article. This is illustrated by the position taken by Turkey as regards the northern part of Cyprus invaded and occupied by her military forces. The Commission in its Report found as follows:

> In its decision on the admissibility of the present applications, the Commission found that the Turkish armed forces in Cyprus brought any other persons or property there 'within the jurisdiction' of Turkey, in the sense of Article 1 of the Convention, 'to the extent that they exercise control over such persons or property'. It follows that, to the same extent, Turkey was the High Contracting Party competent *ratione loci* for any measures of

17 Ibid.

> derogation under Article 15 of the Convention affecting persons or property in the north of Cyprus. The Commission notes that no communication was made by Turkey, under Article 15 of the Convention, with regard to the persons or property under her jurisdiction in the north of Cyprus. The Commission further notes that, at the admissibility stage, the respondent Government submitted that they had no jurisdiction over that area ...[18]

(2) The statement that "Article 15 itself is to be read subject to the 'jurisdiction' limitation enumerated in Article 1 of the Convention" is begging the question which concerns the meaning of the term "jurisdiction" itself. In other words how can the concept of the term "war" be determined through the use of the word "jurisdiction" whose definition and limits are themselves in issue? The meaning of the general term "war" is evident; and any war (which is not expressly limited to civil war) cannot through any imaginative interpretation be applied only to a war within a particular territory. A war by its very nature is capable of spreading to neighbouring or other territories in addition from the one in which it started; and this applies both to wars against or in defence of the sovereignty of any State. Therefore the evident concept of "war" may more usefully be employed as an aid for interpreting the term "jurisdiction" whose meaning was in issue rather than the other way around.

5. *Travaux Préparatoires*

The Court also invoked the *travaux préparatoires* of the Convention in order to confirm the "territorial notion of jurisdiction". In this respect the Court stated:

> ... the Expert Intergovernmental Committee replaced the words 'all persons residing within their territories' with a reference to persons 'within their jurisdiction' with a view to expanding the Convention's application to others who may not reside, in a legal sense, but who are, nevertheless, on the territory of the Contracting States.[19]

Here I cannot but endorse and repeat Lawson's pertinent observation:

18 Paras. 525, 526.

19 (2001) 11 B.H.R.C. 435 at (63].

> Interestingly, the governmental experts did not decide to limit the Convention's reach to 'all persons in the territory' which would have been an obvious choice. Instead they preferred the more flexible notion 'within the jurisdiction'.[20]

Therefore, the reference to the *travaux préparatoires* does not appear to be of any help in confirming the restrictive interpretation supported by the Court. It would tend to confirm instead that a territorial limitation of the obligations of the High Contracting Parties under the Convention was to be excluded. Indeed such limitation would have led to the absurd result of a different standard of behaviour being permissible depending on which soil States conducted their activities.

But the Court invokes another argument:

> Had the drafters of the Convention wished to ensure jurisdiction as extensive as that advocated by the applicants, they could have adopted a text the same as or similar to the contemporaneous Articles 1 of the four Geneva Conventions of 1949.[21]
>
> Article 1 of each of these Conventions ('the Geneva Conventions 1949') requires the Contracting Parties to undertake 'to respect and to ensure respect for the present Convention in all circumstances'.[22]

The argument is devoid of substance because:

- it is made on the assumption that the term "within the jurisdiction" has the restricted meaning given by the Court, in spite of its jurisprudence according to which cases outside the territorial limit of a State do fall within the jurisdiction of the State;
- the argument may be reversed: had the drafters of the Convention wished to ensure jurisdiction as restricted as that supported by the Court they could have adopted the words mentioned above, i.e. "all persons residing within their territories" or introduce a clear ter-

20 Lawson, fn. 2 above, p. 88.

21 (2001) 11 B.H.R.C. 435 at [75].

22 Ibid., at [25].

ritorial limitation to the application of the Convention, but this was not done;[23]

- as rightly observed by Sedley L.J., "[j]urisdiction need equate only with state agency: it does not have to operate 'in all circumstances' as the 1949 Geneva Conventions do".[24]

6. The European Legal Space

In its decision the Court refers to:

> the special character of the Convention as a constitutional instrument of *European* public order for the protection of individual human beings and its role, as set out in Article 19 of the Convention, is to ensure the observance of the engagements undertaken by the Contracting Parties (the above-cited *Loizidou* judgment (preliminary objections), at § 93). It is therefore difficult to contend that a failure to accept the extra-territorial jurisdiction of the respondent States would fall foul of the Convention's *ordre public* objective, which itself underlines the essentially regional vocation of the Convention system, or of Article 19 of the Convention which does not shed any particular light on the territorial ambit of that system ... In short, the Convention is a multi-lateral treaty operating, subject to Article 56 of the Convention, in an essentially regional context and notably in the legal space (*espace juridique*) of the Contracting States. The FRY clearly does not fall within this legal space. The Convention was not designed to be applied throughout the world, even in respect of the conduct of Contracting States.[25]

It is correct that the Convention has an essentially regional character in the sense that it binds only certain countries in Europe and provides a constitutional instrument for those countries. However, that does not mean that the responsibilities undertaken under such an instrument by those countries are confined only to their territories. The extra-territorial "exceptions" accepted by the Court itself prove the contrary. The same is true about the notion of legal space (*espace juridique*) invoked

23 C. Ovey and R. White, *Jacobs and White: The European Convention on Human Rights* (4th ed, Oxford University Press, 2006), p. 32.

24 R. (*on the application of Al-Skeini*) *v. a Secretary of State for Defence* [2005] EWCA Civ 1609; [2006] H.R.L.R. 7 at [201].

25 (2001) 11 B.H.R.C. 435 at [80].

by the Court in the same paragraph in its effort to limit the application of the Convention and to exclude such application in respect of FRY. In this respect the Court makes a plausible statement which at first sight appears reasonable and convincing: "The Convention was not designed to be applied throughout the world, even in respect of the conduct of Contracting States". However, the statement falls apart if one takes into account the unlimited latitude given to the High Contracting Parties under Art.56 to extend its application "to all or any of the territories for whose international relations it is responsible". By virtue of this provision the Convention was extended to many territories all over the world.

In 1953 the United Kingdom extended the Convention to 45 territories which included Aden Colony, Bahamas, Barbados, Basutoland, Bermuda, British Guiana, British Solomon Islands, Falkland Islands, Fiji, Gambia, Ellice Islands, Gold Coasts, Jamaica, Kenya, Federation of Malaya, Mauritius, Nigeria, Northern Rhodesia, Northern Borneo, St Helena, Seychelles, Sierra Leone, Singapore, Tanganyika, Trinidad, Zanzibar and Tonga. Another group of territories declared by Holland included Surinam and the Dutch Antilles.

Looking at the 1953 world map and locating these territories, it is easy to reach the conclusion that the Convention was in fact, according to its drafters, capable of being applied throughout the world since the High Contracting Parties could make use of the express provision allowing unrestricted extension of the Convention to non-metropolitan territories – many of them far distant from Europe – as a result of that extension they belonged automatically to the "*espace juridique*" of the Convention. Equally important in rejecting the validity of the above-mentioned statement of the Court, is the fact that the Convention was open for signature by any members of the Council of Europe, i.e. any European country so long as it accepts the principles of the rule of law and of the enjoyment by all persons within its jurisdiction of human rights and fundamental freedoms. By virtue of these provisions the number of High Contracting Parties to the Convention has now reached 46, including the geographically huge State of Russia. In addition, all those territories which were or could potentially come under the control of the High Contracting Parties through occupation or otherwise were, by virtue of the judgment of the Court in the case of *Cyprus v. Turkey* and the "exceptional cases" of extraterritorial jurisdiction,[26] entitled to the Convention rights. This category could, depending on the facts, include

26 Ibid., at [71].

also FRY. Therefore the practical difficulties or the unrealistic interpretation implicitly relied upon in the judgment in support of the contention that the Convention was not designed to be applied throughout the world is untenable.

7. "Within Their Jurisdiction": Within Their Authority

The view that the expression "within their jurisdiction" means that the High Contracting Parties are responsible for breaches of the Convention wherever they are committed and that this is in line with the object of the Convention is a valid legal interpretation.[27] Whether there is a breach of the Convention should not depend on whether the breach has taken place on the territory of the Contracting Party or in any part of any other territory over which the High Contracting Party concerned has an "overall or effective control", even though in these situations the breach is more easily attributable to such Party. What is decisive in finding whether a High Contracting Party has violated the Convention in respect of any particular person or persons is the question whether such Party has exercised *de facto* or *de jure* actual authority, i.e. the power to impose its will, over the alleged victim.

The correct approach is that the Convention laid down rules of conduct for the States Parties whenever and wherever they exercise effective authority over individuals. Any other interpretation would be contrary to the very object of the Convention and lead to ludicrous results: a breach of the Convention if State agents kill a person inside State borders but no breach if the victim is killed a few metres outside those borders in the territory of a non-High Contracting Party or, to use the admission of the respondent governments in the *Banković* case: an arrest of a person outside the territory of a State Party to the Convention is a "classic exercise of jurisdiction"; yet if a person is killed by the same State without being arrested, that is not exercise of "jurisdiction" and no question of responsibility under the Convention arises. On the basis of what logic should a State which has undertaken to secure respect of human rights to everyone within its jurisdiction apply different standards of conduct to individuals who could claim to be victims of State activity? In this respect it is useful to invoke the opinion of the Human Rights Committee ("HRC") in the *Lopez Burgos* case, according to which Art. 2(1) of the International Covenant on Civil and Political Rights (which

27 See, *inter alia*, *Jacobs and White*, fn. 23 above, p. 33.

in substance corresponds to Article 1 ECHR, though it is arguably more restrictive):

> ... does not imply that the state party concerned cannot be held accountable for violations of rights under the Covenant which its agents commit upon the territory of another State, whether with the acquiescence of the Government of that State or in opposition to it .... It would be unconscionable to so interpret the responsibility under Article 2 of the Covenant as to permit a State party to perpetrate violations of the Covenant on the territory of another state, which violations it could not perpetrate on its own territory.[28]

Interestingly the opinion of the HRC quoted above was referred to by the Court in the *Issa* case[29] which concerned complaints for killings of six Iraqi shepherds by Turkish military forces in the territory of Iraq. The case was declared inadmissible by the Court because of lack of sufficient evidence that Turkish troops actually operated in the area of the victims.

In fact the approach adopted in the *Lopez Burgos* case as regards the extra-territorial extent of the concept of "jurisdiction" has been followed in respect of other human rights treaties to such an extent as to amount to an established tendency in the interpretation of corresponding treaty provisions.[30]

Therefore, like other jurists who criticised the judgment, I would say that "the Court got it all wrong".[31] However, seeking to explain the wrongfulness of the judgment through legal analysis as I, like others, have tried to do, only leaves me with the feeling that the effort is misconceived as the judgment is not explicable in terms of a legal approach but as an effort to avoid engaging in a politically sensitive area with negative impact on contemporary methods of combating terrorism

28 ICCPR, Art. 2(1) reads: "Each State Party to the present Covenant undertakes to respect and to ensure to all individuals within its territory and subject to its jurisdiction the rights recognised in the present Covenant, without distinction of any kind, such as race, colour, sex, language, religion, political opinion, national or social origin, property, birth or other status".

29 *Issa v. Turkey* (2005) 41 E.H.R.R. 27 at [71].

30 See Gondek, fn. 2 above, pp. 378-382.

31 Lawson, fn. 2 above, p. 85.

through bombing and other military activities or, to quote again verbatim Jean-Francois Flauss " ... *on comprend fort bien que la Cour, déjà plus que surchargée, ne veuille pas s'encombre de contentieux 'lointains' et politiquement sensibles*".[32] Cohen-Jonathan tries also to explain the decision "*par les circonstances de l'espèce et le rôle éminent joué par un Etat non membre du Conseil de l'Europe*".[33]

8. A Break in a Substantial Line of Jurisprudence

Furthermore, I would argue that the *Banković* decision departs from the previous case-law regarding the concept of "jurisdiction" commencing with the decisions of the European Commission of Human Rights in the first three interstate cases of *Cyprus v. Turkey*. It is also difficult to reconcile it with the relevant jurisprudence which followed such as *Ilaşcu, Issa,*[34] and *Öcalan.*[35] In the case of *R.* (*on the application of Al-Skeini*) *v. Secretary of State for Defence*[36] before the English Court of Appeal, where the *Banković* decision was discussed and applied on the facts of the particular case before it, Counsel for the Secretary of State supported the view that this decision "is a watershed in the Court's jurisprudence". Sedley L.J., in expressing his doubts regarding the consistency and effect in the light of the *Banković* decision on the concept of "jurisdiction", rightly observed the following:

> I do not accept Mr Greenwood's submission that *Banković* is a watershed in the Court's jurisprudence. *Banković* is more accurately characterised, in my view, as a break in a substantial line of decisions, nearly all of them

32 See fns. 3 and 4 above. Gondek, fn. 2 above, p. 356 states: "The decision addressed a particularly difficult situation whereby the alleged violations of the right to life and freedom of information of the victims of the NATO attack on Serbian TV station were perpetrated during an armed conflict. Moreover, the respondent States Parties to the ECHR took decisions and acted in a framework of an operation undertaken by a military alliance ("NATO") involving also other states, not parties to the Convention (like the USA and Canada)."

33 "A Propos des Arrets Assanidze, Ilaşcu et Issa" (2005) 64 *Revue Trimestrielle des Droits de l'Homme* 767, p. 770.

34 *Issa v. Turkey* (2005) 41 E.H.R.R. 27.

35 *Öcalan v. Turkey* (2003) 37 E.H.R.R. 10.

36 [2005] EWCA Civ 1609; [2006] H.R.L.R. 7.

> relating to the Turkish occupation of northern Cyprus, which hold a member state answerable for what it does in alien territory following a *de facto* assumption of authority. They are not explained, in my opinion, by the fact that but for the occupation the citizens of northern Cyprus (unlike those of Iraq) would have enjoyed the protection of the Convention. This is no doubt the case – the Court more than once draws attention to it – but it is not the legal ground of Turkey's liability. If it were, one would expect to find it in the Court's reasoning in *Banković*, where it would have been straightforward to hold that the citizens of the FRY, unlike those of northern Cyprus, could not complain of the violation of rights which they had never had. But the *Banković* decision turned on the concept of a member state's *espace juridique*. This, the Court held, was limited to its physical territory, with only such extensions as could be exceptionally justified.[37]

Sedley L.J. does not seem particularly content with the *Banković* decision and expresses doubts as regards the effect of its reasoning and its compatibility with the other relevant jurisprudence of the Court. He has also criticised parts of the reasoning of the decision.[38] Finally he feels bound to follow the decision and states the following:

> Taking it into account, as s.2 of the Human Rights Act requires us to do, *Banković* appears for the present to constitute a road-block on the first way out of the dilemma. It is also, I accept, an obstacle to the solution I

37 Ibid., at [193].

38 See, e.g. ibid., at [75]. Sedley L.J. states *inter alia* : "It may be that the Court will sooner or later revisit this passage. The applicants' argument is not one, I would respectfully suggest, which reduces itself to an absurdity in quite the way suggested by the Grand Chamber. Its predicate is not a worldwide *espace juridique* but precisely the kind of state agency illustrated in *Issa v. Turkey* and indeed in the present case, now ex concessis so far as it concerns the British military prison in Basra. The holding that the underlying obligation contained in art. 1 of the Convention cannot be 'divided and tailored' [in the French text, *fractionnée et adaptée*] in accordance with the particular circumstances of the extra-territorial act in question may not flow inexorably from either of the propositions which follow it by way of explanation ... And there may be room for debate whether jurisdiction and breach, even if they are separate admissibility questions, are nevertheless synergistic to the extent that the nature of the breach may condition or determine whether the responsibility of the state is extra-territorially engaged."

have proposed in paragraph 198 above. It stands in striking contrast, in this regard, to the decision of the Inter-American Commission on Human Rights in *Coard v. United States* ... that extra-territorial liability for a state's breach of human rights depended simply on 'whether, under the specific circumstances, the State observed the rights of a person subject to its authority and control' – in other words, that liability is case and fact-specific.

9. My Separate or Dissenting Opinions

Assanidze v. Georgia

As I already mentioned above, I have expressed my disagreement with the *Banković* interpretation of the concept of the "jurisdiction" in Article 1 ECHR in two opinions which I quote below. The first was a concurring opinion in the *Assanidze v. Georgia* case:[39]

> While agreeing with the approach of the majority in this case I would like to say a few words about the notion of 'jurisdiction' within the meaning of Article 1 of the Convention. This issue is dealt with in paragraphs 137 and 138 of the judgment.
>
> To my mind 'jurisdiction' means actual authority, that is to say the possibility of imposing the will of the State on any person, whether exercised within the territory of the High Contracting Party or outside that territory. Therefore, a High Contracting Party is accountable under the Convention to everyone directly affected by any exercise of authority by such Party in any part of the world. Such authority may take different forms and may be legal or illegal. The usual form is governmental authority within a High Contracting Party's own territory, but it may extend to authority in the form of overall control of another territory even though that control is illegal (see *Loizidou v. Turkey* (preliminary objections), judgment of 23 March 1995, Series A no. 310), notably occupied territories (see *Cyprus v. Turkey* [GC], no. 25781/94, ECHR 2001-IV). It may also extend to authority in the form of the exercise of domination or effective influence through political, financial, military or other substantial support of a government of another State. And it may, in my opinion, take the form of any kind of military or other State action on the part of the High Contracting Party concerned in any part of the world (see, by way of contrast, *Banković and Others v.*

39 (2004) 39 E.H.R.R. 32.

Belgium and Others (dec.) [GC], no. 52207/99, ECHR 2001-XII, cited in the judgment).

The test should always be whether the person who claims to be within the 'jurisdiction' of a High Contracting Party to the Convention, in respect of a particular act, can show that the act in question was the result of the exercise of authority by the State concerned. Any other interpretation excluding responsibility of a High Contracting Party for acts resulting from the exercise of its State authority would lead to the absurd proposition that the Convention lays down obligations to respect human rights only within the territory under the lawful or unlawful physical control of such Party and that outside that context, leaving aside certain exceptional circumstances (the existence of which would be decided on a case-by-case basis), the State Party concerned may act with impunity contrary to the standards of behaviour set out in the Convention. I believe that a reasonable interpretation of the provisions of the Convention in the light of its object must lead to the conclusion that the Convention provides a code of behaviour for all High Contracting Parties whenever they act in the exercise of their State authority with consequences for individuals.[40]

10. The *Ilaşcu* Case

In the case of *Ilaşcu v. Moldova and Russia*[41] I expressed the following dissenting opinion:

I would first like to reiterate the view which I expressed in *Assanidze v. Georgia* ([GC] no. 71503/0, ECHR 2004-II) as regards the notion of 'jurisdiction' within the meaning of Article 1 of the Convention, dealt with in paragraphs 310 to 314 and 319 of the judgment in the present case ... I wish to expand on my aforesaid position by adding that a State may also be accountable under the Convention for failure to discharge its positive obligations in respect of any person if it was in a position to exercise its authority directly or even indirectly over that person or over the territory where that person is.

In the light of the above and the facts and circumstances of the case as set out in the judgment, I agree with the majority that the applicants come within the 'jurisdiction' of the Russian Federation for the purposes of Article 1 and that its responsibility is engaged with regard to the acts com-

40 Ibid., at [00].

41 (2005) 40 E.H.R.R. 46.

plained of. As rightly pointed out in the judgment, it has been proved that the 'MRT', set up in 1991-92 with the support of the Russian Federation, vested with organs of power and its own administration, remains under the effective authority, or at the very least under the decisive influence, of the Russian Federation, and in any event that it survives thanks to the military, economic, financial and political support given to it by the Russian Federation.

However I disagree with the majority that the applicants come under the 'jurisdiction' of Moldova and that it is responsible for failure to discharge its positive obligations to take sufficient effective and appropriate measures to secure the applicants' Convention rights. There is nothing to show that Moldova actually had any direct or indirect authority over the territory where the applicants were detained or over the applicants themselves. Moldova was in no way responsible for the illegal detention of the applicants or for the continuation of such detention. There is nothing to show that Moldova acquiesced in or encouraged the existence of the illegal regime which at all material times (with the support of Russia as already explained) exercised actual authority in the area where the violations occurred and where the applicants were detained.

None of the factors set out by the majority in support of their conclusion that Moldova had jurisdiction over the applicants could possibly, in my opinion, be considered as amounting to an exercise or avoidance of exercising effective authority in respect of the applicants. In this respect I also associate myself with the approach of Sir Nicolas Bratza as set out in paragraphs 15 to 26 of his partly dissenting opinion.

In any case, to conclude that there is 'jurisdiction' over certain persons for the purposes of the Convention simply because the government concerned has failed to take judicial, political, diplomatic and economic measures or any other of the measures cited by the majority, with the object of securing the Convention rights of the applicants even though actual authority over these persons on the part of the government was lacking, would be stretching the concept of 'jurisdiction' to an unrealistic and absurd extent. In other words it would, in my opinion, be a fallacy to accept that a High Contracting Party to the Convention has 'jurisdiction' over any person outside its authority simply because it does not take the political or other measures mentioned in general terms by the majority. Such a position would in my view lead, for instance, to the illogical conclusion that all High Contracting Parties to the Convention would have jurisdiction and responsibility for violations of the human rights of persons in any territory of a High Contracting Party, including their own, but outside their actual

> authority (either *de facto* or *de jure* or both depending on the territory), merely by virtue of not pressing to secure the Convention rights in that territory through action against the State which does in reality exercise such authority over these persons. I believe that the interpretation of a treaty should avoid a meaning which leads to a result which is manifestly absurd.
>
> In the *Banković and Others* decision (with which I personally disagree), the Grand Chamber of the Court found that the bombing of buildings in Belgrade resulting in the killing of sixteen civilians was an extraterritorial act outside the 'jurisdiction' of the High Contracting Parties to the Convention responsible for such bombing and for that reason the relevant complaint of the relatives of the deceased was dismissed as inadmissible. It seems to me incomprehensible and certainly very odd for a High Contracting Party to escape responsibility under the Convention on the ground that the throwing of bombs from its aeroplanes over an inhabited area in any part of the world does not bring the victims of such bombing within its 'jurisdiction' (that is to say, authority) while a failure on the part of such Party 'to take all the measures in [its] power whether political, diplomatic, economic, judicial or other measures ... to secure the rights guaranteed by the Convention to those formally [*de jure*] within its jurisdiction but in actual fact outside its effective authority ascribes jurisdiction to that State and imposes on it positive duties towards them ...[42]

I could of course also invoke one of the grounds for finding that Russia in the *Ilaşcu* case had jurisdiction over the region of Moldova claimed by the Transdniestrian regime, i.e. that this regime "remains ... at the very least under the decisive influence of the *Russian Federation*", as another position taken by the Grand Chamber of the Court which undermines the correctness of the restrictive "territorial" interpretation of the term "jurisdiction" upheld by the decision in *Banković*.

11. The Supporters of the Decision

Beside those who disagreed with the *Banković* decision there were a number of jurists who expressed their approval of the decision by adopt-

42 Ibid., at [oo].

ing its reasoning. One of them was Professor Dominic McGoldrick. In his relevant article[43] he concludes by stating, *inter alia*:

> *Banković* was clearly a political case in the sense of its significance in international politics. A decision the other way would have raised additional institutional questions about the appropriateness of the European Court of Human Rights directly or indirectly applying aspects of international humanitarian law through the medium of ECHR rights; and its exercise of the review of military actions by individual states or by an international institution (NATO) and whether a more expansive jurisdictional approach would divert the Court from its hitherto primary focus on the application of the ECHR within the territorial jurisdiction of the states parties. The *Banković* decision avoided these questions for the time being. For some it may be seen as a hard case which made bad law and has to be seen in the context of the attacks on the United States in September 2001. It is submitted that when understood in its proper legal context – as a jurisdictional question within a specific intentional human rights treaty – it is a hard case which made good law. That good law is consistent with the previous jurisprudence on the possible exceptional extraterritorial application of the ECHR in situations of 'authority and responsibility and effective control' and *Banković* should not be read as undermining that jurisprudence. Where there is some degree of extraterritorial application this should be seen as a positive addition to the ECHR regime of protection rather than as merely creating arbitrary distinctions between particular situations where there is or is not effective control.

Here the author adds the following interesting footnote:

> The argument is that if an individual who is arrested and detained is 'within the jurisdiction' because they are under the effective control of the state, but an individual who is simply shot is not 'within the jurisdiction', this creates an incentive to shoot the individuals concerned. *(sic)*

The passage speaks for itself.

---

43 D. McGoldrick, "Extraterritorial Application of the International Covenant on Civil and Political Rights" in Coomans and Kamminga, fn. 2 above, pp. 41 et seq.

Another supporter of the decision in the *Banković* case is Michael O'Boyle.[44] He has, *inter alia*, stated:

> NATO bombed the RTS because it was considered to be used for propaganda purposes. The legal questions which arose under the law of war were: (1) was the station a legitimate military objective; and if it was, were the civilian casualties disproportionate to the military advantage gained by the attack? But – assuming no issue of 'jurisdiction' arose – are these really questions which are fitting for a Court of Human Rights to address? Should the Court really be examining issues concerning what is a legitimate military objective and whether there was military advantage to be gained? The rules of international humanitarian law sit uneasily with the Court's case-law on the right to life.

The answer to that is:

- the argument seems to ignore the provisions of Article 15 ECHR according to which "[n]o derogation from Article 2, *except in respect of deaths resulting from lawful acts of war* ... shall be made under this provision" (emphasis added);
- the Commission and the Court had the opportunity in the past to deal with complaints of violations of the Convention as a result of military operations where issues such as the legality of the operation and other related issues were raised, and they managed successfully to deal with the complaints before them[45];
- it is by now an established principle that during wars human rights must be respected along with the rules of international humanitarian law. As rightly observed by Emanuela-Chiara Gillard, legal adviser of the International Committee of the Red Cross,[46] "in such situations human rights and the rules of international humanitarian law are applicable concurrently and provide important complementary protections ... [This] concurrent application ... in times

44 M. O'Boyle, "The European Convention on Human Rights and Extraterritorial Jurisdiction: A Comment on Life After *Bankoviç*" in Coomans and Kamminga, fn. 2 above, pp. 125 et seq.

45 See the inter-state cases of *Cyprus v. Turkey* and an interesting reference and application of the rules of humanitarian law in para. 313 of the Report of the Commission in the first two applications 678074/74 and 6950/75.

46 E.-C. Gillard, "International Humanitarian Law and Extraterritorial State Conduct" in Coomans and Kamminga, fn. 2 above, p. 25, at p. 35.

of armed conflict is not problematic. On the contrary it enhances protection";
- the Court is only competent to pass judgment on the conduct of a State Party to the Convention, in terms of the Convention; and is not prevented from doing that by other parallel humanitarian or other legal principles.

But both O'Boyle's and McGoldrick's arguments for the difficulties that the Court might have faced if it was accepted that there was jurisdiction over the bombed territory of FRY reinforce the view that the decision of no jurisdiction was influenced by the facts (or difficulties) of the case rather than by purely legal considerations. In the words of McGoldrick, "[t]he *Banković* decision avoided these questions for the time being". At the end of his article O'Boyle states that "*Banković* has underscored the territorial axis of the Convention system while admitting a certain extraterritorial dimension. Given current international developments there can be little doubt that the Court will be faced with further cases which request an elucidation of the Convention's extraterritorial reach ... However I suspect that the law on 'jurisdiction' is still in its infancy".

It seems to me that the Court is not yet ready to meet the challenges of the application of the Convention in respect of modern violations of human rights in consequence of military operations launched in the name of combating terrorism or purporting to establish democratic regimes. In that sense I agree with O'Boyle that the law on "jurisdiction" is still in its infancy.

Personally I endorse Lawson's concluding remark:

> The least one may expect from states who intervene abroad in the name of the great ideals of freedom, democracy and the rule of law, is that they continue to abide by the same universal human rights standards – whether they act at home or abroad.

As such, I believe that the *Banković* decision is a set-back in the effort to achieve the effective promotion of and respect for human rights by the High Contracting Parties to the Convention in relation to the exercise of any State activity within or outside their country.

Chapter 6 The European Convention on Human Rights and the Rights of Persons with Disabilities

1. Introduction

The European Convention on Human Rights guarantees certain human rights for the benefit of individuals in general within the jurisdiction of the contracting parties. The Convention does not deal with any specific rights for the protection of persons with disabilities nor does it address in any way problems concerning such persons. Of course the rights set out in the Convention belong to every individual including persons with one or another kind of disability. Article 14 of the Convention provides "that the enjoyment of the rights safeguarded in the Convention shall be secured without discrimination on any ground such as sex, race, colour ... national or social origin ..., birth or other status". This excludes discrimination at the expense of disabled persons in the enjoyment of any of the rights under the Convention. However, what is of particular interest of the purposes of our topic are the following two questions:

a) Whether the difficulties, practical problems or special situation of the disabled persons are taken into account so as to ensure effective enjoyment of the rights in question and,
b) Whether the States Parties to the Convention have an obligation to take positive measures to assist disabled persons to overcome their problems as much as possible.

The answer to the first question is positive. The Convention has always been considered to be an instrument capable of adapting itself to new developments and, for this reason, it was described in the case-law as a "living instrument".[1] The adaptation and extension of the Convention has been effected through the interpretation of its provisions by the European Commission and the Court of Human Rights in the light of the changing conditions of life and the prevailing conceptions and values in democratic societies. While the Convention does not expressly refer to

1 E.g. *Tyrer v. the United Kingdom*, Series A no. 26, para. 31.

disability (with the single exception of Article 5(1)e *infra.*), applications brought by disabled persons have, over the years, given the Court and the Commission the opportunity to elaborate significant principles of case-law in this area, as the following survey shows.

2. Article 3 – Prohibition of Torture

This provision enshrines one of the fundamental values of democratic society, admitting of no exceptions. In its first judgment under this provision,[2] the Court held that in assessing the severity of the punishment or treatment endured by a person, regard should be had to the victim's personal characteristics, such as their age, sex and state of health. Applying this case-law in a recent judgment,[3] the Court found that the detention of a severely disabled woman for three nights and four days in a prison that lacked adequate facilities constituted degrading treatment and thus a violation of Article 3.

It is established case-law under Article 3 that States are under an obligation to protect the physical and mental health of prisoners and detainees.[4] The Court has laid emphasis on the increased vulnerability in such situations of persons suffering mental illness, who may not be capable of complaining about their treatment. In a recent case the Court found that the failure to ensure adequate psychiatric care for a mentally disturbed prisoner who eventually committed suicide in his cell violated Article 3, since it amounted to inhuman and degrading treatment.[5]

The very fact of being disabled as such makes the person concerned particularly vulnerable to inhuman or degrading treatment. Certain prison conditions, interrogation techniques, deportation measures and similar restrictions of human rights, which are in general permissible under domestic or international human rights law, may amount to inhuman or degrading treatment if applied to a disabled person.[6] The Commission of Human Rights decided that the expulsion of an Algerian

2 *Ireland v. the United Kingdom*, judgment of 18 January 1978, Series A no. 25.

3 *Price v. the United Kingdom*, no. 33394/96, ECHR 2001-VII.

4 *Herzcegfalvy v. Austria*, judgment of 24 September 1992, Series A no. 296-A.

5 *Keenan v. the United Kingdom*, no. 27229/95, ECHR 2001-III.

6 Novak and Suntinger, "The right of disabled persons not to be subjected to torture, inhuman or degrading treatment or punishment" in *Human*

citizen who had lived since his childhood in France constituted a violation of his right to personal integrity and respect for his family life under Articles 3 and 8 of the ECHR. Taking into account the fact that the victim was deaf, the Commission found that his deportation to Algeria would inevitably lead to total sensory isolation constituting inhuman and degrading treatment.

So far as mentally disabled persons are concerned the European Court of Human Rights stressed in the case of *Herczegfalvy v. Austria* that "the position of inferiority and powerlessness which is typical of patients in psychiatric hospitals calls for increased vigilance in reviewing that the Convention has been complied with". As rightly observed by Novak and Suntinger,[7] "thirdly, since the risk of being exposed to inhuman or degrading treatment is much higher for disabled persons, Strates have an increased obligation to protect them against such treatment by affirmative action. Failure to live up to this obligation of conduct or result may constitute a violation by omission".

3. Article 5 – Right to Liberty and Security

The Court has consistently stressed the central importance of Article 5 in the scheme of Convention rights. Persons may be deprived of their liberty only if their situation is one of those set forth in the first paragraph. Of these, one concerns persons of unsound mind (sub-paragraph e). In the course of many judgments, the Court has clarified the substantive and procedural guarantees that must be observed before a person may be detained on the ground of mental disorder:[8] there must be objective medical evidence of the person's condition; the nature of their condition must be such as to necessitate compulsory confinement, i.e. where there is a danger of self harm or harm to others; the confinement may only continue for as long as this condition persists. Furthermore, the place and conditions of detention must relate to the person's disorder.[9] Anyone detained on this basis is entitled to be informed of the

Rights and Disabled Persons, Essays and Relevant Human Rights Instruments, p. 117 at p. 118.

7 Ibid.

8 *Winterwerp v. the Netherlands*, judgment of 24 October 1979, Series A no. 3.

9 *Ashingdane v. the United Kingdom*, judgment of 28 May 1985, Series A no. 93.

reason for the detention in accordance with Article 5 § 2.[10] They must also have the opportunity to challenge the lawfulness of their detention "speedily" and at regular intervals in accordance with Article 5 § 4. The Court has emphasised that a person detained on the ground of mental disorder should receive legal assistance for this purpose, in view of the importance of what is at stake – their liberty – and their diminished mental capacity.[11]

4. Article 6 – Right to a Fair Trial

In ensuring that the right of a fair trial is enjoyed effectively by disabled persons it is submitted that all the necessary facilities for an effective conduct of proceedings on behalf of them and an effective exercise of the right of defence in a criminal case against them should be provided by the State. For instance, if the disabled person concerned is deaf or blind he/she should be given the necessary assistance to follow the judicial proceedings. In a recent judgement of the Court in the case of *S.C. v. the United Kingdom* the 4th Section found that Article 6 § 1 of the Convention has been violated because the Court was not convinced that in the circumstances of the case the 11 year-old applicant charged with attempted robbery was capable of participating effectively in his trial taking into account his young age and limited intellectual capacity. According to the same judgment the applicant should have been tried by "a specialist tribunal which is able to give full consideration to and make proper allowance for the handicaps under which he labours, and adapt its procedure accordingly".[12]

5. Article 8 – Right to Respect for Private and Family Life

The notion of private life within the meaning of Article 8 has been given a broad reading. Indeed the Court has stated that the term is not susceptible to exhaustive definition.[13] The right to respect for private life has been clearly identified with the right to the free development of personality. The case-law has also established that the concept embraces physical and

10 *Van der Leer v. the Netherlands*, judgment of 21 February 1990, Series A no. 170.

11 *Megyeri v. Germany*, judgment of 12 May 1992, Series A no. 237-B.

12 60958/00, judgment 15/06/2004.

13 *Ben Said v. the United Kingdom*, no. 44599/98, ECHR 2001-I.

psychological integrity. A particularly important precedent in this field is the case of *X. and Y v. the Netherlands.*[14] The applicants complained that a lacuna in Dutch law made it impossible to prosecute a man who had raped a mentally disabled girl aged 16 (the second applicant), since a criminal complaint had to be lodged by the victim herself, with no exception made for persons lacking legal capacity. The Court ruled that Article 8 required effective deterrence of such wrongdoing, which could only be ensured through the criminal law. Mere civil remedies were insufficient.

The landmark case of *Pretty v. the United Kingdom*[15] raised fundamental questions about private life, illness, quality of life and personal autonomy. Ms. Pretty was at an advanced stage of a degenerative disease that left her severely physically incapacitated. She argued on the basis of several provisions of the Convention, including Article 8, that she had a "right to die" and that, accordingly, her husband should be permitted to assist her in ending her life. The Court affirmed that "[t]he very essence of the Convention is respect for human dignity and human freedom. Without in any way negating the principle of sanctity of life protected under the Convention, the Court considers that it is under Article 8 that notions of the quality of life take on significance". Although it went on to rule that the ban on assisted suicide was justified, this statement of principle is clearly relevant to the question of disability.

6. Article 1 of Protocol no. 1 – Protection of Property

The case-law regarding property and pecuniary rights has evolved over the years to the point where both contributory[16] and non-contributory[17] benefits are now considered to come within the scope of this provision. Although States enjoy a considerable margin of appreciation regarding the level of payment, the right to social security or social welfare now enjoys the protection of the Convention and so cannot be arbitrarily taken away. Furthermore, since the right to receive such benefits clearly constitutes a civil right within the meaning of Article 6 § 1, legal proceedings concerning them must provide all the guarantees of fairness set forth in that provision: access to an independent and impartial court

14 Judgment of 26 March 1985, Series A no. 91.

15 No. 2346/02, ECHR 2002-III.

16 *Willis v. the United Kingdom*, no. 36042/97, ECHR 2002-IV.

17 *Koua Poirrez v. France.*

of law,[18] equality of arms, right to an oral hearing,[19] legal aid if necessary, etc.

An important case-law of the Court has established the principle that if under the domestic laws parents were entitled to high amounts of compensation for the special burdens arising from their children's disability throughout their life which the medical authorities did not detect before birth on account of negligence, a law abolishing the right to such compensation in respect of pending judicial proceedings amounts to a breach of Article 1 of Protocol No. 1 to the Convention.[20]

7. Article 2 of Protocol no. 1 – Right to Education

The Commission considered an application brought by the parents of a child with mental and physical disabilities.[21] They argued that their son was entitled to be educated in the ordinary school system rather than being referred to specialised institutes and that the authorities should recognise and respect their firm conviction on this point. The Commission noted that under the relevant domestic legislation, children with special needs were educated in ordinary schools as far as possible. However, it observed that in some cases, more specialised education would be necessary. Accordingly, while the authorities had to place weight on the applicants' convictions, they were not under a duty to comply with their wishes regarding the education of their son.

8. Article 14 – Prohibition of Discrimination

By virtue of Article 14, States must secure the enjoyment of all Convention rights without discrimination on any of the listed grounds[22]. The list is not exhaustive, meaning that discrimination based on disability is forbidden within the sphere of the Convention. Article 14 can only be relied on if the facts of the case bring it within the scope of another

18 See *Obermeier v. Austria*, judgment of 28 June 1990, Series A no. 179.

19 See *Lundevall v. Sweden*, and *Salomonsson v. Sweden*, judgments of 12 November 2002, nos. 38629/97 and 38978/97.

20 *Draon v. France*, no. 1513/03, and *Maurice v. France*, no. 11810/03.

21 *Graeme v. the United Kingdom*, Commission decision of 5 February 1990.

22 "[S]ex, race, colour, language, religion, political or other opinion, national or social origin, association with a national minority, property, birth or any other status".

Convention provision. It is not therefore fully autonomous. An example of a case where the discrimination argument succeeded is *Koua Poirrez v. France.*[23] At issue here was the applicant's entitlement to the special allowance for disabled adults. His application had been refused on the basis of his nationality. In finding a violation of Article 14 (and of Article 1 of Protocol No. 1), the Court attached particular weight to the fact that the benefit was intended for persons with a disability, and cited, for further emphasis, other relevant Council of Europe texts in this domain. More generally, the Court has ruled that Article 14 is not confined to cases where similar situations are treated differently. It also requires that States treat differently persons whose situations are significantly different,[24] a principle that could well be relied on by a person with a disability. Furthermore, the Court has affirmed that Article 14 forbids indirect discrimination too.[25]

The scope for raising arguments based on the principle of non-discrimination has been greatly enlarged with the entry into force of Protocol No. 12 to the Convention, which stipulates a fully autonomous right to equality in the enjoyment of any right set forth *by law.*[26]

As regards the second question, namely, whether the States Parties to the Convention have an obligation to take positive measures to assist disabled persons to overcome their problems as much as possible, the answer is that the *approach of the case-law has been so far extremely hesitant.* This is up to a point understandable considering that any precedent to the effect of accepting an obligation on the part of the States to provide special facilities in order to solve general problems of disabled persons resulting from their disability will entail an inestimable burden on the economic capacity of the State concerned.

Several applications have been lodged by disabled persons seeking to establish a positive obligation on State authorities to ensure them increased mobility or autonomy. In *Botta v. Italy,*[27] the applicant, who

23 No. 40892/98, ECHR 2003-X.

24 *Thlimmenos v. Greece* [GC], no. 34369/97, ECHR 2000-IV.

25 *Hugh Jordan v. the United Kingdom,* no. 24746/94, judgment of 4 May 2001, ECHR 2001-III (extracts).

26 The Protocol came into force on 1 April 2005. See Hendriks, "Disabled persons and their right to treatment: Allowing differentiation while ending discrimination", *Health and Human Rights,* Vol. 1, no. 2, p. 152, 1995.

27 *Botta v. Italy,* judgment of 24 February 1998, *Reports of Judgments and Decisions* 1998-I.

had a physical disability, complained of the difficulties of gaining access to a private bathing establishment and to a beach. The Court accepted in principle that there could be a duty on the State to take appropriate measures, but there had to be a direct and immediate link between these measures and the private life of the applicant. In this particular case, the scope of the measures requested was too broad and indeterminate. In the later case of *Zehnalová and Zehnal v. the Czech Republic,*[28] the first applicant, who was confined to a wheelchair, complained that many public buildings in her town were inaccessible for her. Although it reiterated the point that Article 8 may imply a duty "in exceptional cases" for the State to take certain steps, the Court found that there was no direct and immediate link to the applicants' private lives.

In another case the Court was asked to consider whether a severely physically disabled young man in the Netherlands could invoke Article 8 to demand that he be provided with a robotic arm, without which he would remain totally dependent on others for every need.[29] It accepted that, given his very particular circumstances, the applicant had shown a special link between his demand and the needs of his private life. However, the matter was one that fell within the margin of appreciation of the national authorities, especially in the context of the allocation of limited public funds. Moreover, the Court was wary of setting a precedent. It considered that since the applicant already enjoyed a certain level of public assistance, the State had fulfilled its duty under Article 8.[30]

More recently, the Court dealt with a complaint that the applicant was deprived of his right to vote on account of his disability and more specifically with the question whether the facts of the case, in particular the lack of appropriate access for the applicant to a polling station in local elections, fall within the scope of the concept of "respect" for "private life" set forth in Article 8 of the Convention so as to be included in the positive obligations of the State *vis-a-vis* disabled persons.[31] The Court admitted that the effective enjoyment of many of the Convention rights by disabled persons may require the adoption of various positive

28 *Zehnalová and Zehnal v. the Czech Republic* (dec.), no. 38621/97, ECHR 2002-V.

29 *Sentges v. Netherlands* (dec), no. 27977/02, not yet reported.

30 See also *Pentiacova and Others v. Moldova,* no. 14462/03.

31 *Molka v. Poland,* no. 56550/00.

measures by the competent State authorities.[32] In this respect, the Court referred to various texts adopted by the Council of Europe which stress the importance of full participation of people with disabilities in society, in particular in political and public life. The Court observed " ... that it cannot be excluded that the authorities' failure to provide appropriate access to the polling station for the applicant, who wishes to lead an active life, might have aroused feelings of humiliation and distress capable of impinging on his personal autonomy, and thereby on the quality of his private life" and that "in circumstances such as those in the present case, a sufficient link would exist to attract the protection of Article 8". However, the Court stated that the margin of appreciation is even wider as the issue at stake involves the provision of adequate access for the disabled to polling stations, which must necessarily be assessed in the context of the allocation of limited State resources. Finally the Court noted "that the applicant has not shown ... that he could not have been assisted in entering the polling station by other persons". In fact, the domestic legislation provided that a disabled voter may be assisted in voting by another person, but not by members of the electoral commission or election monitors. In the circumstances, taking also into account the fact that the complaint concerned only one isolated incident the Court found that "the respondent State cannot be said, ... to have failed to ensure respect for the applicant's private life".

9. Specific Problems within the Financial Capacity of the State

It is evident that the case-law is reluctant to extend the obligation of the States Parties to the Convention to take positive measures to solve the problems resulting from the disability of a person. In cases where the complaint relates to general problems of indeterminate scope which would cover everything and anything *in abstracto* which could or could not be of direct significance for the life of a particular disabled person the position of the jurisprudence is in my opinion correct. But one could

32 See also *Marzari v. Italy*, no. 36448/97, where the Court *inter alia* stated that "although Article 8 does not guarantee the right to have one's housing problem solved by the authorities, a refusal of the authorities to provide assistance in this respect to an individual suffering from a severe disease might in certain circumstances raise an issue under Article 8 of the Convention because of the impact of such refusal on the private life of the individual".

not exclude an obligation on the part of the State to solve specific problems of a disabled person which are essential for the enjoyment of life in a modern society and are within the financial capacity of the State. I believe that this was in fact the situation in the *Botta* case and that is why I expressed a dissenting opinion, in the report of the European Commission of Human Rights, where I have stressed, *inter alia*, the following:

> The personality of individuals cannot be developed in a vacuum. It goes hand in hand with the developments of the social environment. I believe that the positive obligations of the State for an effective protection of the private life or personality of an individual entail the duty to secure to everyone certain minimum rights and facilities to enable the free development of his or her personality in the context of the conditions of social life ... Things which are essential for the enjoyment of life in a modern society and are intended to be enjoyed through public use (transport, roads, buildings, beaches with facilities, etc) should be made accessible to every individual to develop freely his personality or to meet the essential needs of his personality ... The Court added that 'this is an area in which the Contracting Parties enjoy a wide margin of appreciation in determining the steps to be taken to ensure compliance with the Convention with due regard to the needs and resources of the community and of individuals' ... However, according to the Italian legislation there is an obligation to insert in the State concessionary contracts (such as in the present case) a provision imposing the duty on the relevant beach establishments to make the necessary arrangements to allow handicapped persons to have access to the beach and to the sea. In enacting the legislation in question Italy must have taken into account the needs and resources of its community. Consequently, I find that the omission of the competent authorities to enforce the above-mentioned legislation with the result that persons like the applicant were deprived of the possibility to have access to the public facilities of the beach in question amounts to a breach of the positive obligations of the respondent State to ensure an effective protection of the right to respect for the private life of the applicant, contrary to Article 8 of the Convention.[33]

33 See the observations of Beatrice Maurer on the case, concluding as follows: "... une réponse plus audacieuse de la Cour aurait manifesté l'importance accordée à la requête de M Botta: celle de partager avec d' autres les joies de la plage sur la côte italienne! ", *Revue trimestrielle des droits de l'homme*, Vol. 10, no. 39, pp. 595-618 Bruxelles: Bruyland, 1999 2-0777-3579.

10. Employment of Disabled Persons

The Commission dismissed a complaint that the imposition of a special tax on certain employers who do not employ disabled persons amounts to a criminal sanction under Article 6 of the Convention. The Commission found that "the imposition of the tax in question is clearly linked to an objective factor namely non-employment of disabled persons regardless of whether this is the result of a deliberate policy of the employer or of an impossibility to find suitable disabled persons as employees".[34]

11. Epilogue

I have tried to show how the Convention has been applied in order to meet the special problems of people with disabilities. Although the Convention was not intended to be an instrument aiming specifically at the solution of such problems the jurisprudence has evolved in a way as to give particular attention to these problems and take them into account in applying the rights enshrined in the Convention. The big step would have, of course, been to establish through the case-law a principle of an obligation of the States Parties to the Convention to take positive measures to facilitate the disabled persons to overcome as much as possible their problems and enjoy life under better conditions similar, whenever that is feasible, to those applicable to their fellow human beings who do not suffer from any disability. The legal scope of the Convention makes this step difficult but not impossible. The provisions of Article 2 (right to life), Article 3 (prohibition of torture and inhuman and degrading treatment) and Article 8 (right to respect of private life) may be interpreted in a progressive and liberal manner so as to establish the necessary conditions for a better, more tolerable life for all those who had the misfortune to suffer from disabilities that affect substantially their quality of life. But there will always be the obstacle of the financial capacity of every State to make this objective a reality.

The ECHR has proved that it is particularly sensitive to human problems and has adjusted accordingly on many occasions and in different contexts the interpretation and application of the rights safeguarded by the Convention. The Convention is ... taking into account the needs of human beings and the interest shown by the people themselves as regards such needs. Therefore the demonstration and expression of a

34 *H v. Austria*, appl. no. 17819/91.

constant interest by the society and the persons concerned as well as a co-operation on the part of the High Contracting Parties to the Convention is essential for the achievement of an improved and more extensive protection of the rights and dignity of people with disabilities. The Convention cannot, of course, solve all the problems of the disabled persons but it can certainly contribute greatly to their alleviation.

Chapter 7 The Judgment of the European Court of Human Rights in the Case of *Cyprus v. Turkey*

1. Introduction

On 10 May 2001 the European Court of Human Rights delivered a historic judgment[1] in which it found Turkey responsible for committing grave and continuing violations in Cyprus of a number of human rights guaranteed by the European Convention on Human Rights. The violations had begun as a result of the Turkish invasion of Cyprus in July 1974 and the ensuing occupation of the northern part of the island. The judgment is uniquely important in many respects. Apart from the fact that it deals with a wide spectrum of violations of rare gravity resulting from the military occupation of the territory of one of the High Contracting Parties to the Convention by another High Contracting Party, the judgment decides certain important legal questions in the sphere of international law and of human rights in particular. The judgment is also noteworthy for its various dissenting opinions.

2. Grave Violations

The Court found, *inter alia*:

- a continuing violation of Article 8 of the Convention by reason of the refusal to allow the return of any Greek-Cypriot displaced persons – exceeding 211,000 – to their homes in northern Cyprus;[2]
- a continuing violation of Article I of Protocol No. 1 by virtue of the fact that Greek-Cypriot owners of property in northern Cyprus – again exceeding 211,000 – are being denied access to and control, use and enjoyment of their property as well as any compensation for the interference with their property rights;[3]

---

1 Case of *Cyprus v. Turkey* [GC], Judgment of 10 May 2001, no. 25781/94, *Reports of Judgments and Decisions* 2001-IV.

2 Judgment, paras. 166-175.

3 Ibid., at paras. 178-189.

- a continuing violation of Article 2 of the Convention on account of the Turkish authorities' failure to conduct an effective investigation into the whereabouts and fate of Greek-Cypriot missing persons who disappeared in 1974 in life-threatening circumstances[4] and of Article 5 by virtue of the failure to investigate the fate of the Greek-Cypriot missing persons in respect of whom there is an arguable claim that they were in Turkish custody at the time of their disappearance;[5] and
- a continuing violation of Article 3 of the Convention in respect of the relatives of the Greek-Cypriot missing persons on account of their agony resulting from the silence of the respondent State as to the fate of the missing persons.[6]

This is the first time in the history of the Convention that the Court established and thereunder has found a High Contracting Party responsible for continuing violations of so many rights affecting such a large number of persons over such a long period of time. So far only two inter-state cases have been determined by the Court. The first was the case of *Ireland* v. *the United Kingdom*[7] in 1978, which, however, was not comparable in terms of the scale of violations with the case under consideration.

3. Background to the Case

For a better understanding of the magnitude of the case it is necessary to bear in mind its background, which is set out in the judgment as follows:

> The complaints raised in this application arise out of the Turkish military operations in northern Cyprus in July and August 1974 and the continuing division of the territory of Cyprus. At the time of the Court's consideration

4 Ibid., at para. 136.

5 Ibid., at para. 150.

6 Ibid., at para. 158.

7 Merits and Just Satisfaction, Judgment of 18 January 1978, 1978 ECHR Series A no. 25, at 90-91.

of the merits of the *Loizidou v. Turkey* case in 1996, the Turkish military presence at the material time was described in the following terms [...]:[8]

> Turkish armed forces of more than 30,000 personnel are stationed throughout the whole of the occupied area of northern Cyprus, which is constantly patrolled and has checkpoints on all main lines of communication.

A major development in the continuing division of Cyprus occurred in November 1983 with the proclamation of the 'Turkish Republic of Northern Cyprus' (the 'TRNC') and the subsequent enactment of the 'TRNC Constitution' on 7 May 1985.

This development was condemned by the international community. On 18 November 1983 the United Nations Security Council adopted Resolution 541 (1983) declaring the proclamation of the establishment of the 'TRNC' legally invalid and calling upon all States not to recognise any Cypriot State other than the Republic of Cyprus. [...][9]

[...]The events of July and August 1974 and their aftermath gave rise to three previous applications by the applicant Government against the respondent State. The first [...] and second [...] applications were joined by the Commission and led to the adoption on 10 July 1976 of a report [...] in which the Commission expressed the opinion that the respondent State had violated Articles 2, 3, 5, 8, 13 and 14 of the Convention and Article I of Protocol No. 1 [...].

The third application [...] lodged by the applicant Government was the subject of a further report [...] adopted by the Commission on 4 October 1983 [...]. In that report the Commission expressed the opinion that the respondent State was in breach of its obligations under Articles 5 and 8 of the Convention and Article 1 of Protocol No. 1.[10]

[...] [this is the first occasion on which [the Court] has been seised of the complaints invoked by the applicant Government in the context of an inter-State application [...] as regards the previous applications, it was not open to the parties or to the Commission to refer them to the Court

8 Judgment, para. 13.

9 Ibid., at para. 14.

10 Ibid., at para. 17.

> […]. Turkey only accepted the compulsory jurisdiction of the Court by its declaration of 22 January 1990.[11]

In its report in respect of the first two applications the Commission found Turkey responsible for her refusal to allow the return of more than 170,000 Greek-Cypriot refugees to their homes in the north of Cyprus, the eviction of Greek Cypriots from houses, including their own homes, the separation of Greek-Cypriot families, inhuman treatment of Greek Cypriots including repeated rapes and other forms of ill-treatment, deprivation of life on a large scale, illegal detentions, deprivation of possessions to an indefinite extent, absence of remedies and discrimination on the ground of ethnic origin.[12] In its report regarding the third application the Commission found Turkey responsible for continuing displacement of more than 170,000 Greek Cypriots, separation of families, deprivation of possessions, failure to account for the fate of missing Greek Cypriots unlawfully deprived of their liberty in Turkish custody in 1974, absence of remedies and discrimination as per the first report.[13]

Both reports ended up with the Committee of Ministers, which under former Article 32 of the Convention had the responsibility for deciding whether there had been a violation of the Convention. However, in both cases the Committee of Ministers failed the take a decision in accordance with that Article and confined itself, basically, to declassifying the first report and publishing the second. The Court agreed with the applicant Government's position that "The Committee of Ministers never took any formal decision on the findings contained in either of the Commission's reports under former Article 31."[14]

4. Continuation of Violations

The violations found by the Court reflect a continuation of the violations found by the Commission in the previous cases of *Cyprus* v. *Turkey*, the main thrust of such violations being-the result of a policy pursued by Turkey aiming at the geographical separation of the Greek-Cypriot and

11 Ibid., at para. 66.

12 Report of the Commission (appl. nos. 6780/74 and 6950/75), 10 July 1976, at 163-167.

13 *Decisions and Reports* (DR) 72, 5, at 50-51.

14 Judgment, paras. 64-67.

Turkish-Cypriot Communities. This is borne out by the judgment, *inter alia*, in the following statements:

> The Court further notes that the situation impugned by the applicant Government has obtained since the events of 1974 in northern Cyprus. It would appear that it [...] is enforced as a matter of policy in furtherance of a bi-zonal arrangement designed, it is claimed, to minimise the risk of conflict which the intermingling of the Greek and Turkish-Cypriot communities in the north might engender [...].[15]
>
> [...] the violation at issue has endured as a matter of policy since 1974 and must be considered continuing.[16]

According to the Court, this policy was also applied in respect of the remaining Greek Cypriots in the occupied area and more specifically those residing in the Karpas area, where the living conditions were found by the Court to amount to an administrative practice by Turkey of violating several Convention rights, such as the right to respect for one's family life and home,[17] the right to freedom of religion,[18] the freedom of expression,[19] the right to the peaceful enjoyment of one's possessions,[20] the right to ensure education of one's children[21] and the right to an effective remedy.[22] The Court concluded as follows:

> For the Court it is an inescapable conclusion that the interferences at issue were directed at the Karpas Greek-Cypriot community for the very reason that they belonged to this class of persons. The treatment to which they were subjected during the period under consideration can only be explained in terms of the features which distinguish them from the Turkish-Cypriot population, namely their ethnic origin, race and religion. The Court would further note that it is the policy of the respondent State to pursue discussions within the framework of the inter-communal talks on

15 Ibid., at para. 173.

16 Ibid., at para. 174.

17 Ibid., at paras. 292-296.

18 Ibid., at paras. 243-246.

19 Ibid., at paras. 252 and 254.

20 Ibid., at paras. 269 and 270.

21 Ibid., at paras. 278 and 280.

22 Ibid., at para. 324.

> the basis of bi-zonal and bi-communal principles [...]. The respondent State's attachment to these principles must be considered to be reflected in the situation in which the Karpas Greek Cypriots live and are compelled to live: isolated, restricted in their movements, controlled and with no prospect of renewing or developing their community. The conditions under which that population is condemned to live are debasing and violate the very notion of respect for the human dignity of its members.[23]
>
> In the Court's opinion, and with reference to the period under consideration, the discriminatory treatment attained a level of severity which amounted to degrading treatment.[24]

5. Turkish Cypriots and the Gypsy Community

As regards the alleged violations as a matter of administrative practice of the rights of Turkish Cypriots and the Gypsy community in northern Cyprus, the Court concluded that although there may have been individual cases of interference with the rights of political opponents of the regime in the occupied area, it had not been established that, during the period under consideration,[25] there had been an administrative practice of violation of the rights of Turkish Cypriots[26] or of members of the Turkish-Cypriot Gypsy community.[27]

However, contrary to the conclusions of the Commission, the Court found that there had been a violation of Article 6 of the Convention on account of the legislative practice of authorising the trial of civilians by military courts in the occupied area.[28]

6. Establishment of the Facts

In coming to its conclusions, the Court followed, in practically all respects, the Commission's approach in the case. As regards the establishment of the facts and the assessment of the evidence, the Court did not

23 Ibid., at para. 309.

24 Ibid., at para. 310.

25 22 November – 22 May 1994.

26 Judgment, paras. 346 and 348.

27 Ibid., at para. 353.

28 Ibid., at paras. 354-359.

depart from the findings of the Commission invoking its case-law to the effect that

> prior to the entry into force of Protocol No.11 to the Convention the establishment and verification of the facts were primarily a matter for the Commission and only in exceptional circumstances the Court would exercise its powers to make its own findings of fact.[29]

It is to be noted that the applicant Government disputed the conclusion of the Commission as regards certain of its findings. This was particularly the case with regard to the allegations of violations of the human rights of Turkish Cypriots and members of the Gypsy community. The Court endorsed the approach of the Commission and reaffirmed its case-law to the effect that the standard of proof in relation to complaints of breaches of the Convention should be "beyond reasonable doubt" and "that such proof may follow from the coexistence of sufficiently strong, clear and concordant inferences or of similar unrebutted presumptions of facts."[30] As regards the establishment of the existence of administrative practices, the Court reasserted its position that the burden of proof is not borne by one or the other of the two Governments concerned. "Rather, the Court must examine all the material before it, irrespective of its origin."[31]

The respondent Government, without giving any reasons, did not participate in the proceedings before the Court. They however actively participated in all stages of the examination of the case by the Commission.

7. Preliminary Rulings

The Court rejected four preliminary objections of the respondent Government, which had also been rejected by the Commission. Similar objections were raised by Turkey in the three previous inter-state applications before the Commission and they were likewise rejected by

29 Ibid., at para. 117.

30 Ibid., at paras. 112 and 341.

31 Ibid., at para. 113.

the latter. Some of them had already been rejected by the Court in the individual application in the case of *Loizidou* v. *Turkey*.[32]

In rejecting these objections the Court held that:

- The Government of the Republic of Cyprus is the sole legitimate Government of Cyprus;[33]
- The view of the international community is that the "TRNC" is not a state under international law and is therefore illegal[34] and the Court confirmed this view;[35]
- Turkey, which has "effective overall control over northern Cyprus," is responsible for securing all human rights under the Convention and violations of such rights by her own soldiers, or officials, or by the local administration (the "TRNC") are imputable to her under Article 1 of the Convention;[36]
- If she acquiesces or connives in the acts of private individuals, which violate Convention rights of others, she may also be responsible;[37] and
- "TRNC" remedies are "domestic remedies" of Turkey.[38]

8. Dissenting Opinions

8.1 Individual Opinions

The conclusions of the Court regarding the violations of the rights of Greek Cypriots mentioned above were reached by a majority of 16 votes

32 Merits and Just Satisfaction, Judgment of 18 December 1996, ECHR *Reports* 1996-VI, 2216.

33 Judgment, paras. 61 and 90.

34 Ibid., at paras. 61, 90 and 238.

35 Ibid., at para. 236.

36 Ibid., at para. 77. The Court followed its judgment in the *Loizidou* case where it held that

> the concept of 'jurisdiction' [...] is not restricted to the national territory of the Contracting States [...] the responsibility of Contracting States [...] could also arise when as a consequence of military action – whether lawful or unlawful – [the state] exercises effective control of an area outside its national territory [...].

Ibid., at para. 76.

37 Ibid., at para. 81.

38 Ibid., at paras. 82-102.

to 1. The conclusion that there has been no violation of the rights of Turkish Cypriots, with the exception of the violation of Article 6 as regards the military courts, was reached unanimously. The finding regarding the latter violation and the finding that there has been no violation of the rights of members of the Turkish-Cypriot Gypsy community were adopted by 16 votes to 1.

Judge Fuad disagreed with all the findings of the violations of rights of Greek Cypriots and of the violation on account of the functioning of military courts. He also disagreed with the ruling of the Court that Turkey has jurisdiction in respect of the facts complained of in the application. In his Dissenting Opinion he disagreed with the judgment of the Court in the *Loizidou* case and quoted in this respect the views of Judges Bernhardt, Pettiti and Gölcüklü who dissented in that case. The following points were made:

The establishment of "the border" in 1974 and its closure – not an act of Turkish troops – were responsible for denying Mrs Loizidou access to her property in the northern part of Cyprus. It was not possible to base a judgment exclusively on the assumption that the Turkish presence was illegal and that Turkey was therefore responsible for more or less everything that happened in northern Cyprus. The situation of Cyprus was complex and required a thorough investigation on site. The whole problem of the two communities had more to do with politics and diplomacy than with European judicial scrutiny. The Court was dealing with a political situation and it was not possible to separate the political aspects of the case from the legal aspects. The implementation of the Treaty of Guarantee established the separation of the two communities. The problem of Cyprus went well beyond the dimensions of a mere lawsuit. In view of the prevailing special circumstances of the problem it was not realistic to allow every dispossessed property owner to demand the immediate right to resume possession, of his or her property, wherever situated. The answer to the question of the missing persons was the existing investigation procedure for missing persons from both communities. The northern part of Cyprus did not come under Turkey's jurisdiction. "TRNC" was not subordinate to Turkey. It was democratic and exercised independent and effective control over that area.

Judge Costa disagreed with the majority as regards the religious discrimination against the Greek Cypriots living in the Karpas region and the violation of the rights of the Turkish-Cypriot Gypsy community. In his view there should also be a finding of a violation of Article 9 taken together with Article 14 and of numerous violations of the rights of the

Turkish-Cypriot Gypsy community as a matter of administrative practice.

Judge Marcus-Helmons found, contrary to the majority, a violation of Article 2 of the Convention on account of the refusal to afford to Greek-Cypriots living in the Karpas area sufficient access to medical care, and a violation of Article 14 in conjunction with Article 9 as regards the relevant restrictions imposed on that population. He also, in a Separate Opinion, disagreed with the majority on the subject of the "TRNC" remedies and expressed the view that the courts established illegally in northern Cyprus could not be considered as "established by law" or take an impartial decision in a matter relating to the military occupation.

8.2 Joint Opinions – The "TRNC" Judicial Remedies

8.2.1 The majority

Four of the Court's findings were the subject of a noteworthy disagreement among its members. The findings related to the following matters:

(a) exhaustion of "TRNC" judicial remedies;
(b) no violation of Article 6 of the Convention in respect of Greek Cypriots living in northern Cyprus;
(c) no violation of Article 13 of the Convention by reason of the absence of remedies in respect of interferences by private persons with the rights of Greek Cypriots living in northern Cyprus under Article 8 of the Convention and Article 1 of Protocol No. 1; and
(d) no violation of Article 13 of the Convention by reason of an alleged practice of failing to secure effective remedies to Turkish Cypriots living in northern Cyprus.

The finding as regards (a) was adopted by 10 votes to 7. Findings (b), (c) and (d) were adopted by 11 votes to 6. The issue was whether the remedies of the "TRNC" judicial system could be considered as remedies which qualified for the purposes of Articles 26 (now 35), 6 and 13 of the Convention. The first finding related to a preliminary issue and had to be examined as such. In view of the common questions arising in all four matters the decision of the Court on this preliminary issue automatically determined the core problems raised by the other three matters.

The majority, relying on a principle of international law established by the Advisory Opinion of the International Court of Justice ("ICJ") in the *Namibia* case,[39] adopted the position that the requirement to exhaust domestic remedies applied to the judicial remedies of the "TRNC" courts established in the occupied area, and therefore inhabitants of that area had to exhaust those remedies before applying to the Court unless their ineffectiveness could be proved – a point to be examined on a case-by-case basis.[40] The majority invoked the following passage from the Advisory Opinion:

> In general, the non-recognition of South Africa's administration of the Territory should not result in depriving the people of Namibia of any advantages derived from international co-operation. In particular while official acts performed by the Government of South Africa on behalf or concerning Namibia after the termination of the Mandate are illegal and invalid, this invalidity cannot be extended to those acts, such as, for instance, the registration of births, deaths and marriages, the effects of which can be ignored only to the detriment of the inhabitants of the Territory.[41]

The majority approached the question as follows:

> It appears evident to the Court, despite the reservations the Greek-Cypriot community in northern Cyprus may harbour regarding the 'TRNC' courts, that the absence of such institutions would work to the detriment of the members of that community. Moreover, recognising the effectiveness of those bodies for the limited purpose of protecting the rights of the territory's inhabitants does not, in the Court's view and following the Advisory Opinion of the International Court of Justice, legitimise the 'TRNC' in any way.[42]
>
> It is to be noted that the International Court's Advisory option [...] shows clearly that, in situations similar to those arising in the present case, the obligation to disregard acts of *de facto* entities is far from absolute. Life goes on in the territory concerned for its inhabitants. That life must be made tolerable and be protected by the *de facto* authorities, including their courts; and, in the very interest of the inhabitants, the acts of these

39 Legal Consequences for States of the Continued presence of South Africa in Namibia notwithstanding Security Council Resolution 276, Advisory Opinion, 21 June 1971, 1971 ICJ Repr. 16.

40 Judgment, paras. 90-99.

41 *Ibid.*, at para. 93.

42 *Ibid.*, at para. 92.

> authorities related thereto cannot be simply ignored by third States or by international institutions, especially courts, including this one [...][43]

8.2.2 The joint dissenting opinion

The position of the majority was contested by a weighty opinion of Judge Palm joined by Judges Jungwiert, Levits, Pantîru, Kovler and Marcus Helmons on the following grounds:

The Court should have shown judicial restraint by avoiding an elaboration of a general theory concerning the validity and effectiveness of remedies in the "TRNC" because (a) such a theory in the present case was not at all necessary since the Court did not in fact at any stage reject a complaint for failure to exhaust domestic remedies; (b) "the Court should avoid putting itself in a position where, for supposedly laudable reasons, it is tempted to fashion a semblance of legality out of a clearly illegal situation"; (c) Turkey itself did not claim that the "remedies" in question are Turkish remedies; (d) it could not be for the benefit of Greek Cypriots to require them to exhaust these "remedies."

The dissenting judges accepted that, even in a situation of illegality, it is in the interest of inhabitants to have some form of court system to enable basic everyday disputes to be settled by a source of authority and it is not excluded that the decisions of such courts could be recognised by the courts of other countries. However, Judge Palm's opinion went on to state that:

> [...] it does not follow from my acceptance of the utility of a local court system that this Court should require applicants in northern Cyprus complaining of human-rights violations to exhaust these possible avenues of redress [...] before it has jurisdiction to examine their complaints. Episodic recognition by foreign courts is one thing. The exhaustion requirement is another. To require those subject to the exigencies of an occupying authority to have recourse to the courts as a precondition to having their complaints of human-rights violations examined by this Court is surely an unrealistic proposition given the obvious and justifiable lack of confidence in such a system of administration of justice [...].
>
> [...] The Court accepts that the enclaved Greek Cypriots are 'compelled to live in a hostile environment in which it is hardly possible to lead a normal private and family life' [...]. It also finds that this population is the victim of discriminatory and degrading treatment based on ethnic origin,

43 *Ibid.*, at para. 96.

> race and religion [...] the Court accepts the general picture of a [...] community that has been subjected to a substantial reduction of the Convention rights of its members under colour of a policy of ethnic separation [...].
>
> In such a context, is it realistic to say that the members of this community have access to the courts in respect of their civil claims? Is it a credible proposition that there exists a haven of juridical relief ready and able to defend the rights of this beleaguered population notwithstanding the existence of an official policy of containment and oppression?

It is submitted that that is the better approach. The *Namibia* opinion accepts the recognition of certain transactions which are unavoidable *ex necessitate* in the daily relations of individuals. The opinion does not *require* the inhabitants of an occupied territory to resort to illegal remedies established by the *de facto* organs before they have a right to bring their case before an international court. The more so when it comes to the requirement of exhaustion of domestic remedies for the purposes of the Convention applicable in this case. Such remedies should not be illegal. The Preamble to the Convention reiterates adherence to the "rule of law." It is inconceivable for the Convention to express respect for the rule of law while requiring individuals to exhaust illegal remedies before resorting to the Convention institutions. As rightly observed by the dissenters, "[e]pisodic recognition by foreign courts is one thing. The exhaustion requirement is another."

9. Conclusion

The Court has, for the first time, pronounced on the overall legal consequences of Turkey's invasion and continued military presence in Cyprus. In terms of scale and nature of violations of the Convention the case is unprecedented. The Court has proved once more that it can act judicially and defend the public order of Europe in situations where the violations are intertwined with political issues leading to them.[44]

Of great significance are the international law issues decided by the Court: That a State which has effective control over an area of the territory of another state is responsible for securing all human rights and its responsibility is engaged by virtue of the acts of its local administration; that such state may be also responsible for the acts of private individu-

44 Cf. US Diplomatic and Consular Staff in Teheran, 1980 ICJ Rep. 90.

als if it acquiesces or connives in such acts; that the failure of authorities of a state to conduct effective investigations into the whereabouts of missing persons last seen in the custody of agents of that state and subsequently disappeared in life-threatening circumstances constitutes continuing breach of the obligations to protect life and liberty; that the refusal to allow the return of displaced persons to their homes (after 27 years) amounts to a continuing breach of the Convention.

Equally important in terms of international law and human rights is the finding (albeit disputed by a powerful dissenting opinion) that remedies available by *de facto* organs in an occupied area are to be regarded as remedies of the state which has control over that area and that it is in the interest of the inhabitants to have such remedies which, for that matter, qualify as remedies that in principle have to be exhausted before resorting to an international court. The case is also an outstanding example of the concept of "continuing" violations.

Because of its dimensions and the attitude of Turkey so far, the case is bound to test the efficiency of the Convention system.

Chapter 8 The Protection of the Right to Property in Occupied Territories

1. Introduction

The right to property was accorded the status of a human right as a result of its incorporation in international human rights instruments in the second part of the twentieth century. The right has acquired special importance as part of the freedom of the individual, economic autonomy in modern democratic societies and generally as a significant element for the development of the individual's personality.[1] Its recognition as a separate human right and its legal protection on an international level was the result of gradual efforts. It is still in the process of further legal elaboration, as regards both its scope and effect, by legal theory and jurisprudence.

About a hundred years ago, when basic norms of international law, especially those concerning human rights, were either non-existent or in an embryonic state, human rights did not generally enjoy legal protection. Even more distant from reality was the legal protection of human rights in territories under military occupation. People in such territories were in all respects at the mercy of the occupant power. In those times serious crimes against humanity such as genocide were not even shocking the conscience of mankind into some type of reaction aimed at repressing them. It was only in 1915 that Britain, France and Russia denounced the genocide of Armenians as constituting a "crime against civilization and humanity".

However, paradoxical though it may seem, it is in the context of armed hostilities that we first find the development of principles and rules concerning protection of individuals in international law. This

1 See Marcus-Helmons, "Le Droit de Propriété est-il un droit fondamental au sens de la Convention européenne des Droits de l'Homme?", in *Les nouveaux Droits de L'Homme en Europe* (Bruxelles European Lawyers' Union 1999) 193 paras. 207-8; Meyer-Bisch 194 of the same article: "L'homme tire une partie de son identité de ce qu'il s'est approprié".

may be due to the special need to protect individuals which is felt more intensively at times of excessive suffering of human beings as a result of such hostilities.

The Greeks and Romans customarily observed certain humanitarian principles which have become fundamental rules of the contemporary laws of war.[2] In feudal times a variety of military codes were promulgated listing acts forbidden during war.[3] A significant event in the history of our topic is the trial and execution in 1474 of Peter Hagenbach in that while administering occupied territories he had indulged in murder, rape, and confiscation of private property.[4] This event later influenced the drafting of the Charter of London of 1945 which set up the Nuremberg Court.[5] In the Swedish Articles of War of 1621 there are provisions for the protection of civilians such as the prohibition of assaults on women, theft, and pillage.[6] The so called Lieber Code adopted in 1863 during the American Civil War prescribed among other things that "the unarmed citizen is to be spared in person, property and honour ... The United States acknowledge and protect in ... countries occupied by them, religion and morality; strictly private property; the persons of the inhabitants and the sacredness of domestic relations. Offences to the contrary will be rigorously punished".[7]

Reference should also be made to the Project of an International Declaration concerning the Laws and Customs of War produced in 1874 at the initiative of Czar Alexander II which, *inter alia*, laid down that "family honour and rights, and the lives and property of persons ... must be respected".[8] Equally important, from the point of view of the development of humanitarian law in armed conflict, is the Oxford Manual

2 C. Phillipson, *The International Law and Custom of Ancient Greece and Rome* (London Macmillan 1911) II, 166-384.

3 M.H. Keen, *The Laws of War in the Middle Ages* (London Routledge 1965).

4 G. Schwarzenberger, *International Law as Applied by International Courts and Tribunals II The Law of Armed Conflict* (London Stevens 1968) ch 39.

5 L.C. Green, "Human Rights and the Law of Armed Conflict", in *Essays on the Modern Law of War* (2nd edn. New York Transnational 1999) 446.

6 A. Roberts and R. Guelff, *Documents on the Laws of War* (3rd edn. Oxford OUP 2000) 3.

7 Green (n. 5) 440.

8 Ibid., 441; and D. Schindler and J. Toman, *The Laws of Armed Conflicts* (Geneva Sijthoff-Leiden 1973) 27 Art 38.

adopted by the Institute of International Law in 1880, which reaffirmed the rules of the Lieber Code and the aforementioned Project and included in its rules that "private property whether belonging to individuals or corporations must be respected".[9]

With the development of international law in Europe, priority was given to problems relating to hostility in international relations. Gradually, principles and rules regarding the conduct of armed hostilities were incorporated in a number of texts with binding effect in the form of bilateral and multilateral treaties.

2. The Hague Regulations: General Principles of International Law

The first time that we see a codification of duties for the protection of the individual's rights is in the Hague Regulations annexed to the 1907 Hague Convention. The provisions of the Regulations are still in force as part of the customary international law binding on all States[10] and are applicable not only in cases of occupation as a consequence of war, but also in cases of occupation[11] as a result of any military operations, which include even those carried out by States in accordance with the UN Charter.[12] They contain specific clauses concerning private property in occupied territories. Thus Article 46 stipulates: "Family honour and rights, the lives of persons, and private property, as well as religious

9 D. Schindler and J. Toman (n. 8) 44.

10 P. Daillier and A. Pellet, *Droit International Public* (6th edn. Paris Nguyen Quoc Dinh 1999) 481 para. 314; the International Military Tribunal at Nuremberg in 1946, and a report of the UN Secretary-General to the Security Council in May 1993 concerning the establishment of the International Criminal Tribunal for the former Yugoslavia, expressly recognised 1907 Hague Convention IV as declaratory of customary international law: A. Roberts and R. Guelff (n. 5) 68, 178; it was on this premise that the Tribunal found that the rules in that Convention applied in respect of Czechoslovakia even though that country was not a party to the Convention; see also *Oppenheim's Internationnl Law II: Disputes, War and Neutrality* (7th edn. Lauterpacht (ed.) London Longmans 1952) 234-5.

11 Whether there is occupation is a question of fact. Occupied territory means "any territory under the overall control of a party to the conflict". *Naletilic and Martinovic Case (Judgment)* ICTY-98-34 (31 Mar 2003) para. 211.

12 J.G. Starke, *An Introduction to International Law* (11th edn. Shearer (ed.) London Butterworths 1994) 500, 517-18.

convictions and practice, must be respected. Private property cannot be confiscated."

Commenting on this Article, Oppenheim states:

> Immovable private enemy property may under no circumstances or conditions be appropriated by an invading belligerent. Should he confiscate and sell private land or buildings, the buyer would acquire no right whatever to the property ... if the occupant has appropriated and sold such private or public property as may not legitimately be appropriated by a military occupant, it may afterwards be claimed from the purchaser without payment of compensation.[13]

The same applies to movable property which does not consist of war material.

Movable private property which may be used for military purposes and immovable government property may only be requisitioned and not confiscated (Article 53 para 2; and Article 55).[14] Title to such property shall not pass to the occupying State. Upon termination of the war, the items and real estate seized shall be restored.

The protection of the property of municipalities and certain institutions and of works of art and science and historical monuments is under the same Regulations absolute. Thus according to Article 56 thereof,

> [t]he property of municipalities, that of institutions dedicated to religion, charity and education, the arts and sciences, even when State property, shall be treated as private property. All seizure of, destruction or wilful damage done to institutions of this character, historic monuments, works

13 Ibid., at 403, 619.

14 The Israeli High Court has approved acquisitions by private persons of privately owned land in the territories occupied by Israel for the settlements of Israeli civilians, with the explanation that such settlements increased the security of the occupying power and could therefore be justified on the basis of military interest (*Beth El Case, Israel Yearbook on Human Rights* 9 (1979)). As rightly observed by Dr Hans-Peter Gasser, Senior Legal Adviser to the International Committee of the Red Cross: "This extension of the concept of security as an exception to the guarantee of property should be rejected as excessive, since it nullifies the guarantee of property based in international law": "Protection of the Civilian Population" in D. Fleck (ed.), *The Handbook of Humanitarian Law in Armed Conflicts* (Oxford OUP 1995) 209, 262.

> of art and science, is forbidden, and should be made the subject of legal proceedings.

Article 52 of the Regulations provides that "requisitions in kind ... shall not be demanded from ... inhabitants except for the needs of the army of occupation". All requisitions must be paid for in cash, and if this is impossible they must be acknowledged by receipt and the payment of the amount must be made as soon as possible. As rightly observed by Oppenheim, "from the rule that requisitions must always be paid for, it again becomes clear and beyond all doubt that private property is, as a rule, exempt from appropriation by an invading army".[15]

In this respect Article 43 of the Hague Regulations appears also to be relevant inasmuch as it provides that the occupant must respect, unless absolutely prevented, the laws in force in the country under occupation.

The Hague Regulations have been partly supplemented by the fourth Geneva Convention of 1949[16] which provides, *inter alia,* that

> any destruction by the Occupying Power of real or personal property belonging individually or collectively to private persons or to the State or to other public authorities, or to social or co-operative organisations, is prohibited, except where such destruction is rendered absolutely necessary by military operations . (Article 53)

Article 147 of the 1949 Convention defines the "grave breaches" of its provisions that should be criminally punishable and includes therein "the extensive destruction and appropriation of property not justified by military necessity and carried out unlawfully and wantonly".

In the Charter of the International Military Tribunal for the trial of war criminals of 1945, "plunder of public or private property" is expressly included in the group of war crimes punishable by the Court (Article 6). This is also considered as representing general international law.[17]

15 *Oppenheim's International Law* (n 10) 410.

16 This Convention reflects principles of international customary law: see T. Meron, *Human Rights and Humanitarian Norms as Customary Law* (Oxford Clarendon Press 1991) 45-9.

17 I. Brownlie, *Principles of Public International Law* (5th edn. Oxford OUP 1998) 566.

The International Military Tribunal at Nuremberg condemned as a war crime the plunder by Germans of private property in occupied territory during the Second World War. Moreover, the criminal responsibility of private individuals participating in acts of plunder was affirmed in a number of war crime trials, thus extending responsibility of a criminal character for such acts to individual members generally.[18]

The Statute of the International Criminal Tribunal for the former Yugoslavia (1993) (ICTY) provides that the Tribunal shall have the power to prosecute persons committing or ordering to be committed grave breaches of the Geneva Conventions of 12 August 1949, which expressly include extensive destruction and appropriation of property, not justified by military necessity and carried out unlawfully and wantonly, and to prosecute persons violating the laws or customs of war including plunder[19] of public or private property.

In the more recent Statute of the International Criminal Court (1998), "extensive destruction and appropriation of property, not justified by military necessity and carried out unlawfully and wantonly" is also included as one of the war crimes within the Court's jurisdiction and in

18 See, e.g., *War Crimes Reports*: the Flick trial 9 (1949) 48; the IG Farben trial 10 (1949) 1; the Krupp trial 10 (1949) 69 and more recently the ICTY trials of *Blaskic Case (Judgment)* ICTY-95-14 (3 Mar 2000), *Naletilic and Martinovic Case (Judgment)* ICTY-98-34 (31 Mar 2003), *Milutinovic et al Case* and *Gotovina Case*.

19 It has been held that "plunder" within the meaning of the Statute encompasses "all forms of unlawful appropriation of property in armed conflicts for which individual criminal responsibility attaches under international law" and extends to both cases of "organised" and "systematic" seizure of property from protected persons in occupied territories, as well as to "acts of looting committed by individual soldiers for their private gain". Furthermore, the terms "pillage", "plunder", and "spoliation" varyingly have been used to describe the unlawful appropriation of public and private property during armed conflicts. See the *Simic et al Case (Judgment)* ICTY-95-9 (17 Oct 2003) paras. 98 and 99. It may also be pointed out here that in so far as any forced displacement of any person to another location may entail the loss of the use and enjoyment of that person's property, this may amount to an impermissible interference with the right to property contrary to the required protection according to the instruments under consideration: See ibid., paras. 123 and 126 and *Loizidou v. Turkey (Merits)*, *Reports of Judgments and Decisions* 1996-VI, pp. 2237-8.

respect of which it can impose a sentence of imprisonment of up to 30 years of a term of life imprisonment in cases of extreme gravity.[20]

These are the main legal provisions in international law instruments which expressly provide for the protection of private property in occupied territories or during hostilities.

3. The European Convention on Human Rights

In parallel a body of international law instruments on human rights has been adopted and is applicable in the territories in respect of which the Contracting Parties exercise jurisdiction. The adoption of such instruments was triggered and inspired by the Universal Declaration of Human Rights adopted and proclaimed by the UN General Assembly Resolution of 10 December 1948. In this Declaration a number of human rights were declared to be part of a common standard of achievement for all peoples and all nations. The list of these rights includes the right of everyone to own property alone as well as in association with others. Arbitrary deprivation of property is prohibited.

There followed the European Convention on Human Rights, which came into force in 1953. It represents the most important regional instrument on human rights. Over a period of 50 years it has become the most sophisticated and effective human rights treaty in the world.

The Convention safeguards the right to property in Article 1 of Protocol No. 1 in the following terms:

> Every natural or legal person is entitled to the peaceful enjoyment of his possessions. No one shall be deprived of his possessions except in the public interest and subject to the conditions provided for by law and by the general principles of international law.
>
> The preceding provisions shall not, however, in any way impair the right of a State to enforce such laws as it deems necessary to control the use of property in accordance with the general interest or to secure the payment of taxes or other contributions or penalties.

The language used guarantees the protection of a wide range of proprietorial interests. It covers immovable and movable property and corporal and incorporeal interests such as shares and patents, as well as contractual rights including leases and judgment debts. Furthermore,

20 Arts. 5, 77.

the concept of "possession" is autonomous, which means that other economic interests may be found to be sufficient to enjoy protection by virtue of this right.[21] However, it should be noted that the right is not a right to have or acquire property, but a right to the protection of a person's existing property.[22] Evidently the importance of the right in relation to specific cases depends on the nature, extent, and value of the particular property in respect of which the right is invoked. Certainly, a property which is at the same time the home of its owner – and therefore afforded additional protection by virtue of the right to respect for one's home[23] – is of much greater value than a piece of land of no special utility.

The Convention allows measures derogating from the obligations under the Convention in time of war or other public emergency threatening the life of the nation.[24] However, in order for a derogation to be valid the High Contracting Party resorting to it must establish that the measures derogating from the obligations were strictly required by the exigencies of the situation and that they are not inconsistent with its other obligations under international law.

No derogation concerning the right to property has been invoked until now at the instance of any High Contracting Party to the Convention. The UK and Turkey have however derogated in respect of Article 5 on the ground of the need to counter domestic terrorism.[25]

Given that under Article 15 the measures of derogation must not be inconsistent with other obligations under international law of the High Contracting Party resorting to them, the latter is precluded from relying on Article 15 in order to justify any interference with any property right in any territory occupied by it contrary to its obligations under custom-

21 See *Gasus Dosier- und Fordertechnik GmbH v. the Netherlands,* Series A no. 306-B (1995), where the Court also observed that "possession" is not limited to ownership of physical goods: other rights and interests constituting assets can also be regarded as property rights.

22 See D. Rook, *Property Law and Human Rights* (London Blackstone 2001) 60-1, where it is also stated that the guarantee does protect the "peaceful enjoyment of possessions which embraces the right to own, possess, use, lend or dispose of the property as one so desires without interference by the state".

23 Art. 8 of the Convention.

24 Art. 15 of the Convention.

25 No derogation concerning a state of war has yet been in issue.

ary international law such as those provided in the Hague Regulations.[26] But even if there is no derogation, there is no possibility in law for an occupying country to interfere with any property in such territory in exercise of any rights under the provisions of Article 1 of Protocol No. 1 of the Convention (e.g. deprivation of possessions "in the public interest") contrary to the relevant rules of international law, because these provisions cannot reasonably be interpreted as bestowing on an occupant country any more rights than those found in the Hague Regulations, or as abrogating the protection provided by these Regulations.[27] It is submitted that it is evident from the wording and object of the provisions in question that the possibility of an occupying country exercising the rights of a lawful government for the purposes of the same provisions is excluded. Reference to the "law" or "laws" could only mean the laws adopted and enforced by the lawful government of that territory. Moreover, the express reference to "the conditions provided for ... by the general principles of international law" for any deprivation of possessions[28] brings in the legal restrictions on the rights of occupying States in the territories occupied by them.

It is now universally recognised that in time of armed conflict, civilian populations are in special need of increased protection and the fundamental human rights recognised by international law continue to apply

26 Cf. D.J. Harris, M. O'Boyle and C. Warbrick, *Law of the European Convention on Human Rights* (London Butterworths 1995) 502. See also Art. 53 of the Convention: "Nothing in this Convention shall be construed as limiting or derogating from any of the human rights and fundamental freedoms which may be ensured under the laws of any High Contracting Party or under any other agreement to which it is a party."

27 Art. 53 of the Convention.

28 This requires that any taking of property must conform with international law, and it is submitted that the better view is that this requirement applies to nationals as well as to aliens: C. Russo, "L'application aux nationaux des principes généraux du droit international vise l'article 1 du Protocol N° 1" in *Mélanges Wiarda* (Cologne Carl Heymann Verlag 1988) 547 et seq., and the references appearing at 522 n. 5; L. Condorelli, "Article 1 of the Additional Protocol" in Pettiti, Decaux and Imbert (eds.), *La Convention européenne des Droits de l'Homme* (Paris Economics 1995) 986-8. See to the contrary *Lithgow v. the United Kingdom*, ECHR Series A no. 102 (1986) and *James and Others v. the United Kingdom*, ECHR Series A no. 98 (1986).

fully. This has been stressed by the United Nation's General Assembly in its Resolution of 9 December 1970.[29]

Generally effective legal protection of human rights, including the right to property, can be achieved in territories under the *de jure* or *de facto* control of States which are parties to the European Convention on Human Rights, which provides efficient machinery in respect of breaches of its provisions. No comparable machinery exists in respect of non-compliance with the Hague Regulations, the Geneva Conventions or the UN Resolutions including those of the Security Council, whose implementation depends on the political will of its permanent members.

4. Case-law under the European Convention

The European Convention on Human Rights has in fact been applied in specific cases concerning interference with property belonging to individuals in occupied territories. These cases are the four interstate cases of *Cyprus v. Turkey*[30] and the individual applications of *Loizidou v. Turkev*,[31] *Demades v. Turkey*,[32] and *Eugenia Michaelidou Developments Ltd and Michael Tymvios v. Turkey*.[33] They all concerned complaints by or on behalf of Greek-Cypriot owners of immovable property in the northern part of Cyprus occupied by Turkey since the invasion of the island in 1974, on account of being prevented by the respondent govern-

29 Res 2675 (XXV) "Noting that in the present century the international community has accepted an increased role and new responsibilities for the alleviation of human suffering in any form and, in particular, during armed conflicts ... Convinced that civilian populations are in special need of increased protection in time of armed conflicts ... Affirms the following basic principles for the protection of civilian populations in armed conflicts, without prejudice to their future elaboration within the framework of progressive development of the international law of armed conflict: 1. Fundamental human rights, as accepted by international law and laid down in international instruments, continue to apply fully in situations of armed conflict ..."

30 Applications nos. 6780/74, 6950/75, 8007/77, and 25781/94 respectively.

31 Application no. 15318/89.

32 Application no. 16219/90.

33 Application no. 16163/90.

ment from having access to, control, use and enjoyment of their properties.

The first three interstate cases resulted in reports adopted by the European Commission of Human Rights in 1976 and 1983 in which Turkey was found responsible *inter alia* for continuing violations of the right to property in the form of deprivation of possessions of Greek Cypriots without this being justified by any of the aims mentioned in Article 1 of Protocol No. 1.[34] At that time the respondent government had not recognised the jurisdiction of the Court and therefore the proceedings ended in ineffective, politically motivated and worded resolutions of the Committee of Ministers of the Council of Europe.[35]

The fourth interstate case of *Cyprus v. Turkey*, as well as the three individual applications of *Loizidou, Demades*, and *Michaelidou*, present a greater legal interest inasmuch as they were finally decided in 1996, 2001, and 2003 respectively by the European Court of Human Rights, whose jurisdiction had in 1989 been accepted by Turkey, and whose judgments are legally binding on the parties. The following points made in the judgment in the *Loizidou* case, which was the first of the relevant group to be decided by the Court, are particularly important for the topic under consideration.

(a) Turkey occupied through its military forces the northern part of Cyprus where the immovable property of the applicant was situated.[36] As a consequence Turkey was considered as exercising *de*

34 See the Commission's Report in *Cyprus v. Turkey* applications nos. 6780/74 and 6950/75, 151 and 166, "there has been deprivation of possessions of Greek Cypriots on a large scale, the exact extent of which could not be determined" and Report in application no. 8007/77, 42-3, 47. The reference to possible justification "by any of the aims mentioned in Article 1 of Protocol No. 1" was made without any consideration of the question of whether such justification can in law apply to any interference with property rights by an occupant country contrary to the Hague Regulations. Such question was not raised in the relevant proceedings and it is submitted that the answer should be in the negative (see 5-6 in the present Article). It may be added that in any event no justification in terms of Article 1 of Protocol No. 1 was invoked by the respondent government. Therefore the reference to possible justification under the Article in question was *obiter* as well as wrong.

35 ResDH(79)1 and ResDH(92)12.

36 *Loizidou v. Turkey (Preliminary Objections)* ECHR Series A no. 310 (1995) 24 para 63, and *Loizidou v. Turkey (Merits)* (n 19), 2223, 2234.

facto jurisdiction over that part of Cyprus and therefore it was, by virtue of Article 1 of the Convention, accountable for any violations of any rights safeguarded thereby in respect of the same area.

(b) The administration established in the occupied area and known as "TRNC", itself being legally invalid and amounting simply to a subordinate administration of Turkey, the expropriation of the applicant's property through the Constitution of the "TRNC" was of no legal effect. Accordingly, the applicant could not be deemed to have lost title to her property as a result of the "TRNC" Constitution.[37]

(c) As a consequence of the fact that the applicant was refused access to her land by the Turkish troops since 1974, the applicant effectively lost all control over, as well as all possibilities to use and enjoy, her property.[38]

(d) Neither the fact that the property rights were the subject of inter-communal talks, nor the need to re-house displaced Turkish Cypriot refugees in the years following the Turkish intervention in the island in 1974, could justify the total and continuing denial of access and purported expropriation without compensation in this case.[39]

In these circumstances the Court concluded that there was and continued to be a breach of the right to property under the Convention.[40]

A similar approach was adopted by the Court in the 4th interstate case and in the individual applications of *Demades* and *Michaelides* in respect of complaints about interference with property rights of the same nature as in the *Loizidou* case. It is important to note that in the interstate case the Court dealt with a complaint concerning interference with the property rights of more than 200,000 Greek Cypriots. The Court found

> that there has been a continuing violation of Article 1 of Protocol No. 1 of the Convention by virtue of the fact that Greek Cypriot owners of property in northern Cyprus are being denied access to and control, use and enjoy-

37 Ibid., at 2231-2.

38 Ibid., at 2237.

39 Ibid., at 2237-8.

40 Ibid., at 2238.

ment of their property as well as any compensation for the interference with their property rights.

In this respect it should be borne in mind that the property or "possessions" to which the interstate case referred and the relevant finding of the Court of a continuous violation of the Convention applied, was the same property covered by the first three interstate applications viz the houses and other property belonging to the displaced Greek Cypriots (about 200,000) and legal persons, which included extensive agricultural, commercial and industrial enterprises, tourist industries (hotels and other tourist accommodation), etc.[41]

In the *Loizidou* case the Court awarded 300,000 CY pounds for pecuniary damage, 20,000 CY pounds non-pecuniary damage (for the anguish and feelings of helplessness and frustration which the applicant must have experienced over the years in not being able to use her property as she saw fit) 137,000 CY pounds for costs and expenses and interest at an annual rate of 8 % on the amounts in question.[42]

This jurisprudence covers fully the question as to the kind of legal protection of the right to property in occupied territories guaranteed by the European Convention on Human Rights when no derogation is made, as provided by the Convention.

5. Expropriations Contrary to *Jus Cogens*

On the basis of the current international law, expropriation of private land by the occupying power during an armed conflict or otherwise either directly or through a subordinate administration is illegal and invalid, whether that expropriation is accompanied by compensation or not. It is the more so if the purpose of such expropriation is the violation of peremptory norms of general international law or the commission of crimes against humanity, such as the implementation of a plan of ethnic

41 See the Commission's Report in respect of applications nos. 6780/74 and 6950/75, 141 et seq.; and in respect of application no. 8007/77, 38-43; and the judgment of the Court in *Cyprus v. Turkey*, application no. 25781/94 ECHR 2001-IV, 49-52.

42 *Loizidou v. Turkey (just satisfaction), Reports of Judgments and Decisions* 1998-IV.

cleansing or persecution,[43] or prevention of the exercise of the right to return of displaced persons to their homes and properties from which they were forcibly expelled by the occupying army,[44] or a breach of the rule against racial discrimination. Indeed, to hold otherwise would be tantamount to accepting that a wrongdoing State may be allowed, by the payment of compensation, to purchase the benefits of breaches of rules of international law having a status of *jus cogens* with the ultimate result of endorsing the original wrong and entrenching its character and its consequences: This approach is also expressly adopted by the eminent professors of international law, Georges Abi-Saab, Dieter Blumenwitz, James Crawford, John Dugard, Christopher Greenwood, Gerhard Hafner, Francisco Orrego-Vicuna, Alain Pellet, Henry Schermers and Christian Tomuschat, in a joint opinion dated 30 June 1999.[45]

6. The Position of Third Parties

This leads to another question: Does the illegality and invalidity of appropriations by occupying States of properties affect the subsequent transfer of such properties to third persons who retain possession

43 See *Blaskic* (n 18) para. 233. According to Art 5(h)of the Statute of the Tribunal, persecution on political, racial and religious grounds amounts to a crime against humanity punishable under the same Statute.

44 As to the right of return of refugees and in internally displaced persons to their former homes, lands or places of habitual residence in safety and dignity, see also the final report of the Special Rapporteur of the Commission on Human Rights (Sub-Commission on the Promotion and Protection of Human Rights) Paulo Sergio Pinheiro on the "Principles on housing and property restitution for refugees and displaced persons" (28 June 2005 E/CN.4/Sub.2/2005/17), especially paras. 10.1 and 10.2. See also: Alfred de Zayas, *Heimatrecht ist Menschenrecht,* Universitas, München 2001. See also the Statement by the first United Nations High Commissioner for Human Rights, Jose Ayala Lasso, to the "Expert Meeting on Human Rights Dimensions of Population Transfers including the implantation of settlers and settlements", 17-21 February 1997 and Resolution on the right to return, UN Sub-Commission on Promotion and Protection of Human Rights, Doc. E/CN.4/Sub.2/Res/2002/30.

45 See at 12 of the opinion entitled "Legal Issues arising from Certain Population Transfers and Displacements on the Territory of the Republic of Cyprus in the Period since 20 July 1974" <htttp://www.attorney-general.gov.cy>.

thereof for a substantial length of time? We can answer this question with reference to the typical example of appropriation of properties by occupying countries for the housing of settlers transferred to the occupied areas from their own territories. For my part, I repeat here the views that I have expressed in a relevant article published in 1992:

> Where a choice must be made between two hardships, the one which accords more to the rule of law and justice must be remedied at the expense of the other. This is generally the objective of the law whenever a solution must be found in respect of conflicting claims, interests or situations. And although it is correct to admit that *fait accompli* through the passage of time may establish situations that may become materially impossible to be reversed, the law should retain as much and as long as possible its constructive role as an instrument to deter or avert the prevalence of force over justice. This must be so if the rule that the limits of aggression must not be recognised is to have any meaning. *Ex injurio jus non oritur* is an inescapable principle of law. The forcible transfer of populations and the implantation of settlers are prohibited by international law and qualify as international crimes. These methods entail by definition long-term situations. If it is accepted a priori that passage of time legalises the effects of such methods the role of law becomes pathetic. Law must strive to avert breaches of its rules. If such breaches occur, their continuation or their acceptance should not be a choice of the law.[46]

The principle supported consistently by international jurists, especially after the end of the Second World War, has been, as Oppenheim puts it: "There is little room for doubt that acts of deprivation of property in disregard of International Law are incapable of creating or transferring title."[47] The same jurist proceeds to support the view that

> [neutral] States which by failing to take the requisite and practicable steps for preventing their subjects from acquiring the property in question connive indirectly in the unlawful measures of the occupant and incur a responsibility whose novelty probably does not preclude it from being enforced by appropriate international remedies.[48]

46 L.G. Loucaides, *Essays on the Developing Law of Human Rights* (Dordrecht Nijhoff 1995).

47 *Oppenheim's International Law* (n. 10) 411.

48 Ibid.

In line with these principles, many governments of countries occupied or about to be occupied by the Germans during the Second World War issued decrees notifying that measures of confiscation of private properties by the occupant country as well as transactions deriving from these acts were illegal.[49] There followed a warning issued in 1943 by the USA, Great Britain, Russia, China, and certain other countries to persons in neutral countries, that they intended "to do their utmost to defeat the methods of dispossession" practised in the occupied territories.[50] It is true that these measures did not serve as a deterrent to the occupying power, nor did they restrain "collaborationist" elements in the local population from engaging in prohibited property deals under enemy occupation.[51] Nevertheless, these measures may have certain positive legal effects upon withdrawal of the occupant. In any event, such measures are useful in that they warn both nationals and agents in the occupied territories or abroad as regards the legal consequences of their transactions or investments with respect to properties in such territories.

It is useful to add here that according to the final report of the Special Rapporteur Paulo Sergio Pinheiro referred to above (op. cit.), "[s]tates should ensure that the safeguards of due process extended to secondary occupants do not prejudice the rights of legitimate owners, tenants and other rights holders to repossess the housing, land and property in question in a just and timely manner" (para. 17.2). Secondary occupants are persons who take up residence in a home after the home's rightful occupants have fled due to, *inter alia*, forced displacement, forced eviction, violence or threat of violence, or natural or human-made disasters. Secondary occupation may at times occur when the perpetrators of human rights abuses forcibly evict residents and subsequently loot property and move into the abandoned homes themselves. Yet, often, secondary occupiers are themselves displaced persons.[52]

---

49 Robinson, "Transfer of Property in Enemy Occupied Territory", *AJIL* 39, 221 et seq.

50 *Oppenheim's International Law* (n. 10) 410-11, and Robinson (n. 48) 228-9.

51 Robinson (n. 48) 223.

52 See para. 63 of the *Explanatory Notes on the Principles on Housing and Property Restitution for Refugees and Displaced Persons,* 11 July 2005.

7. The Breaches of the Principles

It is sad to admit that the sound principles of international law to which I have referred have in fact been disregarded by those expected to respect them. The relevant Hague Regulations were entirely ignored by the Germans while they occupied European countries during the Second World War, for they made requisitions, not only for the needs of the army of occupation; but for the needs of Germany in general, and they confiscated without compensation the property of special categories of persons, such as those belonging to the ruling family, those who left the country, Jews, and citizens of annexed territories.[53] For example, the houses and possessions of 1,500,000 Poles, who were forcibly deported from the annexed territories during the first year of German occupation, were turned over to Germans, mostly new settlers; and in Alsace and Lorraine all property of enemies of Germany was confiscated.[54]

The practice of "Aryanization" of property, that is, transfer of property defined as Jewish to Germans, was also adopted. As pointed out by Robinson, "this practice clearly violates Article 43 of the Hague Convention because it conflicts with the constitutional safeguards of equality of all citizens irrespective of race or creed".[55]

Similar breaches of the Hague Regulations and other principles of international law prohibiting appropriation of properties by occupying powers were committed by the Soviet troops in the Second World War, culminating in the widespread organised system of "nationalising" private properties, even without any compensation, in countries occupied by these troops in order to implement the communist system of government. Such nationalisation lasted for half a century until the communist regimes collapsed. Afterwards, in certain ex-communist countries it was recognised that a remedy should be provided for the restoration of the properties to their lawful owners, even though the solution adopted in some of these countries was not entirely satisfactory in terms of fulfilling the international law obligation of restitution *in integrum*. Certain discriminatory conditions referring, for example, to the residence or the nationality of the lawful owners, etc., were attached to the possibility of returning the properties. It must, however, be mentioned that the

53 Ibid., at 219.

54 Ibid., n. 10.

55 Ibid., at 220.

nationalisation of the private properties in these cases was maintained by the local communist governments, which enjoyed international recognition and, for that matter, the view may be taken that the resulting appropriations were thus legalised in terms of the domestic legal order.

8. Case-law Regarding the Expropriation in the Occupied Zone of Germany

Expropriations effected in the German Democratic Republic without compensation subsequent to 1949 fell, according to the Unification Treaty, under a specific Act which provided, in principle, for the return of confiscated property, where this was still possible and did not violate user rights acquired in good faith. If a return was excluded compensation had to be paid.

However, properties expropriated by the Soviet Union between 1945 and 1949 in the Soviet occupied zone of Germany, were, according to the same Treaty, not to be returned. The lawful owners of these properties applied to the European Commission of Human Rights complaining against Germany about this regulation concerning their property.[56] They argued that the expropriation of their property was invalid under public international law, in particular the Hague Convention on the Laws and Customs of War, and that it resulted in a continuous violation of their property rights. Therefore the Unification Treaty, by excluding both restitution and full reparation, amounted in their submission to a violation of Article 1 of Protocol No. 1 of the European Convention on Human Rights. They denied that in the unification negotiations the former Soviet Union demanded that property taken between 1945 and 1949 should not be given back to its former owners. They considered that the only concern of the Soviet Union was that the legality of the expropriations concerned should not be put into question. The respondent Government submitted that in the light of the history of the unification negotiations as a whole, there could be no doubt that the Soviet Union accepted German unification only on the condition that expropriations carried out between 1945 and 1949 should not be reversed. Furthermore, the respondent Government considered that Germany also had to respect its obligations under the Unification Treaty *vis-à-vis* the Russian Federation. In this respect it has been submitted that from

56 *Weidlich and Others v. Germany*, applications nos. 19048/91, 19049/91, 19342/92, 19549/92, and 18890/91.

the Russian point of view the expropriations in question were meant as a punishment for war criminals and Nazis.

In 1996 the Commission, by majority, rejected the complaints of the applicants. The Commission noted that the original deprivation of the applicants' property occurred at the instance of the Soviet occupying forces in Germany, more than 40 years ago, at a time when the Federal Republic of Germany did not even exist. Even if it was true that the authorities of both German States subsequently recognised the validity of the expropriations in question, the German authorities could in no way be held responsible for the deprivation of property as such, which was not imputable to them. Despite the applicants' claim that the expropriations were contrary to international law and thus unlawful, in the German legal order these expropriations were being considered as legally valid even before the conclusion of the Unification Treaty. The provisions of the Treaty could not therefore be seen as legalising the deprivation of the applicants' property and thereby as being the source of the deprivation for the purposes of German law. As regards any possible compensation claim generated by the loss of the property, the Commission referred to its jurisprudence, according to which it is not competent *ratione temporis* and *ratione materiae* to examine complaints relating to the refusal or denial of compensation claims based on facts that occurred prior to the entry into force of the Convention with respect to the State concerned. The Commission observed that the expropriations took place before the entry into force of the Convention and before the ratification of Protocol No. 1 by the Federal Republic of Germany. In this respect the Commission applied its case-law, according to which a deprivation of ownership or other rights *in rem* is in principle an instantaneous act and does not produce a continuing situation of "deprivation of right".

As a member of the Commission at that time, I disagreed with this decision because I considered that the acts of confiscation were contrary to international law. Other members of the Commission also disagreed.

It may be pointed out that this case is distinguishable from the *Loizidou* case in many respects including the fact that the acts of confiscation of the German properties had taken place before the date of entry into force of the Convention and the ratification of Protocol No. 1 by the respondent Government and that such acts were considered legally valid, according to the German legal order.[57]

What is of additional interest about the German properties case in question is the fact that, pending the decision of the Commission, the German authorities felt duty bound to compensate the applicants for the loss of their properties in the Soviet occupied zone, and this was done through a law enacted in 1994. To complete the history of this case up to this moment, I must add that there are now pending before the European Court applications on the part of those concerned by which they complain that their right to their properties is again violated, inasmuch as the compensation provided in this law is inadequate.[58]

9. Concluding Remarks

There are also more recent serious and systematic interferences with property rights by occupying countries, which continue without any foreseeable remedy. Reference must be made here to the confiscation and expropriation of private and public Arab property in the territories occupied by Israel, which has been repeatedly strongly condemned by the UN General Assembly,[59] and the confiscation and exploitation of the properties of more than 200,000 Greek Cypriots by Turkey, which has been continuing since the Turkish invasion of Cyprus in 1974 contrary to the Rules of International Law already referred to, and the European Convention on Human Rights, and in utter disregard and contempt of the reports of the European Commission of Human Rights and the judgments of the European Court of Human Rights.

Generally States are not prepared to admit that they have the status of an occupying power. As pointed out by Roberts and Guelff:

> [a]t various times, certain States have put forward arguments purporting to show that the situations in which their forces are involved are not mili-

57 See also *Prince Hans Adam II of Liechtenstein v. Germany*, application no. 42527/98, ECHR 2001-VIII.

58 Applications nos. 71916/01, 71917/01, and 10260/02.

59 E.g. A/RES/41/63[D] (3 Dec. 1986). The UN Commission on Human Rights followed the same approach in a series of Resolutions entitled "Question of the violation of human rights in the occupied Arab territories, including Palestine", see, e.g., Resolutions 1985/1 A and B (19 Feb. 1985) and Resolution 1986/1 A and B (20 Feb. 1986).

> tary occupations, or at least differ in significant respects from the understanding of occupation in the Regulations annexed to 1907 Hague Convention IV and 1949 Geneva Convention IV.[60]

This is an additional element, albeit not a principal one, of the problem of non-implementation of the rules protecting properties in occupied territories.

In the light of the above, one may doubt the usefulness of the existence and invocation of the relevant rules and judicial decisions of international law prohibiting or condemning interference with the right to property by an occupying country. One may understandably say: Beautiful rules, excellent judgments, clearly defined human rights, impartial courts, but at the end of the day all these are completely disregarded. The more serious the breach of international law, the less effective are its norms and the competent international institutions.

In response to that, I can only say that in an ever increasingly interdependent world, especially in the European Continent, obedience or disobedience to established rules of international law, Conventional obligations and respect for human rights do matter and can affect the relations between States and even the fate of their political objectives. The international community is nowadays, more so than many years ago, sensitive to breaches of the rule of law and human rights. We have witnessed certain positive reactions to efforts for the prevalence of law in international relations, even though such reactions originated more from the people, rather than their governments. Let us not allow our disappointment to suspend a continuous fight for justice. If we give up, we will be deprived of all possibilities for improving the standards of behaviour of States or, to be more precise, the standards of treatment of human beings by other human beings.

---

60 A. Roberts and R. Guelff (n. 6) 300. Turkey, for example, although it occupies the northern part of Cyprus since the invasion of the island in 1974, resists the terms "invasion" and "occupation" and uses instead the terms "peaceful action" and "peaceful operation"; more specifically, as regards the status of the occupied area, this has been described by Turkey as the "Turkish Federated State of Cyprus" and later as the "Turkish Republic of Northern Cyprus" ("TRNC"); see the Commission's Report in applications nos. 6780/74 and 6980/75 (n. 34) 6-7 and at 10 of the admissibility decision attached as an appendix to the same Reports, the admissibility decision in application no. 8007/77 at 150 and the judgment of the Court in *Cyprus v. Turkey* (n. 41) 22-3.

Chapter 9 Freedom of Expression and the Right to Reputation

Freedom of expression as safeguarded in various constitutional and international law instruments has been developed and expanded by the case-law and the doctrine of western countries in a dynamic and progressive manner in line with the liberal trends and ideas of democracy that have emerged during the years following the Second World War. The concept of freedom of expression was enlarged with an idealistic approach to such an extent that other legitimate interests or rights such as the right to privacy and reputation had to be subjected to inroads and lost, to some substantial degree, and unnecessarily, the required protection which those values deserve.

Taking as examples for our topic the case-law of the US Supreme Court and the European Court of Human Rights, i.e. two judicial institutions which command international respect and which have been particularly active in the field of freedom of expression, a comparable evolution can be discerned.[1] Both institutions began pursuing a case-

1 It is correct that the structure of the US constitutional protection regarding freedom of expression defers from the corresponding protection under Article 10 of the European Convention on Human Rights (see Harris, O'Boyle, Warbrick, *Law of the European Convention on Human Rights*, p. 375). However, the comparison, for the purposes of the topic under consideration, between the relevant case-law in both systems is still useful considering that the US protection of freedom of expression (like the Strasbourg protection), is not absolute but is qualified, such qualification being founded on opposing societal interests or social values. The reputation of individuals has long being recognised as deserving protection. The US Supreme Court as early as 1922 indicated that there was to be no blanket First Amendment protection from either civil action or criminal prosecution for those who defame others (*Balzac v Porto Rico*, 66 L. Ed. 627, 1922). In *Beauharnais v. Illinois*, 343 US 250 (1952) the Court declared that: "Libelous utterances [are] not within the area of constitutionally protected speech." In *Resenblatt v. Baer* (15 L. Ed. 2nd 597, 1966) the Court stated that "important social values ... underlie the law of defamation" and

law approach which adopted an extended protection of freedom of expression especially where the mass media are concerned, as compared with the protection of personal reputation.

1. The Approach of the US Supreme Court

Freedom of speech is safeguarded under the US Constitution through its First Amendment as follows: "Congress shall make no law ... abridging the freedom of speech or of the press."

In 1964, in *New York Times Co. v. Sullivan*,[2] the US Supreme Court engaged in a major doctrinal shift when it had to examine whether the "archaic, rigid and arbitrary"[3] rules of the common law and the privileges they accorded to the press, were incompatible with the First Amendment which protects freedom of speech. The Supreme Court found that the required defence of truth in libel actions did not allow sufficient "breathing space" to free expression, because of the "self-censorship" resulting from the difficulty and expense of proving it.[4] The Supreme Court stated:

> ... libel can claim no talismanic immunity from constitutional limitations. It must be measured by standards that satisfy the First Amendment.
>
> ... [We] consider this case against the background of a profound national commitment to the principle that debate on public issues should be uninhibited, robust, and wide-open, and that it may well include vehement, caustic, and sometimes unpleasantly sharp attacks on Government and public officials.

Erroneous statement is protected, the Supreme Court asserted, there being no exception "for any test of truth". Error is inevitable in any free

---

acknowledged that "[s]ociety has a pervasive and strong interest in preventing and redressing attacks upon reputation". See also Antieau, *Modern Constitutional Law*, 2nd ed. Vol. I, pp. 117 et seq. and The Constitution of the United States of America prepared by the Congressional Research Service, Library of Congress, 1987, pp. 1005 et seq. and 1979, pp. 1003-1007.

2 376 US 254 (1964).

3 Elder, "Kentucky Criminal Libel Law and Public Officials – An Historical Anachronism?" (1981) 8 *N. Ky. L. Rev.* 37.

4 376 US 279 (1964).

debate and to place liability upon that score and especially to place on the speaker the burden of proving truth would introduce self-censorship and stifle the free expression which the First Amendment protected. To take account of factual error, inevitable in robust debate, the Supreme Court adopted exacting constitutional conditions of civil liability in defamation for criticism of "official conduct" of a "public official" – i.e. proof[5] of "actual malice" namely "with knowledge that it was false or with reckless disregard of whether it was false or not" established by evidence of "convincing clarity".[6]

While recognising a societal interest in protecting the good name and reputation of individuals,[7] the US Supreme Court continued, in the name of freedom of speech, to restrict the level of liability for defamatory statements, especially for the press, always on the premise that the press is a pillar of democracy which should be left free to disseminate information and criticise people, particularly those in public positions or in respect of matters of public concern.[8] The latitude given to journalists by the US Supreme Court extended up to the abolition of the common law presumption that defamatory speech is false in cases where a plaintiff seeks damages against a media defendant for speech of public

5 *Idem*, pp. 279-280.

6 *Idem*, pp. 285-286; for this case-law and generally on the subject of the development of the relevant American jurisprudence see David Elder, "Freedom of Expression and the Law of Defamation: The American Approach to Problems Raised by the *Lingens* Case", in *International and Comparative Law Quarterly*, Vol. 35, pp. 891 et seq.; see also Eleni Micha, "Defamation: Dignity Lost?", in *Netherlands Quarterly of Human Rights*, Vol. 16, No. 3, pp. 261 et seq. Certain Judges have gone as far as to express the view that the First Amendment affords "an absolute, unconditional privilege to criticise official conduct" (Justice Goldberg joined by Justice Douglas).

7 See fn. 1 above.

8 In the case of *Gertz v. Robert Welch Inc.* 418 US 323 (1974) the Court held that the *New York Times* standards should not apply to libels of private individuals, if the defamatory falsehoods concerned matters of general or public interest, but even in their case they are required to prove some degree of culpable conduct on the part of the publisher such as intentional or reckless falsehood or negligence. Moreover, the Court found that even if the plaintiff succeeds in such case recovery for loss of reputation will be conditioned upon "competent" proof of actual injury to his standing in the community and in any event no punitive damages will be awarded in his favour.

concern.[9] Justice Stevens, in his dissenting opinion, pointed out that the majority "grossly undervalues the strong state interest in redressing injuries to private reputations". "I simply do not understand" he added "why a character assassin should be given an absolute license to defame by means of statements that can be neither verified nor disproved". This was further described by the same judge as an "obvious blueprint for character assassination".[10] The US Supreme Court's approach towards an over-extensive protection of the mass media from liability for defamatory statements may be further exemplified by references to case-law such as *Masson v. New Yorker Magazine* [11] where the Supreme Court held that a deliberate misquotation of the words uttered by a plaintiff "does not equate with knowledge of falsity for purposes of New York Times unless it results in a material change in the meaning conveyed by the statement". In his dissenting opinion Justice White convincingly points out that the use of quotation marks in reporting what a person said asserts that the person spoke the words as quoted. "Malcom [the reporter] wrote that Masson said certain things that she knew Masson did not say. By any definition of the term this was 'knowing falsehood'".[12] The same Judge added that according to the decision in this case "the reporter may lie a little but not too much".[13] Another line of case-law has lowered the severity of the test of "reckless disregard" by defining it as the serious doubts which the defendant in fact entertained of the truth of his publication. If the acquired information was believed to be true,

9 *Philadelphia Newspapers Inc. v. Heppa*, 89 L Ed 2d 783 (1986).

10 Idem, p. 799 (per J. Stevens with C.J. Burger, J. White and J. Rehnquist joining, dissenting). "... the Court today seems to believe that the character assassin has a constitutional license to defame", idem, p. 798.

11 115 L Ed. 2nd, 501 US, 496.

12 With regard to the majority view that misquotations that do not materially alter the meaning inflict no injury to reputation Justice White observed "This may be true but this is a question of defamation or not, and has nothing to do with whether the author deliberately put within quotation marks and attributed to the speaker words that the author knew the speaker did not utter", op. cit., p. 478. For a criticism of the Masson judgement see W.P. Marshall and S. Gilles, "The Supreme Court, the Ist Amendment and Bad Journalism", *Supreme Court Review*, 1994, pp. 169-208. It is useful to note here that there were no statements-opinions in the Masson case but a tape-recorded interview which was published within quotation marks with material alterations.

13 Op. cit., p. 479.

or even doubted but not seriously, then the statements at issue were protected under the First Amendment, even if the defendant neglected to confirm the relevant facts; it was also held that failure to comply with "professional standards" is not in itself sufficient to establish "actual malice".[14]

The American case-law adopted a distinction between statements of facts and statements of opinions the truth or falsity of the latter not being capable of proof thus allowing any statement of opinion to enjoy immunity from liability for defamation. Thus in the *Gertz v. Robert Welch Inc.*,[15] we find the following dicta:

> We begin with the common ground. Under the First Amendment there is no such thing as a false idea. However pernicious an opinion may seem, we depend for its correction not on the conscience of judges and juries but on the competition of other ideas.

An extension of this approach was the adoption of a broad constitutional absolute immunity rule for pure opinion in the second Restatement of Torts as follows:

> A simple expression of opinion based on disclosed or assumed non-defamatory facts is not itself sufficient for an action of defamation, no matter how unjustified and unreasonable the opinion may be or how derogatory it is.[16]

2. Criticism of the Case-law

The line of case-law in support of an extensive protection of the freedom of speech was accompanied by strong dissenting opinions and critical comments such as: "It makes no sense" to accord the most protection to press-disseminators who cause the widest "misinformation and do

14 *Harte Hawks v. Connaughton*, 491 US, 562.

15 Op. cit., pp. 339-340. This "opinion" doctrine is also found in the case-law of the European Court of Human Rights. It poses practical and legal problems especially when it gives rise to the difficulty of distinguishing a pure opinion from an opinion which contains a factual connotation. Regarding some of the problems arising from the application of this doctrine see Elder, op. cit., pp. 921-922. See also Micha, op. cit., p. 264.

16 See Elder, op. cit., p. 921.

the most damage to private reputation".[17] The *New York Times* judgment necessarily, through its exacting standards, left many deserving plaintiffs without a remedy.[18] "The Court would now shift this risk [of falsehood] to the victim, even though he has done nothing to invite the calumny, is wholly innocent of fault and is helpless to avoid his injury. I doubt that jurisprudential resistance to liability without fault is sufficient ground for employing the First Amendment revolutionise the law of Libel, and in my view, that body of legal rules poses no realistic threat to the press and its service to the public. The press today is vigorous and robust. To me, it is quite incredible to suggest that threats of libel suits from private citizens are causing the press to refrain from publishing the truth. I know of no hard facts to support that proposition, and the Court furnishes none."[19] "New York Times undervalues the individual's interest in reputation. The Court too readily exalts the constitutional interest in free expression over the competing constitutional interest in reputation."[20] *New York Times* may actually reduce "the quality of information [available to the public by eliminating jury judgments] as to the truth or falsity of some accusations".[21]

It is useful to add here the views of two writers on the subject under consideration. Professor Elder in his article cited above states as part of his conclusion the following:

> The Court, in roughly the first decade of its decisions, crafted broad rules of protection for the media with the net result that almost all plaintiffs encountered the exacting requirements of New York Times. Unfortunately, this media oriented spate of decisions resulted in the near demise of an effective remedy for libel (at least against the media), unnecessarily diminished protection of the quasi-constitutional interest in individual reputation, and inadequately protected the quite legitimate interest of the states in deterring defamatory falsehood.[22]

17 Per Justice White quoted by Elder, op. cit., p. 911.

18 *Gertz* case, op. cit., p. 807.

19 Per Justice White in his dissenting opinion in the *Gertz* case.

20 Stone, Seidman, Sunstein, Tushnet, *Constitutional Law*, 2nd ed., p. 1152.

21 Nagel "How Useful Is Judicial Review in Free Speech Cases?" 69 *Cornell L. Rev*. 302. 323 (1984).

22 Op. cit., p. 923. However, the writer points out that the trend of the case-law began to change direction after 1974 with an inclination generally to limit the sphere of applicability of *New York Times* and *Gertz.*

Dr. Eleni Micha in her article cited above states the following:

> ... one cannot overlook the fact, that the Supreme Court follows a track towards an extended protection of free speech especially where the media are concerned, in contrast to the protection of personal reputations ...
>
> ... the dominant position in both systems (US Supreme Court and Strasbourg Court) during the last years is in favour of a free press, even though incidents of bad journalism increase at an alarming rate, forcing us to wonder whether personal reputation still retains its value.[23]

One cannot disagree with the importance of the freedom of speech, especially that of the media, as an essential factor of the democratic society. However, the question is whether the protection accorded to such a freedom may, under any circumstances, be so excessive as to deprive the victims of false defamatory statements of the necessary effective remedy.

3. The Case-law of the European Court of Human Rights

An attempt will now be made to deal with the topic under consideration on the basis of the provisions of the European Convention on Human Rights ("the Convention") and in the light of relevant case-law of the European Court of Human Rights ("the Court").

Freedom of speech is safeguarded by Article 10 of the Convention. The relevant parts on which we need to concentrate are as follows:

> 1) Everyone has the right to freedom of expression. This right shall include freedom to hold opinions and to receive and impart information and ideas without interference by public authority ...
>
> 2) The exercise of these freedoms, since it carries with it duties and responsibilities, may be subject to such formalities, conditions, restrictions or penalties as are prescribed by law and are necessary in a democratic society, ... for the protection of the reputation or rights of others ...

In *Handyside v. the United Kingdom*,[24] the Court, in a much quoted passage, said:

---

23 Op. cit., at pp. 275 and 284.

24 Series A no. 24, § 49 (1996).

> Freedom of expression constitutes one of the essential foundations of a [democratic] society, one of the basic conditions for its progress and for the development of every man. Subject to paragraph 2 of Article 10, it is applicable not only to 'information' or 'ideas' that are favourably received or regarded as inoffensive but also to those that offend, shock or disturb the state or any sector of the population. Such are the demands of that pluralism, tolerance and broadmindedness without which there is no 'democratic society'.[25]

In a recent case[26] the Court reiterated the general principles developed by its case-law as follows:

> The test of 'necessity in a democratic society' requires the Court to determine whether the 'interference' complained of corresponded to a 'pressing social need', whether it was proportionate to the legitimate aim pursued and whether the reasons given by the national authorities to justify it are relevant and sufficient. In assessing whether such a 'need' exists and what measures should be adopted to deal with it, the national authorities are left a certain margin of appreciation. This power of appreciation is not, however, unlimited but goes hand in hand with a European supervision by the Court, whose task it is to give a final ruling on whether a restriction is reconcilable with freedom of expression as protected by Article 10.
>
> One factor of particular importance for the Court's determination in the present case is the essential function the press fulfils in a democratic society. Although the press must not overstep certain bounds, in particular in respect of the reputation and rights of others and the need to prevent the disclosure of confidential information, its duty is nevertheless to impart – in a manner consistent with its obligations and responsibilities – information and ideas on all matters of public interest. In addition, the Court is mindful of the fact that journalistic freedom also covers possible recourse to a degree of exaggeration, or even provocation. In cases such as the present one the national margin of appreciation is circumscribed by the interest of democratic society in enabling the press to exercise its

25 It should be noted that the case-law has been more reluctant to find violations of freedom of expression in cases of defamatory statements concerning judges. See e.g. *Prager and Oberschlick* (26/04/1995, Series A no. 313), But see *De Haes and Gijsels,* judgment 24/02/1997.

26 *Bladet Tromsø and Stensaas v. Norway,* no. 21908/93, ECHR 1999-III.

> vital role of 'public watchdog' in imparting information of serious public concern.
>
> In sum the Court's task in exercising its supervisory function is not to take the place of the national authorities but rather to review under Article 10, in the light of the case as a whole, the decisions they have taken pursuant to their power of appreciation.

In the *Lingens* case[27] the Court pointed out that it is incumbent on the press "to impart information and ideas on political issues just as on those of other areas of public interest" and added that "... freedom of the press affords the public one of the best means of discovering and forming an opinion of the ideas and attitudes of political leaders". Which is why in this context "... the limits of acceptable criticism are accordingly wider as regards a politician as such than as regards a private individual. Unlike the latter, the former inevitably and knowingly lays himself open to close scrutiny of his every word and deed by both journalists and the public at large, and he must consequently display a greater degree of tolerance."

This approach is similar to the one followed in the American jurisprudence on the freedom of speech.[28] The same is true as regards the distinction established by the Court in defamation cases between facts and value-judgments: "The existence of facts can be demonstrated, whereas the truth of value-judgments is not susceptible of proof."[29]

The Court has adopted a balance of interests approach which in certain cases has resulted in greater protection for persons targeted by crit-

27 ECHR, *Lingens* judgement of 8 July 1986, Series A no. 103, 41.

28 The American Judge Brennan in his dissenting opinion in the *Rosenbloom* case (403 US 29,48) criticised the relevant proposition as follows: "[Thus] the idea that certain 'public' figures have voluntarily exposed their entire lives to public inspection, while private individuals have kept theirs carefully shrouded from public view is, at best, a legal fiction."

29 *Lingens* case, op. cit., see also *Oberschlick* (*no 1*) case, Series A no. 204. See however the recent judgement of the First Section of the Court in the *Tammer v. Estonia* case (6 February 2001) where the Court, although accepting that the impugned words "amounted to value judgements", did not extend protection to them by virtue of the freedom of speech because these words "amounted to value judgements couched in offensive language, recourse to which was not necessary in order to express a 'negative' opinion" (§ 67).

icism of journalists, especially when such criticism was aimed at private persons not holding any public office.

It is however important to draw attention to the fact that in defamation cases the Court has been placing freedom of speech in the position of a right expressly guaranteed by the Convention while the protection of reputation has been simply considered as a ground of permissible restriction to the right in question which could only be found as a justified interference to any expression if it was "necessary in a democratic society", in other words if it corresponded to "a pressing social need", was "proportionate to the aim pursued" and "the reasons given were relevant and sufficient". Moreover, judged as a restriction to a right under the Convention it had to be (like any other restriction to such rights) strictly and narrowly interpreted. The State has the burden to assert grounds for interfering with expression and then to demonstrate the existence of "relevant and sufficient" grounds for doing so. As stated in the *Sunday Times* case:

> The Court is faced not with a choice between two conflicting principles but with a principle of freedom of expression that is subject to a number of exceptions which must be narrowly interpreted.[30]

4. The Right to Reputation as a Human Right

However, this approach does not seem to be in line with a correct interpretation of the Convention. It is submitted that the right to reputation is safeguarded by Article 8 of the Convention as part and parcel of the right to respect for one's private life. Professor Velu in a treatise of 1970 expressed the view that the right to respect for private life was, in effect, a miscellany of rights covering a wide field of individual activities, and added:

> In particular, this right protects the individual against:
> 1) Attacks on his physical or mental integrity or his moral or intellectual freedom.
> 2) Attacks on his honour and reputation and similar torts…[31]

30 Series A no. 30, para. 65 (1979).

31 "The European Convention on Human Rights and the Rights to Respect for Private Life, the Home and Communications" in Robertson (ed.), *Privacy and Human Rights* (1973), p. 12 at p. 92. See also Van Dijk and Van Hoof,

The European Commission of Human Rights has implicitly recognised that attacks on a person's reputation may constitute a breach of Article 8.[32] Moreover, it is submitted, that it is reasonable to assume that the case-law of the Commission and the Court to the effect that respect for private life comprises the right to the "free development of the personality" cannot but cover the right to reputation as part of the concept of "private life".[33] This assumption is strengthened by the personalised approach of the Commission and the Court in interpreting and applying the right to privacy. It is useful to add here that the Consultative (Parliamentary) Assembly of the Council of Europe in its Resolution 428 (1970) defined the right to privacy as concerning, *inter alia,* "honour and reputation".

Indeed, it would have been inexplicable not to find a direct protection of the reputation and dignity of the individual in a Convention on Human Rights drafted in the aftermath of the Second World War and intended to enhance the protection of the individual as a person after the abhorrent experiences of Nazism. The Convention expressly protects rights of lesser importance, such as the right to respect of correspondence. It is therefore difficult to accept that the basic human value of a person's dignity[34] is deprived of direct protection by the Convention and instead simply recognised, under conditions, as a possible restriction to

---

Theory and Practice of the European Convention on Human Rights, 2nd ed., pp. 368-369, Harris, O'Boyle, Warbrick, *Law of the European Convention on Human Rights,* p. 304, and Francoise Tulkens, *Freedom of expression and information in a democratic society and the right to privacy under the European Convention on Human Rights: comparative look at Articles 8 and 10 of the Convention in the case-law of the European Court of Human Rights,* p. 28.

32 See appl. no. 2413/65, *X v. Federal Republic of Germany,* Coll. 23 (1967), p. I (7), and *N v. Sweden,* 50 DR 173 (1986). Cf. judgments in *Niemietz v. Germany* (Series A no. 251-B, p. 36), and *Rotaru v. Romania* (ECHR 2000-V, § 44).

33 Loucaides, *Essays on the Developing Law of Human Rights,* pp. 85-88 and 99-102.

34 In this respect the following well-known words of Shakespeare come to our mind: "Good name in man and woman, dear my lord, is the immediate jewel of their souls (...) who steals my purse, steals trash (...) but he that filches from me my good name (...) makes me poor indeed." (*Othello,* Act III, scene 3). The right of redress for harm to reputation "reflects no more than our basic concept of the essential dignity and worth of every human

the freedom of expression with the result that a person's reputation is "allowed" by the Convention to be destroyed should a High Contracting Party decide not to give adequate legal protection against libel. Of course in such a situation one could argue that the obligation of the contracting States to implement the prohibition of degrading treatment would not possibly permit the exercise of a freedom to defame persons at will. Nevertheless a person's dignity requires more extensive and direct protection against false defamatory accusations which may destroy persons or may amount (to use the words of an American judge quoted above) to "character assassinations" – and we have plenty of examples of such tragic results.

In my dissenting opinion, in the report of the Commission concerning the case of *Bladet Tromsø A/S* and *Pal Stensaas v. Norway* (09/07(1998); I stated the following:

> The press is, in our days, an important and powerful means of influencing public opinion. The impressions that may be created through a publication in the press are usually more decisive than the reality because until the reality is found out the impressions prevail. And the reality may never be discovered or when it is disclosed it may be too late to remedy the damage done by the original impressions.[35] The press is in effect exercising a significant power and should be subject to the same restraints applicable to any exercise of power, namely, it should avoid abuse of its power, it should

being – a concept at the root of any decent system of ordered liberty" per J. Stewart. in *Rosenblatt v. Baer*. 383 US 75, 92 (1966) (concurring opinion).

35 As rightly observed by the US Supreme Court in the *Gertz* case, op. cit. (n. 9): "Of course, an opportunity for rebuttal seldom suffices to undo harm of defamatory falsehood. Indeed, the law of defamation is rooted in our experience that the truth rarely catches up with a lie." Pertinent to the same point are also the following observations in the dissenting opinion of Justice Stevens joined by Burger White and Rehnquist in the *Philadelphia Newspapers lnc. v. Hepps* (op. cit.): "The destruction that defamatory falsehood can bring is, to be sure, often beyond the capacity of the law to redeem ... a host of factors may make it impossible for an honourable person to disprove malicious gossip about his past conduct, his relatives, his friends, or his business associates." See also Thomas David Jones, *Human Rights: Group Defamation, Freedom of Expression, and the Law of Nations*, Chap. III, "The Myth of Absolutism: The First Amendment Right to Freedom of Expression" at p. 68: "Once tarnished, reputation is virtually impossible to restore."

act in a fair way and respect the rights of others. Therefore, whenever it engages in imparting information of a defamatory nature it should respect basic rules of natural justice such as the rule of *audi alteram partem*.

Accepting that respect for reputation is an autonomous human right, which derives its source from the Convention itself, leads inevitably to a more effective protection of the reputation of individuals *vis à vis* the freedom of expression. As rightly pointed out by Judge Tulkens:[36]

> More fundamentally, this right is guaranteed by Article 8 § 1 of the Convention, which protects individuals not only against interference by the public authorities but also against interference by individuals and private institutions, including the media .... This brings us to the heart of a situation of virtual conflict between two rights ... in addition to the exception in Article 10 § 2, which ... gives the 'protection of the reputation or rights of others' as a legitimate ground for restricting freedom of expression, Article 8 § 1 requires the State to take the measures necessary to protect the reputation of persons within its jurisdiction.

In the light of the above, it is submitted, that protection of reputation is an obligation cast on the State to enforce a corresponding right guaranteed by the Convention with the same status as the freedom of expression.[37] Any defamatory statement amounts to an interference with the right guaranteed by the Convention and can only be justified if it satisfies the requirements of permissible restrictions on the exercise of such right, i.e. be prescribed by law, be necessary in a democratic society, correspond to a pressing social need, be proportionate to the aim pursued, etc. Therefore, it will be more difficult to defend a defamatory statement in terms of the Convention when examined as an interference with a right recognised thereunder than when examined as a necessary restriction of freedom of expression.

When there is a conflict between two rights under the Convention neither of them can neutralise the other through the adoption of any

36 Op. cit. at pp. 27-28.

37 The view was propounded that the right to reputation enjoys the status of a constitutional right in the US on the ground that the interest in reputation is protected as part of the "liberty" guaranteed by the 14th Amendment. See Monaghan, "Of 'Liberty' and 'Property'", 62 *Cornell L. Rev*. 405 (1977).

absolute approaches. Both must be implemented and survive in harmony through the necessary compromises, depending on the facts of each particular case. Consequently, the position, for instance, that free speech, especially by mass media, allows any false defamatory statement under any circumstances so long as it concerns a politician in the exercise of his public duties or a matter of public interest is, it is submitted, incompatible with the required proper balancing between the two competing rights[38] and their co-existence.

The Court has not as yet adopted a clear position on the question of whether Article 8 protects reputation as part of the concept of private life. There is case-law to the effect that the right to reputation is protected by Article 8 of the Convention.[39] On the other hand a later judgment of the Court went to the other direction by stating that "... to date, in no case brought under Article 8 of the Convention has the Court ruled that this provision embodies a right to protection of reputation and honour as such, albeit that these are interests that may be taken into account in the determination of complaint about a State's failure to ensure 'the right to respect for ... private ... life'".[40] This state of the law is not at all satisfactory and the matter must be brought before the Grand Chamber for a clear and final determination.

5. Over-protection of the Freedom of Expression

Like the American jurisprudence, the Strasbourg case-law on the subject of freedom of speech has on occasions shown excessive sensitivity and granted over-protection in respect of interferences with freedom of expression as compared with interferences with the right to reputation. That may be explained to a certain extent by the fact that the Court has not, so far, recognised the right to reputation as a right guaranteed by the Convention. As pointed out above, reputation has always been considered as a ground for legitimate restriction to freedom of speech provided it satisfied the strict requirements of such restriction. Freedom of speech was a value of primary importance which in many cases could neutralise the legitimate demands for respect for an individual's dig-

38 See Tulkens, op. cit., pp. 32-33 and the relevant references therein to Fr. Rigaux and R. Ergerc.

39 *Chauvy and Others v. France*, no. 64915/01 ECHR 2004 and *Abeberry v. France*, no. 58729/00, 21/09/2004.

40 *Gunnarsson v. Ireland*, appl. no. 4591/04.

nity. There has been a lot of praise of the concept of freedom of speech and its significant role in a democratic society. Reputation was simply referred to in general terms as a category of possible limitations. On occasions – more often in dissenting or separate opinions[41] than in the judgments themselves – one can find certain acknowledgements of the right to reputation as a value worthy of specific protection, but even then reputation is not assessed as a right under the Convention.

The recent case of *Bladet Tromsø and Stensaas v. Norway*[42] illustrates clearly the over-protective approach of the Court as regards freedom of speech in contrast to the right to reputation. The relevant facts of the case may be summed up as follows:

The applicant's newspaper had published an interview with a certain Mr Lindberg who on the instructions of the Ministry of Fisheries had carried out an inquiry and prepared a report in relation to allegations that certain seal hunters of a seal hunting vessel ("*Harmoni*") had used illegal hunting methods. The report was by order of the Ministry in question exempted from public disclosure, the ground being that it contained allegations of statutory offences. The applicant's newspaper reproduced some of the statements of Mr Lindberg included in his report concerning the alleged breaches of the seal-hunting regulations by members of the crew of the *Harmoni*. Defamation proceedings were instituted by the persons concerned against the applicant seeking compensation and requesting that certain of the statements in question be declared null and void. Judgment was entered in favour of the plaintiffs for certain statements which were found to be false and defamatory. These statements included the following:

> "At 11:45 [a crew member] beat to death a female harp seal which was protecting her pup." "At 14:40 [a crew member] beat to death a female harp seal which was protecting her pup." "At 15:00 (a crew member] beat to death a female harp seal." "At 19:00 (a crew member) killed a female which was protecting her pup." "Seals skinned alive." "Not least the report includes an

41 See e.g. dissenting opinion of Judges Palm, Fuhrmann and Baka in the *Stenaas v. Norway* case, *infra*; concurring opinion of Judge Rozakis joined by Judges Baka and Lorenzen in the *Maronek v. Slovakia* case (Second Section, 19 April 2001); dissenting opinion of Judge Rozakis in the case of *Nilsen and Johnsen v. Norway* (25 November 1999).

42 No. 21908/93, ECHR 1999-III.

> account of his (Mr Lindberg) being beaten up by furious hunters, who also threatened to hit him on the head with a gaff if he did not keep quiet."

The Court, by a majority, found that the judgment against the applicant declaring null and void the above statements and awarding compensation to the plaintiff amounted to a violation of Article 10 of the Convention which safeguards freedom of expression. The majority referred to the relevant case-law principles set out above. It found that the impugned judgment served the legitimate aim of protecting the reputation of the crew members but came to the conclusion that such a judgment was not necessary "in a democratic society". In this respect, the majority stressed that the publications in question concerned a matter of public interest[43] and pointed out the duty of the Court to conduct a careful scrutiny of measures interfering with the freedom of speech when such measures are capable of "discouraging the participation of the press in debates over matters of legitimate public concern". Reference was also made to the duty of journalists "to act in good faith in order to provide accurate and reliable information in accordance with the ethics of journalism".[44] It was also accepted that the impugned expressions consisted of factual statements.

Nevertheless, the Court found that the applicant's newspaper was dispensed from the "obligation to verify factual statements that were defamatory for private individuals" because such statements "did not emanate from the newspaper itself" (§ 66) but originated in a report drawn up by Mr Lindberg in an official capacity and could in the cir-

43 It is useful here to repeat the words of Dr. Micha (op. cit., 272). The argumentation of the US Supreme Court "overlooks one cardinal disadvantage: the subjectivity of the distinction between matters of public and private concern. Who could really decide on the issue when the mass media – having a really mighty role today – are able to manipulate people's opinions and promote as matters of public concern, issues really insignificant?" cf. Justice Brennan's criticism of the "public-private dichotomy created by the majority" with "almost no guidance" concerning its extent with the consequence of containing an impoverished definition of "public concern": *Dan & Bradstreet v. Greenmoss Builders*, 472 US 749 (1985).

44 In the case of *Fressoz and Roire v. France*, 21 January 1999, the Court confirmed the principle that Article 10 "protects journalists' rights to divulge information on issues of general interest provided that they are acting in good faith and on an accurate factual basis and provide 'reliable and precise' information in accordance with the ethics of journalism".

cumstances of the case be considered as reliable without being necessary for the newspaper to carry out its own research into the accuracy of the facts reported".

As regards the nature of the defamation, the Court found that although the four impugned statements "implied reprehensible conduct they were not particularly serious". The other two allegations – that seals had been skinned alive and that furious hunters had beaten up Mr Lindberg and threatened to hit him with a gaff – "were more serious but were expressed in rather broad terms and could be understood by readers as having been presented with a degree of exaggeration".

The majority concluded that "on the facts of the present case, the Court cannot find that the crew members' undoubted interest in protecting their reputation was sufficient to outweigh the vital public interest in ensuring an informed public debate over a matter of local and national as well as international interest".

6. The Contrary View

Four members of the Court dissented (Judges Palm, Fuhrmann, Baka and Greve). In the dissenting opinion of the first three Judges it was stated *inter alia* that:

> It is the right to the protection of reputation aspect of the present case which has been given insufficient attention in the Court's judgment and which motivates the present dissent ... for the first time the Court is confronted with the question of how to reconcile the role of newspapers to cover a story which is undoubtedly in the public interest with the right to reputation of a group of identifiable private individuals at the centre of the story. In our view the fact that a strong public interest is involved should not have the consequence of exonerating newspapers from either the basic ethics of their trade or the laws of defamation.
>
> The crux of the Court's reasoning involves essentially a new test that newspapers can be dispensed from verifying the facts of a story depending on (1) the nature and degree of the defamation and (2) whether it was reasonable in the circumstances to rely on the details of the Lindberg report. On both points we find the Court's reasoning to be flawed. The majority has tried to minimise the extent of the defamation in the present case but eventually considers that 'some of the accusations were relatively serious'. However it reaches the rather vague conclusion that 'the criticism was not an attack against all the crew members or any specific crew member'.

> This approach of the majority illustrates the main fault-line running through the judgment, namely that the Court does not give sufficient weight to the reputation of the seal hunters. The effort to balance the respective public and private interests is thus defective front the start.
>
> We observe, in passing, that newspapers can generally be expected to carry out checks on controversial stories before rushing into print.
>
> ... the newspaper did nothing at all to check the story.
>
> ... They could have been expected, at the very least, to ask the crew members for their version of the events and their reaction to the various accusations made by Mr Lindberg and given them an opportunity to answer the accusations at the same time as the impugned articles were printed.
>
> ... The present judgment's conclusion, that the newspaper was exonerated from the verification of basic factual information by virtue of the degree of defamation involved and the supposedly 'official' nature of the Lindberg report, appears to suggest an exceptionally low threshold for the protection of the right to reputation of others where there is an important public interest involved and no public figures.
>
> ... the judgment sends the wrong signal to the press in Europe. Few stories can be so important in a democratic society or deserving of protection under Article 10 of the Convention, that the basic ethics of journalism – which require, *inter alia*, journalists to check their facts before going to press with a story in circumstances such as the present – can be sacrificed for the commercial gratification of an immediate scoop. We are not persuaded that the Court's approach in the case which has exonerated the applicant newspaper from this elementary requirement will actually advance the cause of press freedom since it undermines respect for the ethical principles which the media voluntarily adhere to. Article 10 may protect the right for the press to exaggerate and provoke but not to trample over the reputation of private individuals.

It is submitted that the over-protection of freedom of speech, in an almost unqualified manner, when it concerns a matter of public interest is demonstrated adequately in the above case bearing in mind in particular the response of the dissenters to the approach of the majority.

7. Active Involvement in a Public Discussion

One could also refer to other cases manifesting the same trend. The case of *Nilsen and Johnsen v. Norway* [45] contains basic elements of such a trend. In that case the applicants were police officers representing the Norwegian and the Bergen Police Associations respectively. They were found responsible for having published false defamatory statements concerning Professor Bratholm who, in a book published by him, attributed to the police incidents of unlawful violence, brutality and other forms of misconduct. The impugned statements amounted to allegations that Professor Bratholm "with the intent of harming the police is deliberately imparting false information on police brutality, that he has dishonest motives and that he is taking part in a private investigation for the purpose of fabricating allegations of police brutality". The domestic court found that these allegations were assertions of fact the truth of which could be tested by evidence. In finding in favour of the plaintiff, the Norwegian Supreme Court rightly observed, *inter alia*, that:

> The statements sought to be declared null and void were made in a public debate concerning police brutality.
>
> However, freedom of expression does not go as far as [allowing] every statement in a debate, even if the debate relates to matters of public concern. Freedom of expression must be weighed against the rights of the injured party. The limit between statements which may be permissible and statements which may be declared null and void must in principle be drawn at statements which relate to the other person's personal honesty or motives
>
> ... Nor do accusations of lies, improper motives, dishonesty ... serve to promote the freedom of expression but, perhaps, rather to suppress or prevent debate which should have been allowed to take place.
>
> ... it was natural that Mr Johnsen and Mr Nilsen as representatives looked after the interests of the police officers in the debate ... their freedom of expression should be protected to the same extent as the freedom of those who direct the attention towards possible questionable circumstances within the police force. But as already pointed out there is a limit also in respect of them. That limit has been overstepped in this case.

45 ECHR 1999-VIII (25/11/99).

The Court found by majority that there has been a violation of Article 10 of the Convention as a result of the judgment against the applicants. As regards the statements which imputed improper motives or intentions to Professor Bratholm, the Court found that they should not be regarded as allegations of facts requiring the applicants to prove their truth because, according to the Court, those statements "were intended to convey the applicants' own opinions and were thus rather akin to value judgments". As regards the other statements, the majority found that because "there was some factual basis for such statements, to the effect that false and fabricated allegations of police brutality had been made" the inaccuracies were excused. The majority took into account the fact that the applicants were speaking on behalf of the members of the police associations criticised by Professor Bratholm and therefore they "were not entirely unjustified in claiming that they were entitled to 'hit back in the same way'". The Court also found that a "greater weight should be attached to the plaintiff's own active involvement in a lively public discussion[46] than was done by the national court. In the Court's view, 'a degree of exaggeration should be tolerated in the context of such a heated and continuing public debate of affairs of general concern, where on both sides professional reputations were at stake'".

Five Judges who dissented (Rozakis, Kuris, Turmen, Straznicka and Greve) upheld the approach of the national court and endorsed the protection of the right to reputation in issue because of the falsity and defamatory nature of the impugned statements. In the dissenting opinion of the last four of the aforesaid dissenters certain statements of the Norwegian Supreme Court are expressly adopted: "I accept that there is a need to provide the best possible terms for a debate on 'matters of public concern' and that [such a debate] might suffer if statements such as those dealt with in this case are not declared null and void, even if their background is taken into consideration." In concluding, the dissenters in question stated that they agreed with the Norwegian Supreme Court and that a "contrary conclusion will in our opinion have

46 This test is comparable to a similar test established by the American caselaw according to which individuals who do not hold public office may become "public figures" with a lower level of protection from defamatory statements as per the *New York Times* standards if they happen to be intimately involved in the resolution of important public questions or, by reason of their fame, shape events in areas of concern to society at large; *Curtis Publishing Co. v. Butts; Associated Press v. Walker*, 388 US 130 (1967).

the consequence in practice of allowing debates on matters of public concern to be suppressed by defamatory remarks and as such does not contribute to enhancing freedom of expression in the States Parties to the Convention."

8. Adverse Consequences of Over-protection

This brings me to the problem of the adverse consequences resulting from an extensive protection of the freedom of expression at the expense of the right to reputation.

The main argument in favour of protecting freedom of expression, even in cases of inaccurate defamatory statements, is the encouragement of an uninhibited debate on public issues.[47] But the opposite argument is equally strong: the suppression of untrue defamatory statements, apart from protecting the dignity of individuals, discourages false speech and improves the overall quality of public debate through a chilling effect on irresponsible journalism.[48] Moreover, as rightly pointed out above, such debates may be suppressed if the potential participants know that they will have no remedy in case they become the object of false defamatory accusations. Also, the prohibition of defamatory speech eliminates misinformation by public media and protects effectively the right of the public to truthful information. Furthermore, false accusations concerning public officials including candidates for public posts may drive capable persons away from government service thus frustrating rather than furthering the political process.

---

47 "Erroneous statement is inevitable in free debate and it must be protected if the freedoms of expression are to have the breathing space that they need to survive": *New York v. Sullivan*, op. cit.

48 "... such statements serve no purpose whatsoever in furthering the public interest or the search for truth but, on the contrary, may frustrate that search and at the same time inflict great injury on the defenceless individual", per Justice White in the *Gertz* case (*op. cit.*). "But there is no constitutional value in false statements of fact. Neither the intentional lie nor the careless error materially advances society's interest in 'uninhibited, robust, and wide-open' debate on public issues." *New York Times Co. v. Sullivan*, op. cit. at 270. They belong to that category of utterances which "are no essential part of any exposition of ideas, and are of such slight social value as a step to truth that any benefit that may be derived from them is clearly outweighed by the social interest in order and morality" *Chaplinsky v. New Hampshire*, 315 US 568, 572, 86 L Ed 1031.

9. Conclusion

I believe that a trend emerges from the case-law of the US Supreme Court and the European Court of Human Rights of placing the concept of freedom of expression above the right to reputation and enlarging the same concept to the extent of leaving without a remedy many individuals whose reputation has been "trampled over" by the mass media. The right to reputation having the same legal status as the freedom of speech, as explained above, is entitled to effective protection so that under any circumstances, any false defamatory statement, whether malicious or not, inevitable for an uninhibited debate on public issues or for the essential function of the press or not, should not be allowed to remain unrescinded. Even if it is accepted that a "self-censorship" of mass media in respect of the accuracy of defamatory statements, may, in certain cases, deter unnecessarily freedom of speech and therefore should be tolerated, and for that matter the mass media should be exonerated from liability to pay damages or compensation, that should not entail elimination of the right of the defamed person to vindicate himself by obtaining a judicial declaration of the falsity of the relevant statements. In this respect, we endorse Justice Brennan's suggestion in the *Gertz* case that States could enact statutes, "not requiring proof of fault, which provide for an action for retraction or for publication of a court's determination of falsity if the plaintiff is able to demonstrate that false statements have been published concerning his activities".[49]

In any event, publication of false information or allegations should not enjoy absolute immunity by virtue of the right to freedom of expression. The contrary position would amount to an unjustified restriction on the right of reputation as safeguarded by Article 8 of the Conven-

49 Mr. Justice White in his dissenting opinion in the *Gertz* case rightly pointed out the following: "In any event if the Court's principal concern is to protect the communications industry from large libel judgements, it would appear that its new requirements with respect to general and punitive damages would be ample protection. Why it also feels compelled to escalate the threshold standard of liability I cannot fathom, particularly when this will eliminate in many instances the plaintiff's possibility of securing a judicial determination that the damaging publication was indeed false, whether or not he is entitled to recover money damages."

tion.[50] Furthermore, one should not lose sight of the fact that mass media are nowadays commercial enterprises with uncontrolled and virtually unlimited strength, interested more for profitable, flashy news than for proper information of the public, control of government abuses or other idealistic objectives. And although they may be achieving these objectives incidentally, accidentally or occasionally even deliberately they should be subject to certain restraints out of respect for the truth and the dignity of individuals.[51] These restraints should include the duty "to carry out checks on controversial stories before rushing into print"[52] and the obligation to give an opportunity to the persons affected by their defamatory stories to react and give their own version. Furthermore they should remain legally accountable to the persons concerned for any false defamatory allegations. Like any power, mass media cannot be accountable only to themselves. The contrary position would lead to arbitrariness and impunity which are factors undermining democracy itself.[53]

---

50 In the *Gertz* case the US Supreme Court again made explicit its conclusion that "there is no constitutional value in false statements of fact". Nonetheless, in its *New York Times/Gertz* line of authority, the Court granted substantial first amendment protection to false statements of fact in the libel context to avoid "self-censorship" and "to protect speech that matters".

51 According to Principle 7 of Resolution No. 2 adopted at the 4th European Ministerial Conference on Mass Media Policy "the practice of journalism in a genuine democracy has a number of implications. These implications which are already reflected in many professional codes of conduct, include: a) respecting the right of the public to be accurately informed about facts and events; b) collecting information by fair means; c) presenting fairly information, comments and criticism, avoiding unjustified infringement of private life, defamation and unfounded accusations."

52 Dissenting opinion in *Tromsø and Stensaas*, op. cit.

53 Cf. David Riesman, "Democracy and Defamation: Fair Game and Fair Comment", 1. 42 *Col L Rev* 1085, 1088 (1942) in relation to the fascists' effective use of defamatory attacks on their opponents. In the Writings of B. Franklin quoted by Justice White in the *Gertz* case (n. 19) we find the following apposite passage: "If the Liberty of the Press were understood merely the Liberty of discussing the Propriety of Public Measures and political opinions, let us have as much of it as you please: But if it means the Liberty of affronting, calumniating, and defaming one another, I, for my part, own myself willing to part with my Share of it when our Legislators shall please so to alter the Law, and shall cheerfully consent to exchange my *Liberty* of Abusing others for the Privilege of not being abused myself."

Chapter 10 Environmental Protection through the Jurisprudence of the European Convention on Human Rights*

1. Introduction

The European Convention on Human Rights ("the Convention") does not expressly protect the environment nor does it address environmental issues in any way – it does not provide for any relevant rights in respect of the environment as such. At the time of the drafting of the Convention, the environment was not one of the values that were intended to be protected. The basic objective of the Convention was to set out a corpus of legal rules aiming at the protection of democracy and of the basic rights and liberties of the individual versus the state. The traditional notion of individual human rights was not concerned with the protection of ecosystems, the atmosphere, or with environmental problems. In an early decision the European Commission of Human Rights ("the Commission") stated that "no right to nature preservation is as such included amongst the rights and freedoms guaranteed by the Convention" with the result that an organisation set up to protest against military use of marshland was unable to claim infringement of any protected right.[1] The Commission repeatedly stated that the provision regarding protection of property (Article 1 of Protocol No. 1) cannot be interpreted as guaranteeing a particular quality of environment.[2] More recently the European Court of Human Rights ("the Court") stated that "neither Article 8 nor any of the other Articles of the Convention are

* On the same topic see M. de Salvia, "Droits et devoirs en matière d'environnement selon la Convention européenne des Droits de l'Homme", in Symposium of the European Lawyers' Union, "Les nouveaux Droits de l'Homme en Europe", Majorca, May 1997, 253-68; K. Reid, *A Practitioner's Guide to the European Convention on Human Rights,* (1998) 212-14.

1 *X and Y v. Germany,* application no. 7407/76, *Decisions and Reports* (hereafter DR) 5, 161; Reid, p. 212.

2 *Rayner v. the United Kingdom,* application no. 9310/81, 47 DR 5; *S v. France,* DR 65, 250.

specifically designed to provide general protection of the environment as such; to that effect, other international instruments and domestic legislation are more pertinent in dealing with this particular aspect.[3]

However, the Convention has always been considered to be an instrument capable of adapting itself to new developments and, for this reason, it is described in the case-law as a "living instrument".[4] The adaptation and extension of the Convention has been effected through the interpretation of its provisions by the Commission and the Court in the light of the changing conditions of life and the prevailing conceptions and values in democratic societies. As rightly observed by Karen Reid[5] "it is a reflection of the growing recognition of the importance of environmental issues that matters of environmental protection, quality of the environment and assertions of the need for protection against, or information concerning, environmental threats are increasingly appearing in cases".

It should also be recalled that according to the Court's jurisprudence the High Contracting Parties to the Convention are not only obliged to abstain from interfering with the protected rights of individuals but they also have positive obligations to secure those rights.

The case-law has extended protection of the environment under the Convention by means of two different methods: (a) as part of individual rights, and (b) as a legitimate restriction on the exercise of such rights.

2. Individual Rights

2.1 The Requirement of Being a "Victim"

The rights that have been extended to encompass environmental values are mainly the right to life (Article 2), the right to respect for private life and home (Article 8), and the right to property (Article 1 of Protocol No. 1). However, in order to be able to invoke any of these rights in the context of the environment, the individuals have to prove that they are victims in a particular situation. The Convention does not allow an *actio popularis*. To put in motion the machinery of judicial supervision, it is a prerequisite that the individual complainant be a direct or indirect vic-

3 *Kyrtatos v. Greece*, judgment of 22 August 2003, application no. 41666/98, para. 52.

4 E.g. *Tyrer v. the United Kingdom*, Series A no. 26, para. 31.

5 Reid, 212.

tim of a violation of the Convention by an act or omission attributable to the State.[6] This principle, which has been reaffirmed in many cases in the context of complaints relating to environmental problems, also implies that no complaint relating to a violation of the Convention can be entertained except *a posteriori*, i.e. when the violation has already taken place, unless the complainant establishes a real probability of a violation concerning him.[7]

In the *Gounaridis* case the applicants contended that the construction of a new peripheral road would amount to a violation of their rights under Article 8 of the Convention because of the consequences the construction was liable to have. In rejecting the application the Commission pointed out that the simple reliance on damage to the environment inherent in the construction of a new road is not sufficient to allow the applicants to claim that they are victims of a violation of the Convention. They must be able to claim in a defensible and detailed way that the degree of probability of potential harm affecting them directly is such that it can be considered as amounting to a violation. The case of the applicants failed because they confined themselves to relying on a future risk without any proof of their allegations.

In the *Tauira* case,[8] where the applicants were complaining of violations of their rights to life, private life, and property as a result of the nuclear tests by France in the Pacific Ocean in 1995, the Commission noted that the applicants did not furnish any evidence that such tests affected their health. The Commission found that since the applicants lived at considerable distances their complaints referred only to potential consequences, which were too remote to be considered as directly affecting them personally. A similar conclusion was reached by the Commission and the Court in *LCB v. the United Kingdom*[9]. In that case the applicant was the daughter of a member of the army who had taken part in the British nuclear tests in the Pacific in 1957 and 1958. She suffered from leukaemia and she alleged violations of Articles 2 (life) and 3 (prohibition of inhuman treatment) of the Convention on the ground that the authorities did not inform her parents that her father was exposed to

6 *Times Newspapers v. the United Kingdom,* DR 65, 307.

7 *Gounaridis and Others v. Greece,* application no. 41207/98.

8 *Tauira and Others v France,* application no. 28204/95, decision of 4 December 1995.

9 Judgment of 9 June 1998, *Reports of Judgments and Decisions* (hereafter *Reports*) 1998-111, pp. 1391 et seq. and 1407 et seq.

radiation caused by the nuclear tests, and that their daughter was therefore at risk of genetic consequences. She argued that her sickness was a direct consequence of radiation to which her father had been exposed and that advance information would have facilitated the diagnosis of her problem in a way that would have improved her medical treatment. The Commission rejected the application on the ground that it was not proved that any information, whether pre-natal or post-natal, could have changed the fatal nature of the applicant's condition or have had any positive impact in respect of her physical condition. The Court also found no violation on the ground that no causal link between the radiation of the applicant's father and her sickness had been established.

In *Balmer-Schafroth and Others v. Switzerland,*[10] the applicants complained that it had not been open to them under Swiss law to seek judicial review contesting the lawfulness of the decision of the Federal Council granting to a company a limited operation licence for a nuclear power plant. Although the Court accepted that the applicants were victims for the purposes of their complaint under Article 6 of the Convention, the Court's finding that there was no direct link between the operating conditions of the power station and the right of the applicants to protection of their physical integrity was fatal to their application. More specifically the Court found that Article 6 was not applicable in that case because the applicants

> ... failed to show that the operation of the power station exposed them personally to a danger that was not only serious but also specific and, above all, imminent. In the absence of such a finding, the effects on the population of the measures which the Federal Council could have ordered to be taken in the instant case therefore remained hypothetical. Consequently, neither the dangers nor the remedies were established with a degree of probability that made the outcome of the proceedings directly decisive within the meaning of the Court's case-law for the right relied on by the applicants. In the Court's view, the connection between the Federal Council's decision and the right invoked by the applicants was too tenuous and remote.

10 Judgment of 26 August 1999, *Reports* 1997-IV.

The same approach was adopted by the Court in respect of a similar complaint in *Athanassoglou v. Switzerland.*[11] The Court proceeded to state that the applicants were in fact alleging "not so much a specific and imminent danger in their personal regard as a general danger in relation to all nuclear power plants; and many of the grounds they relied on related to safety, environmental and technical features inherent in the use of nuclear energy".[12] Of particular interest is the joint dissenting opinion of Judges Costa, Tulkens, Fischbach, Casadevall, and Maruste where it is pointed out that "the dangers presented to the environment and the population by such installations make it, if anything, more necessary for such decisions to be subject to review by an independent and impartial tribunal in adversarial proceedings" and that "it is virtually impossible to prove imminent danger in the case of inherently dangerous installations: the catastrophes that have happened in a number of countries were obviously unforeseeable or, in any event, unforeseen". In order to qualify as a victim of the environmental nuisance complained of the level of such nuisance must exceed the "limits of tolerable inconvenience".[13]

2.2 The Development of the Case-law (Noise, Smoke, Household Waste, and other Pollution)

The fact remains that in the case-law developed during the 1980s, the Commission came to recognise that damage to the environment or environmental problems like excessive noise, pollution, etc., may affect the rights to private life, home, or property of individuals. The starting-point of this development is the *Arrondelle* case.[14] In that case the applicant, who was the owner of a house situated near the runway of Gatwick Airport in London and in the proximity of a highway, complained that she was seriously affected by excessive aircraft noise and

11 [GC], application no. 27644/ 95, ECHR 2000-IV. See also the decisions of 29 June 1999 in the cases of *Asselbourg and Others and Greenpeace-Luxembourg v. Luxembourg*, application no. 29121/95, and *Bernard and Others and Greenpeace-Luxembourg v. Luxembourg*, application no. 2919797/95.

12 *Athanassoglou*, cited above, para. 52.

13 *Moe and Others v. Norway*, application no. 30966/96, Commission decision of 14 December 1999: smell from gas resulting from the operation of waste-treatment plant.

14 *Arrondelle v. the United Kingdom*, DR 26, 5.

noise from the motorway and alleged that her health had been badly affected as a result. She alleged an infringement of her right to respect for her private life and the right to property. The Commission impliedly accepted that the complaints in question fell under the scope of Article 8 of the Convention and Article 1 of Protocol No. 1. The case was later settled amicably with the government paying the difference between the value that the property would have had without the noise problems and its actual value.

The *Powell and Rayner*[15] and *Baggs*[16] cases are of particular importance because in those cases the Commission and the Court for the first time expressly accepted that the right to respect for private life and home protected by Article 8 of the Convention may be interfered with as a result of environmental problems such as noise nuisance. In all three cases, house-owners complained of serious interferences with their private lives on account of aircraft noise. Although the cases were never decided on the merits we have the following pronouncements as regards the effects of noise nuisance on the rights in question:

> ... it has to be noted that a State has not only to respect but also to protect the rights guaranteed by Article 8 § 1 ... Considerable noise nuisance can undoubtedly affect the physical well-being of a person and thus interfere with his private life. It may also deprive a person of the possibility of enjoying the amenities of his home ... The average noise level of aircraft flying over the applicant's home attains, according to the Government's admissions, peaks of about 110 PNdB ... such noise level is likely to awaken persons sleeping in an insulated room. The Commission considers that in the given circumstances the level of noise amounts to an interference with the above-mentioned rights ...[17]

The Court also accepted that "the quality of the applicant's private life and the scope for enjoying the amenities of his home have been adversely affected by the noise generated by aircraft using Heathrow Air-

15 Series A no. 172.

16 DR 44, 13.

17 DR 47, 12.

port ..."[18] As regards the responsibility of the State the Commission in its admissibility decision in the *Rayner*[19] case stated that

> ... Article 8 § 1 of the Convention which guarantees this right (respect for private life and home) cannot be interpreted so as to apply only with regard to direct measures taken by the authorities against the privacy and the home of an individual. It may also cover indirect intrusions which are unavoidable consequences of measures not at all directed against private individuals. In this context it has to be noted that a State has not only to respect but also to protect the rights guaranteed by Article 8 § 1 ....

In respect of the complaint of the applicant under Article 1 of Protocol No. 1 (right to peaceful enjoyment of possessions), the Commission observed:

> ... this provision is mainly concerned with the arbitrary confiscation of property and does not, in principle, guarantee a right to the peaceful enjoyment of possessions in a pleasant environment. It is true that aircraft noise nuisance of considerable importance both as to level and frequency may seriously affect the value of real property or even render it unsaleable and thus amount to a partial taking of property. However, the applicant has not submitted any evidence showing that the value of his property was substantially diminished on the ground of aircraft noise so as to constitute a disproportionate burden amounting to a partial taking of property necessitating payment of compensation ...[20]

More recently aircraft noise also became the subject of a complaint before the Court through an application on behalf of persons living in the vicinity of Heathrow Airport. The applicants alleged a violation of Article 8 § 1 by virtue of the increased level of noise in their homes caused by aircraft using Heathrow Airport at night after the introduction of a new scheme of night flights. The government invoked the "economic well-being of the country" as a justification for the scheme. The case was examined by the Third Section of the Court which found a breach of the positive obligation of the State to take reasonable measures to secure

18 Series A no. 172, para. 40.

19 DR 47, 12.

20 Ibid., 14.

the applicants' rights under Article 8 § 1 of the Convention. The Court took into account the margin of appreciation enjoyed by the State in determining the steps to be taken to ensure compliance with the Convention and that a fair balance had to be struck between the competing interests of the individual and of the community as whole. The Court adopted the following important approach:

> The Court would, however, underline that in striking the required balance, States must have regard to the whole range of material considerations. Furthermore, in the particularly sensitive field of environmental protection, mere reference to the economic well-being of the country is not sufficient to outweigh the rights of others. It considers that States are required to minimise, as far as possible, the interference with these rights, by trying to find alternative solutions and by generally seeking to achieve their aims in the least onerous way as regards human rights. In order to do that, a proper and complete investigation and study with the aim of finding the best possible solution which will, in reality, strike the right balance should precede the relevant project.

At the time this statement was a major step forward for the protection of the environment. The Court finally found that the government had failed to take "the measures necessary" to protect the applicants' position. There was, according to the judgment, absence of any serious attempt to evaluate the extent or impact of the interferences with the applicants' sleep patterns and, generally, absence of a prior specific and complete study with the aim of finding the least onerous solution as regards human rights. However, the result of this judgment was reversed by the Grand Chamber of the Court to which the case was referred.[21] The Grand Chamber was satisfied that appropriate investigations and studies were carried out by the government and that in these circumstances the authorities had not overstepped their margin of appreciation by failing to strike a fair balance between the competing interests. The position of the majority of the Grand Chamber was contested by a weighty opinion of Judges Costa, Ress, Türmen, Zupančić, and Steiner. In their dissenting opinion they referred to "... the close connection between human-rights protection and the urgent need for a decontami-

21 *Hatton and Others v. the United Kingdom*, application no. 36022/97, judgment of 8 July 2003.

nation of the environment".[22] As they said: "after all ... as in this case, what do human rights pertaining to the privacy of the home mean if day and night, constantly or intermittently, it reverberates with the roar of aircraft engines?" The dissenters went on to invoke the "evolutive" interpretation of the Convention and criticised the judgment of the majority as taking "a backward step" for, *inter alia*, "it gives precedence to economic considerations over basic health conditions in qualifying the applicants' "sensitivity to noise" as that of a small minority of people (§ 118). The trend of playing down such sensitivity – and more specifically concerns about noise and disturbed sleep – runs against the growing concern over environmental issues, all over Europe and the world".[23] Finally having found that the government did not make any serious attempt to assess the impact of aircraft noise on the applicants' sleep and that it failed to show "that it has explored all the alternatives, such as using more distant airports" the dissenters found that there had been a violation of Article 8 of the Convention.[24]

It may be added that both the Third Section and the Grand Chamber found that there had been a violation of Article 13 of the Convention because the scope of review by the domestic courts was not sufficient to comply with Article 13.

It is suggested that the difference between the judgment of the Third Section and that of the Grand Chamber concerns more the assessment of the relevant factual situation than the applicable legal principles. In any event the expression and emphasis of the relevant legal principles and the solution given by the Third Section and the dissenters of the Grand Chamber are to be preferred.

In *Moreno Gómez v. Spain*, the applicant complained of noise and being disturbed at night by nightclubs near her home. She alleged that the Spanish authorities were responsible and that the resulting noise pollution constituted a violation of her right to respect for her home, as guaranteed by Article 8 of the Convention. The Court, in its judgment of 16 November 2004, noted that the applicant lived in an area that was indisputably subject to night-time disturbances that clearly unsettled her as she went about her daily life, particularly at weekends. The existence of the disturbances had been noted on a number of occasions. In the

22 Ibid., dissenting opinion (introduction).

23 Ibid., para. 5.

24 Ibid., para. 15.

circumstances, there appeared to be no need to require, as the Spanish authorities had done, a person from an acoustically saturated zone to adduce evidence of a fact of which the municipal authority was already officially aware. In view of the volume of the noise, at night and beyond permitted levels, and the fact that it had continued over a number of years, the Court found that there had been a breach of the right protected by Article 8. Although the City Council had adopted measures intended to secure respect for the rights guaranteed by the Convention, it had tolerated, and thus contributed to, the repeated flouting of the rules that it had itself established. The Court found that the applicant had suffered a serious infringement of her right to respect for her home as a result of the authority's failure to take action to deal with the night time disturbances and held that the respondent State had failed to discharge its obligation to guarantee her right to respect for her home and her private life, in breach of Article 8 of the Convention.

The case-law has developed beyond noise pollution and has also addressed the issue of offensive smell as one of the problems that could be dealt with under the Convention. In *López Ostra v Spain*[25] the applicant, who lived with her husband and children in a house near a waste-treatment plant, complained about the smell, noise, and smoke pollution caused by that plant. The Court seemed to accept that actual damage to health was not required for Article 8, since "naturally, severe environmental pollution may affect individuals' well-being and prevent them from enjoying their homes in such a way as to affect their private and family life adversely, without however seriously endangering their health". The Court concluded that there had been a violation of Article 8 in that "the State did not succeed in striking a fair balance between the interests of the town's economic well-being –that of having a waste treatment land – and the applicant's effective enjoyment of her right to respect for her home and her private and family life". The Court did not rule out the possibility of a breach of the prohibition of inhuman and degrading treatment under Article 3 of the Convention where the nuisance complained of will have reached a certain level of gravity. However, it considered that the pollution in the circumstances at issue did not amount to such a breach.

In the case *Fadeyeva v. Russia*[26] the applicant lived in a "sanitary security zone" around the steel-plant and suffered from its noxious

25 Series A no. 303-C.

26 Application no. 55723/00.

emissions. The Court found that the State had failed to protect the applicant's private life and home from the industrial activities of the steel-plant, and, thus, the State's positive obligation under Article 8 had not been met

In *Öneryildiz v. Turkey*[27] the Third Section of the Court found a violation of Article 2 with regard to the loss of lives caused by a gas explosion in a municipal waste tip. As regards the applicability of Article 2, the Court reiterated

> ... that the first sentence of Article 2 §1 of the Convention enjoins the State not only to refrain from the intentional and unlawful taking of life, but also guarantees the right to life in general terms and, in certain well-defined circumstances, imposes an obligation on States to take appropriate steps to safeguard the lives of those within their jurisdiction ...[28]

The Court proceeded to hold that

> ... a violation of the right to life can be envisaged in relation to environmental issues relating not only to the spheres mentioned by the Government, but also to other areas liable to give rise to a serious risk for life or various aspects of the right to life. In that connection it should be reiterated that the recent development of European standards in this respect merely confirms an increased awareness of the duties incumbent on the national public authorities in the environmental field, particularly with regard to installations for the storage of household waste and the risks inherent in operating them.[29]

---

27 Judgment of 18 June 2002. This case has been referred to the Grand Chamber which through its judgment of 30 November 2004 confirmed the judgment of Third Section of the Court.

28 Para. 62. See also, *inter alia, LCB v. the United Kingdom* (no. 9) 1403 para. 36; *Calvelli and Ciglio v. Italy* [GC], application no. 32967/96 para. 48, ECHR 2002-I; *Eriksson v. Italy* (Dec.), application no. 37900/97, 26 October 1999; *Leray and Others v. France* (Dec.), application no. 4461/98, 16 January 2001; and *Paul and Audrey Edwards v. the United Kingdom*, application no. 46477/99, para. 54, ECHR 2002-II.

29 Para. 64. In this respect the Court referred to various texts adopted by the Council of Europe in the field of the environment and the industrial activities of the public authorities, such as the Parliamentary Assembly's Resolution 587 (1975) on problems connected with the disposal of urban and industrial waste, Resolution 1087 (1996) on the consequences of the

The Court found that no distinction should be drawn between acts, omissions, and "negligence" by the national authorities when examining whether they have complied with their positive obligations under Article 2. In order to assess whether the State in question had met this requirement, the Court examined if (i) preventive regulations had been implemented, (ii) the public's right to information with regard to the relevant risks had been respected, and (iii) the procedural obligation of setting up a judicial system, based on the implementation of investigations which are efficient and not arbitrary as to the assessment of the facts causing the death, was satisfied. The Grand Chamber in its recent judgment stated that this system "must be capable of ensuring that criminal penalties are applied where lives are lost as a result of a dangerous activity if and to the extent that this is justified by the findings of the investigation".[30]

In *Taskin and Others v. Turkey*[31] the Third Section of the Court found that the granting of a licence authorising the exploitation of gold mines with cyanide, the use of which according to expert evidence exposes the inhabitants of the nearby region, like the applicants, to a permanent risk to their health, was in breach of Article 8 of the Convention.

2.3 Access to Information about Environmental Hazards

The jurisprudence has dealt with the issue of access to information about environmental problems under various Articles of the Convention. Thus in the *Guerra* case[32] the Commission found a violation of

Chernobyl disaster, and Recommendation 1225 (1993) on the management, treatment, recycling and marketing of waste and the Committee of Ministers' Recommendation No. R (96) 12 on the distribution of powers and responsibilities between central authorities and local and regional authorities with regard to the environment. The court also took into account the Convention on Civil Liability for Damage Resulting from Activities Dangerous to the Environment (ETS No. 150 – Lugano, 21 June 1993) and the Convention on the Protection of the Environment through Criminal Law (ETS No. 172 – Strasbourg, 4 November 1998), which have to date been signed by nine and thirteen States respectively.

30 Para. 94 of the judgment.

31 Application no. 46117/99, judgment of 10 November 2004.

32 *Guerra and Others v. Italy*, judgment of 19 February 1998, *Reports* 1998-I, 238 et seq.

Article 10 of the Convention on the ground that the competent authorities of the respondent government did not take the necessary measures to inform the applicants about the hazards of the environment which could have consequences for their health. In this respect the Commission invoked the positive obligations of the State under Article 10 of the Convention:

> ... not only to make environmental information accessible to the public ... but also to collect, process and disseminate information which, by its very nature, is not directly accessible and which cannot be known to the public unless the public authorities act accordingly ...

The Commission also invoked "the current state of European law" which according to the Commission "confirms that public information is now an essential tool for protecting public well-being and health in situations of danger to the environment" and pointed out that "the importance of the role which public information now plays in the interdependent fields of environmental protection and of the protection of the health and well-being of persons cannot be overlooked". In this regard the Commission recalled that "the Convention must be interpreted in the light of the present day conditions ... and it is designed to safeguard the individual in a real and practical way as regards those areas with which it deals".[33] Furthermore, the Commission recalled the statement adopted by the Court in *Fredin (no. 1)*[34] according to which "preserving nature is commonly recognised in all Contracting States as being of great importance in present-day society.

In the *Guerra* case[35] the Court also found that the State had an obligation to provide information to individuals so as to enable them to assess risks which they and their families might run if they continued to live in a town particularly exposed to dangers of severe environmental pollution. However, the Court based its findings regarding the existence of the obligation in question on the provisions of Article 8 of the Convention and in particular on the "positive obligations inherent in effective respect for private and family life". The Court held that Article 10 could not in the circumstances of the case impose an obligation on the State

33 *Guerra and Others v. Italy*, judgment of 19 February 1998, *Reports* 1998-I, p. 242.

34 Series A no. 192, 16.

35 Ibid., 210, 227-8.

to collect and disseminate information of its own motion because the Article in question relates basically to information which others wish to impart.

The *McGinley and Egan* case[36] concerned applicants who served in the army and received orders to stay outside the shelter during nuclear tests. In the absence of any individual monitoring, they were left in doubt as to whether or not they had been exposed to radiation at levels engendering risk to their health. The Commission accepted that the applicants should have access to documentation considered by the State as confidential in order that they support their claims arising out of the 1957 to 1958 nuclear tests which, according to the applicants, had caused them many serious health problems. By not having such documentation the applicants were denied access to the court where they were pursuing their claims. Therefore, according to the Commission's report, Article 6 of the Convention was violated. The Commission has also examined the same problem under Article 8 and found that the authorities, by refusing the documentation in question, "have not responded in a proportionate manner to the applicants' strong and legitimate interest in obtaining access to the relevant records and accordingly they failed to fulfil their positive obligation inherent in the applicants' right to respect for their private lives".

In the same case[37] the Court accepted that the facts raised questions under Articles 6 and 8 of the Convention but found that none of those Articles had been violated. As regards Article 6 the Court found that it was not established that the respondent State had in its possession documents relevant to questions at issue in pending proceedings and in any case that it was open to the applicants to use a specific procedure for disclosure of relevant documents. As regards Article 8 the Court found that "where a government engages in hazardous activities (nuclear tests) ... which might have hidden adverse consequences on the health of those involved in such activities, respect for private and family life under Article 8 requires that an effective and accessible procedure be established which enables such persons to seek all the relevant and appropriate information". However, the Court found that the State has fulfilled its obligation in question by providing a procedure which would have enabled the applicants to have secured the necessary docu-

36 *McGinley and Egan v. the United Kingdom*, judgment of 9 June 1998, *Reports* 1998-III, p. 1371.

37 Ibid., p. 1337.

ments. In *LCB v the United Kingdom*[38] the Court did not question the applicability of Article 2 but it did not find it established that, given the information available to the State at the relevant time concerning the likelihood of the applicant's father having been exposed to dangerous levels of radiation and of this having created a risk to her health, it could have been expected to act of its own motion to notify her parents of these matters or to take any other special action in relation to her.

In *Öneryildiz v. Turkey* the Court reasserted the principle enunciated in the *Guerra* case according to which the public had a right to be informed of the risks from the environment that could have consequences on their health and found that on the facts of the case the authorities "failed to comply with their duty to inform the inhabitants of the Kazim Karabekir area of those risks, which might have enabled the applicant –without diverting State resources to an unrealistic degree – to assess the serious dangers for himself and his family in continuing to live in the vicinity of the Hekimbasi rubbish tip.[39]

3. Restrictions on Rights

The second method through which the case-law has extended protection of the environment under the Convention was through upholding restrictions on relevant individual rights and liberties in cases where such restrictions were aiming at the protection of the environment. The same considerations which led to the expansion of the legal protection of the environment through the first method have made it necessary to accept restrictions on relevant rights under the Convention. As stated by the Commission in the *Fredin (no. 1)* case,[40] "the interest of preserving nature is commonly recognised in all Contracting States as being of great importance in present-day society ..." It should also be recalled that the Court in the same case recognised for its part "that in today's society the protection of the environment is an increasingly important consideration".[41] The case concerned restrictions regarding the exploitation of gravel. The Court, while admitting that the applicants suffered a severe prejudice as regards the potential of the gravel, found that a

38 Ibid., (fn. 9).

39 Op. cit., (fn. 29) paras. 84, 87 of the judgment.

40 Op. cit., (fn. 31) 30.

41 Ibid., (fn. 31) 16.

just balance had been struck between the interests of the proprietors and the imperatives of the general interest concerning the protection of nature.

There are other cases adopting a similar approach and at the same time accepting a wide margin of appreciation on the part of the States as regards the imposition of restrictions for the protection of nature. Reference may be made in this connection to *Uuhiniemi and Others v. Finland*[42] where the proprietors of land were complaining about a programme of protecting rivers and lakesides. The Commission found that the programme had certain repercussions on the rights of the complainants but a balance was kept between the interests involved and the object of the programme in question which reflected the exigencies of the general interest of the community on the subject of the preservation of the environment – the protection of the environment constituting an increasingly important consideration in today's society.[43]

There are many cases concerning complaints by persons of restrictions on the use of their land, where the Commission has held that measures of town planning, building restrictions, and sometimes even more drastic measures such as a general prohibition to develop land or even outright confiscation have been justified for the protection of the environment, such protection being considered necessary in the "general interest" or for "the protection of the rights of others". Thus in *Herrick v. the United Kingdom*[44] the applicant was not allowed to continue using as a residence a bunker on her property which was within a green zone in the island of Jersey. With regard to the complaint of the applicant that the relevant restrictions violated her right to property under Article 1 of Protocol No. 1, the Commission found that a proper balance had been struck between the applicant's and the general interest and that consequently the control of the use of applicant's property was in accordance with the requirements of Article 1 of Protocol No. 1. In upholding the restriction the Commission recognised that planning controls are necessary and desirable in order to preserve areas of outstanding natural beauty for the enjoyment of both the inhabitants of Jersey and visitors to the island".

42 Application no. 21343/93.

43 Ibid., 45.

44 DR 42, 275.

Furthermore, in rejecting the complaint under Article 8 of the Convention, the Commission stated:

> ... the existence and operation of planning controls which delimit areas where domestic development may be extended is a legitimate control measure to protect the amenity value of rural areas and thereby to protect the rights of others ....

Reference should also be made to *Photiades Ltd v. Cyprus*,[45] which concerned a complaint under Article 1 of Protocol No. 1 concerning various legislative measures "for the protection of nature", preventing any development of the applicant's property except for works which would assist in the preservation of the special characteristics of the area, agriculture and forestry, the creation of "nature paths" and of small projects that would enable access for the public. The Commission, in declaring the application inadmissible, took into account the judgment of the Supreme Court of Cyprus to the effect that the applicant's property lay within an area of great environmental and ecological importance. The Supreme Court found that the applicant's property was on a coast which was one of the main places where the green turtle – a protected species – laid its eggs. It was also adjacent to the Avaka and Farkona Gorges, which were of great environmental and ecological importance.

The European Court's jurisprudence under consideration goes as far as accepting as legitimate restrictions on the right to property obligations imposed on landowners to plant certain species which favour the protection of the environment.[46]The relevant case concerned the imposition of a duty on the applicant to plant 2,500 Swedish pine plants per hectare on a two-hectare area of his forest land, under a penalty of 10,000 Swedish kronor. The Commission considered that this duty constituted an interference with the applicant's rights under Article 1 of Protocol No. 1. This interference was a measure of control of the use of property aiming at "ensuring the protection of the environment and other public interests, notably that of providing a permanently high and valuable timber yield". The Commission was satisfied that this measure was lawful and in accordance with the "general interest" within the meaning of the second paragraph of Article 1 of Protocol No 1.

45 Application no. 41117/98, Commission decision of 21 October 1998.

46 *Denev v. Sweden*, DR 59, 127.

4. Fair Balance and Margin of Appreciation

The individual right to an environment of a certain quality is subject to restrictions which may be imposed having regard to the needs of the collective life. In that respect the Court has stated that "whether the question is analysed in terms of a positive duty on the State to take reasonable and appropriate measures to secure the .... applicant's rights under paragraph 1 of Article 8 ... or in terms of an 'interference by a public authority' to be justified in accordance with paragraph 2, the applicable principles are broadly similar. In both contexts regard must be had to the fair balance that has to be struck between the competing interests of the individual and of the community as a whole, and in any case the State enjoys a certain margin of appreciation".[47]

In fact the Court allows a wide margin of appreciation to national authorities as regards the assessment of, on the one hand, the particular needs of the person concerned and, on the other hand, the rights of the local community to environmental protection. In this respect reference may be made to *Chapman v. the United Kingdom,* a case decided by the Grand Chamber of the Court.[48] The applicant, a Gypsy by birth, complained that the refusal of planning permission to park caravans on her land and the enforcement measures implemented in respect of her occupation of her land disclosed a violation of Articles 8 and Article 14 of the Convention and of Article 1 of Protocol No. 1. Although she admitted that the impugned measures pursued the legitimate aim of protecting the "rights of others" in the sense of environmental protection she submitted that, in assessing the necessity of the measures in this case, the importance of what was at stake for her weighed very heavily in the balance, as the issue concerned not only the security of her home but also her right to live, with her family, in the traditional Gypsy lifestyle.

The Court stated that "although the fact of belonging to a minority with a traditional lifestyle different from that of the majority does not confer an immunity from general laws intended to safeguard the assets

47 *López Ostra,* ibid., (fn. 25) 54-5.

48 Application no. 27238/95, judgment of 18 January 2001. See also the similar cases of *Jane Smith v. the United Kingdom,* application no. 2554/94; *Beard v. the United Kingdom,* application no. 24882/94; *Coster v. the United Kingdom,* application no. 24876/94; and *Lee v. the United Kingdom,* application no. 25289/94 decided on the same day and on the same lines as *Chapman.*

of the community as a whole, such as the environment, it may have an incidence on the manner in which such laws are to be implemented". There was evidence that the use of the site for the stationing of caravans was seriously detrimental to the environment, and would "detract significantly from the quiet rural character" of the site.[49] In dismissing the applicant's complaints the Court noted that the applicant's personal circumstances had been taken into account in the decision-making process of the responsible planning authorities and held that "the decisions were reached by those authorities after weighing in the balance the various competing interests. It is not for this Court to sit in appeal on the merits of those decisions, which were based on reasons which were relevant and sufficient ... to justify the interferences with the exercise of the applicant's rights".[50] Referring to the margin of appreciation under consideration in *Powell and Rayner*, the Court stated:

> ... it is certainly not for the Commission or the Court to substitute for the assessment of the national authorities any other assessment of what might be the best policy in this difficult social and technical sphere. This is an area where the Contracting States are to be recognised as enjoying a wide margin of appreciation ...

From this review of the case-law it would seem that in striking the balance between individual rights and the "economic well-being of the country" or the "general interest" in cases involving important projects affecting the environment, the Commission and the Court are rather reluctant to find that considered governmental policies are incompatible with their obligations under the Convention.[51]

G. and E. v. Norway[52] provides an example of the application of the fair-balance test by the case-law and of the margin of appreciation allowed to States, especially in the field of measures taken for the "economic well-being" of a country. In that case the Commission accepted that the construction of a hydroelectric plant which would flood an area of 2.8 sq. km traditionally used for reindeer herding and would also affect

49 Ibid., para. 108.

50 Ibid., paras. 114, 129.

51 See P. Cullet, "Definition of an Environmental Right in a Human Rights Context", in *Netherlands Quarterly of Human Rights*, Vol. 13, no. 1, 1995, 25 at 39.

52 DR 35, p. 30.

the neighbouring environment of the plant, constituted an interference with the private life or lifestyle of the two Norwegian Lapp applicants, as members of a minority, who moved their deer herds around over a considerable distance. However, the Commission found that "after the careful consideration of the necessity of the project by the national organs, the interference could reasonably be considered as justified under Article 8 § 2, as being necessary ... in the interests of the economic well-being of the country".

Khatun and Others v. the United Kingdom[53] provides another example. In that case the Commission accepted that as a result of the construction of a road and other projects carried out with the purpose of regenerating the Docklands area the applicants, who were residents in the same area, were unable, for a period of three years, to use their gardens or open their windows without being covered in dust emanating from the construction work or dry their laundry outside. However, the Commission found that although this situation severely impaired the right of the applicants to enjoy their homes and private or family lives, a fair balance had been achieved between the general interest of the community and the applicants' rights. According to the Commission:

> ... the regeneration of the Docklands area pursued a legitimate and important aim. The construction of the road, providing a link to central London was essential to the development of the area. Against this important public interest must be weighed the applicants' own position. They suffered a considerable degree of inconvenience from dust, and it was apparently not open to them to pursue any remedy in respect of that inconvenience ... However, the Commission notes that the inconvenience, whilst undoubtedly unpleasant, has not been claimed to have given rise to health problems for any of the applicants ... Given the importance of the public interest in the present case together with the limits on the extent to which the applicants suffered from the dust caused, the Commission cannot find that a fair balance has not been achieved.

It is submitted that the *Hatton and Others* case referred to above, as decided by the Grand Chamber of the Court, provides another example of the reluctance of the Court to find a breach of the Convention in respect of big projects for which the "economic well-being of the country" is invoked. As rightly pointed out by the dissenters in the same case,

53 Application no. 38387/97, Commission Decision of 1 July 1998.

the judgment "gives precedence to economic considerations over basic health conditions in qualifying the applicants' 'sensitivity to noise' as that of a small minority of people".

An interesting application of the margin of appreciation is found in the case of *Wöckel v. Germany*[54] in which the applicant complained about the lack of effective protection of non-smokers through the enactment of relevant legislation. In dismissing the application the Commission invoked the Contracting States' margin of appreciation regarding "the choice of the means calculated to secure compliance with the Convention ... depending on the aspects of the relevant right at issue". The Commission took into account that German law contained provisions limiting the advertising of tobacco products and prohibiting smoking in certain public areas and that the German authorities have given preference to a public information campaign on the injurious effects of smoking. The Commission concluded that "... bearing in mind the competing interests of the applicant as a non-smoker and of the interests of other individuals to continue smoking ... the absence of a general prohibition on advertising of tobacco products and on smoking does not amount to a failure on the part of the German State to ensure the applicant's rights under Articles 2 and 8".

5. Competing Jurisdictions

The increased awareness of the need to protect the environment is reflected in many other international law instruments and/or their application. This gives rise to the problem of the competing jurisdictions of the organs established under these instruments. Overlaps between the jurisdictions of different international courts and tribunals resulting from the proliferation of new judicial and quasi-judicial bodies have become a widespread phenomenon in recent years and present real and practical problems such as forum shopping, parallel or successive proceedings, lack of finality, and conflicting jurisprudence. These problems, which go beyond the scope of this article, have been the subject of specific studies.[55] The difficulty in finding the right solution lies in the

---

54 Application no. 32165/96, 16 April 1998.

55 See in particular Yuval Shany, *The Competing Jurisdiction of International Courts and Tribunals*, (2003) and Hugh Thirlway, "The Proliferation of International Judicial Organs: Institutional and Substantive Question – The International Court of Justice and Other International Courts" in *Prolif-*

fact that international courts and tribunals do not form a coherent judicial system comparable to the national court system. They constitute "self-contained" regimes governed by autonomous legal norms of different juridical, sociological, and geographical origin and context. In any event, the private international law principle of stay of proceedings on the ground of *forum non conveniens* in cases where a more appropriate alternative forum exists for deciding a dispute in parallel proceedings may, with the necessary adjustments, be adopted in respect of different international law proceedings on the same matter.[56] However it is too early for an effective general solution to be implemented, as such a solution presupposes a universal application with the consent of all those countries that are already parties to the various relevant instruments.

The existing provisions relating to *lis alibi pendens* or *electa una via* may prevent parallel proceedings in different international courts in respect of the same case or dispute and avoid possible incompatible judgments. Such provisions are to be found in the Convention. Article 35 provides that the Court "shall not deal with any application ... that ... is substantially the same as a matter that has already been examined by the Court or has already been submitted to another procedure of international investigation or settlement and contains no relevant new information". Article 55 provides for the exclusion of other means of settlement of a dispute arising out of the interpretation or application of the Convention other than those provided therein.

It should be noted that no real problems of conflicting jurisprudence between different judicial organs of international instruments have as yet appeared in the field of human rights. This may to a certain extent be due to the fact that the different specialised human rights forums follow similar principles developed by the jurisprudence in examining human rights issues, for instance with regard to the margin of appreciation, the positive duties of the States and the onus of proof.

Cases concerning environmental problems in the context of human rights emanating from the same situation have been brought before different judicial institutions on the basis of similar treaty provisions. As a result of France's decision in 1995 to resume underground nuclear test-

---

eration of International Organisations (Niels M. Blokker and Henry G. Schermers, eds., 2001).

56 Cheshire and North's, *Private International Law*, 12th edn. (1992), 220 et seq., and Elbert A. Ehrenzweig and Erik Jayme, *Private International Law*, Oceana Publications, Vol. 2, 1973, 41, 42.

ing in the South Pacific, two cases were brought by different individuals against France before the UN Human Rights Committee (HRC) under the International Covenant on Civil and Political Rights and the European Commission of Human Rights under the Convention, the allegation in both cases being that the tests represented a threat to the claimants' right to life and family life and to the environment through the contamination of agricultural products and fish caught in proximity of the testing area. Both the Commission and the HRC declared the cases inadmissible on the ground that the applicants did not qualify as victims, as they had failed to show that there was a real threat of a violation of their right to life or to respect for their family life.[57] Considering the nature of the case one may justifiably assume the existence of a certain reluctance to accept the arguments of the individual applicants.

6. Concluding Remarks

The jurisprudence summarised above indicates a certain trend to accept the protection of the environment as an important value of modern society and, for that reason, to link it with the well-being of individuals and to encompass it within the scope of relevant rights. It is expected that the protection of the environment will he increasingly enhanced through the protection of various individual rights safeguarded by the Convention. It is suggested that an important contribution to such a progressive approach will be the adoption of a wider meaning of the concept of "home", in relation to the right to respect for one's home (Article 8) so as to include not only the building in which people reside and its amenities but also the natural environment surrounding the place where one lives.[58] In fact this point was raised by the applicant government in the interstate case of *Cyprus v. Turkey* as regards its complaint that the respondent government was responsible for a policy of deliberate destruction and manipulation of the human, cultural, and

---

57 *Tauira v. France*, op. cit., and *Bordes v. France*, decision of the HRC, 1996. Related claims based on the same situation and disputing the legality of the French experiments were submitted against France to the ICJ by New Zealand and to the ECJ by a group of individuals residing in the vicinity the testing area. Both these claims were again dismissed for procedural reasons.

58 L.G. Loucaides, *Essays on the Developing Law of Human Rights* (Dordrecht, Netherlands: Martinus Nijhoff Publishers, 1995) 128.

natural environment and conditions of life in northern Cyprus based on the settling of a massive number of people from Turkey with the intention and the consequence of eliminating Greek presence and culture in northern Cyprus. "In the view of the applicant government, the notions of 'home' and 'private life' were broad enough to subsume the concept of sustaining existing cultural relationships within a subsisting cultural environment. Having regard to the destructive changes being brought to that environment by the respondent State, it could only be concluded that the rights of the displaced persons to respect for their private life and home were being violated in this sense also".[59] The Court did not reject this argument; it considered that it was not necessary to examine the relevant complaint in view of its finding of a continuing violation of Article 8 in respect of the same persons by reason of the refusal to allow the return of any Greek-Cypriot displaced persons to their homes in northern Cyprus.[60]

However, a certain support for the proposition that the concepts of "home" and/or "private life" do embrace the surrounding environment of one's house may be found in the *Kyrtatos* judgment[61] where the Court, in dismissing the applicant's complaint of a violation of Article 8 due to the damage to the birds and other protected species living in the swamp as a result of the urban development, added that:

> ... it might have been otherwise if, for instance, the environmental deterioration complained of had consisted in the destruction of a forest area in the vicinity of the applicants' house, a situation which could have affected more directly the applicants' own well-being.

An even more progressive step in the same direction would be the adoption of an interpretation of the "right to life" broad enough to encompass a positive duty incumbent on the states concerned to secure to everyone within their jurisdiction a healthy environment[62]. After

59 *Cyprus v. Turkey* [GC], application no. 25781/94, para. 167, ECHR 2001-IV.

60 Ibid., para. 176.

61 Ibid., (fn. 3) 53.

62 For the efforts to establish an international legal protection of a right to a healthy environment and generally for the link between an environmental protection and human rights through international instruments see M. Pallemaerts, "The human right to a healthy environment as a substantive

all, the obligation to protect the life of individuals, as envisaged by the Convention, would be deprived of a substantial part of its content and meaning if it did not include the duty to provide protection against environmental conditions which adversely affect human health and which either are the product of human activity or, if foreseen, can be prevented through human effort.

The case-law will continue to develop to meet the changing needs of effectively protecting the environment through the two methods already mentioned, that is, by extending the protection of individual rights *vis-à-vis* the dangers emerging from damage to the environment and by accepting restrictions and limitations on the rights and liberties under the Convention as indicated. However, an essential prerequisite for such development is, on the one hand, a genuine and constant concern by individuals for the protection of their natural environment as part of their private life and home and as a necessary condition for their well-being and, on the other hand, a steady policy by States to preserve nature and protect the environment.

right" in M. Pons and M. Pallemaerts, *Human Rights and the Environment*, 11-21, Council of Europe with the collaboration of the Ministry of Social Affairs, Public Health and Environment of Belgium (2002). See Cullet, op. cit., at 39.

Chapter 11 Questions of Fair Trial under the European Convention on Human Rights

1. Introduction

I will deal with some questions regarding the right to a fair trial under the European Convention on Human Rights which I consider of special interest either because I think that the relevant case-law is not satisfactory or that it has not yet developed sufficiently to cover particular issues. I will adopt a critical approach and I will refer to some of my dissenting opinions.

The right to a fair trial is safeguarded by Article 6 (1) of the European Convention on Human Rights in the following terms: "In the determination of his civil rights and obligations or of any criminal charge against him, everyone is entitled to a fair and public hearing within a reasonable time by an independent and impartial tribunal established by law."

Article 6(1) goes on to impose an obligation for a public pronouncement of judgments, to allow exceptions to the rule for a public hearing, and for minimum rights in criminal cases, including the presumption of innocence.

I will confine myself to certain questions regarding the following topics:

- the meaning of the term "civil rights and obligations" in respect of which the fair trial requirements are applicable;
- the nature and extent of the protection provided by the requirement of a fair hearing, with special reference to the competence of the European Court of Human Rights to review the findings of the national courts, including the assessment of the evidence by such courts;
- the obligation to provide access to the courts;
- the requirement as to the legality of the courts;
- the test regarding the required impartiality of the courts;
- the obligation for a public pronouncement of judgments; and
- the question of waiver by the litigants of the guarantees of a fair trial.

It should be recalled that the right to fair trial provides guarantees for the benefit of individuals and not for the benefit of the Member States. This means that the European Court will not entertain any complaint for a breach of the guarantees for fair trial that might have occurred at the expense of the State whether in civil or criminal proceedings.

It has been repeatedly stated by the European Court of Human Rights that the Convention is a living instrument which must be interpreted in the light of present day conditions. As a consequence of this approach, an extensive jurisprudence of the Court interpreting and applying the right to fair trial to specific cases has defined, clarified and to a certain degree even enlarged the scope of the right. However the interpretative role of the Court through its jurisprudence has been in certain respects problematic. There are topics where the case-law is inconsistent, in some cases it is vague and uncertain and there are also areas where it has caused confusion.

2. Civil Rights and Obligations

One of the most controversial areas of the jurisprudence of the Court concerns the meaning of the term "civil rights and obligations" in Article 6(1). The argument has prevailed that this term could not cover all rights and obligations because of the word "civil" which is used in the text to designate the rights and obligations in respect of which the right to a fair trial applies. This argument is reinforced by the fact that in other international human rights instruments safeguarding the right to a fair trial such as the Universal Declaration of Human Rights (Article 10) and the International Covenant on Civil and Political Rights (Article 14) there is no qualification regarding the rights and obligations in respect of which the relevant guarantee applies. The word "civil" concerning such rights and obligations is only found in the Convention and it seems that it was intentionally inserted during its drafting. Yet not much help can be derived from the preparatory discussions of the relevant draft as to the object and purpose of inserting this word or even as to its meaning.

Many articles have been written on this subject, supporting one or another interpretation.[1] Both the Commission and the Court have tried

1 See, for example, Van Dijk, "The Interpretation of 'civil rights and obligations' by the European Court of Human Rights – one more step to take", in

to distinguish the rights and obligations which should be treated as "civil" from those that are, in contrast, non-"civil" rights. The result has been most unsatisfactory because until now no specific clear meaning or definition of the word "civil" has been adopted in the Court's jurisprudence. Nor has that jurisprudence given any clear guidance as to which rights and obligations can be considered "civil". The Court has used the private law nature of a right or obligation as a criterion of the term "civil".[2] In some cases, it has spoken about the predominant private law features of a right or obligation.[3] At the same time, it has held that the mere fact that the right or obligation at issue is governed by public law is not enough to deprive it of its civil character.[4] Other qualifications or considerations have been adopted, such as the capacity in which a person claims a right or the economic or pecuniary character of the claim. Furthermore a number of proceedings have been considered as determining civil rights or obligations without regard to any particular criterion but simply on a case by case basis. There have also been contradictory solutions; for instance a claim for social benefits[5] and a claim for a judge's pension[6] might qualify as a civil right, but not a claim for tax relief or a claim against unjustified taxation.[7] In one particular area, that concerning claims by civil servants related to their public service, the Court admitted recently that its case-law created uncertainty due to the adoption of a number of different unsatisfactory criteria to bring the civil service within the scope of Article 6 or to exclude it therefrom. In the words of the Court, in *Pellegrin v. France*,[8] in order to "put an end to [this] uncertainty" it has adopted a new criterion based on the nature of the employee's duties and responsibilities. According to this criterion, "no disputes between administrative authorities and employees who oc-

Matscher and Petzold (eds.), *Protecting Human Rights: The European Dimension (Studies in Honour of Gerald J. Wiarda)* (Kohn: Heymann, 1988), 131.

2 *Ringeisen v. Austria*, Series A no. 13 (1971): 1 *EHRR* 445.

3 For example, *Feldbrugge v. Netherlands*, Series A no. 99 (1986; 8 *EHRR* 425.

4 Ibid.

5 Ibid.

6 *Lombardo v. Italy*, Series A no. 249-B (1992).

7 *Ferrazzini v.* Italy, 2001-VII; 34 *EHRR* 1068.

8 1999-VIII 207; 31 *EHRR* 651.

cupy posts involving participation in the exercise of powers conferred by public law" concern civil rights and obligations. I find this criterion unsatisfactory and unjustified and I agree with the joint dissenting opinion[9] in that case in saying that the concept of civil rights and obligations should cover "all dispute that are decisive for a person's legal position, even if he or she is a civil servant".

To my mind, all this effort to distinguish civil rights and obligations from other legal rights and obligations is contrary to the letter and object of the Convention. As I stated in my dissenting opinion in the case of *Maaouia v. France*[10] which concerned an exclusion of an alien from French territory:

> [T]aking into account the object and purpose of Article 6 § 1, combined with the context of the words under consideration, ... it becomes quite clear that the term "civil" should be interpreted as covering all other legal rights which are not of a criminal law nature. If this teleological interpretation is not adopted, then the object and purpose of Article 6 § 1 would be frustrated. It is, I believe, evident that the object and purpose of Article 6 was to ensure, through judicial guarantees, a fair administration of justice to any person in the assertion or determination of his legal rights or obligations. It would be absurd to accept that the judicial safeguards were intended only for certain rights, particularly those between individuals, and not to any legal rights and obligations including all those vis-à-vis the administration where an independent judicial control is especially required for the protection of the individuals against the powerful authorities of the State.

I believe that the *Pellegrin* judgment cannot be the last word on the subject of "civil rights and obligations". It is not convincing and it complicates matters. Already the issue is being re-examined in other case-law pending before the Court and in particular in the case of *Vilcho Eskelinen and Others v. Finland.* I hope that the Court will come up with a more fair and simple solution.

9 By Judges Tulkens, Fischbach, Casadevall and Thomassen.

10 2000-X; 33 *EHRR* 1037.

3. The Extent of the Right to a Fair Hearing

3.1 Unfair Judgments

I will now deal with the nature and extent of the protection provided by the requirement of a "fair hearing" in Article 6(1).

The view has been propounded that the provisions of Article 6 regarding the right to a fair hearing relate exclusively to procedural guarantees.[11] In other words, that the right to a fair hearing means only a right to have a trial conducted according to certain procedural requirements such as, for instance, the opportunity to examine witnesses or to produce relevant evidence. In fact, a literal interpretation of Article 6 does not go beyond that. This has led to the view that if such procedural requirements are satisfied the European Court of Human Rights cannot interfere with the result of a trial. Indeed, the Court itself has established a practice of not interfering with the result of a trial on the ground that such an interference would transform the Court into a Court of "fourth instance". As a consequence, we find the following reasoning in the judgments or decisions of the Court rejecting a complaint relating to the result of a trial:

> ... this Court is not a court of fourth instance and will not intervene generally on the basis that a domestic court has come to a wrong decision. The domestic courts heard all the evidence against the applicant and were therefore in the best position to rule on the admissibility of evidence.[12]

---

11 Strasser, "The Relationship between Substantive Rights and Procedural Rights Guaranteed by the European Convention on Human Rights" in Matscher and Petzold (eds.), *Protecting Human Rights: The European Dimension (Studies in Honour of Gerard J. Wiarda)* (Kohn: Heymann, 1988) 595 and Stavros, *The Guarantees for Accused Persons under Article 6 of the European Convention on Human Rights* (Dortrecht: Nijhoff, 1993), 1.

12 See for example, the decision as to the admissibility in *Anderson v. the United Kingdom,* no. 44958/98 at p.8. See also the decision as to admissibility in *Johnson v. the United Kingdom,* no. 42246/98 at p.10: "It is not for this Court to act as a court of appeal, or as sometimes is said, as a court of fourth instance from the decisions taken by domestic courts. It is the role of the domestic courts to interpret and apply relevant rules of procedural or substantive law. Furthermore, it is the domestic courts which are best placed for assessing the credibility of witnesses and the relevance of evidence to the issues in the case."

Another general formula used in the judgments of the Court in respect of both complaints relating to the assessment of the evidence and the result of the proceedings, is the following:

> In so far as the applicant's complaint may be understood to concern assessment of the evidence and the result of the proceedings before the domestic courts, the Court reiterates that, according to Article 19 of the Convention, its duty is to ensure the observance of the engagements undertaken by the Contracting Parties to the Convention. In particular, it is not its function to deal with errors of fact or law allegedly committed by a national court unless and in so far as they may have infringed rights and freedoms protected by the Convention. Moreover, while Article 6 of the Convention guarantees the right to a fair hearing, it does not lay down any rules on the admissibility of evidence or the way it should be assessed, which are therefore primarily matters for regulation by national law and the national courts. In the light of the foregoing considerations, the Court notes that the applicant had the benefit of adversarial proceedings. At the various stages of those proceedings he was able to submit the arguments he considered relevant to his case. The factual and legal reasons for the first-instance decision dismissing his claim were set out at length.[13]

From this reasoning it is obvious that the Court does not want to interfere with the findings of the national court or, to say the least, it is extremely reluctant to do so. This attitude of the Court is limited to complaints under Article 6 of the Convention, in other words complaints alleging an unfair trial. In such cases any interference by the Court with the findings of the national court would inevitably amount to a finding that the decision of the national court has been unjust. Hence the reluctance of the European Court of Human Rights to review such findings. An additional reason for such reluctance is the restraint of the Court in criticising domestic courts as regards the interpretation of their own law and procedures.

But there remains the question whether the guarantees of a fair hearing under the Convention are confined to procedural guarantees or whether they also extend to substantive guarantees regarding the result of a trial, that is the "determination" itself.

My personal view is that the right to a fair hearing implies also a right to a fair result or a fair judgment. I repeat here what I said in my recent

13 *Garcia Ruiz v. Spain*, 1999-I 87; 31 *EHRR* 589, paras. 28-9.

dissenting opinion in the case *Göktan v. France*,[14] which related to a complaint against a two-year imprisonment fixed by the law without any judicial discretion for adjustment of the sentence to the particular facts of each case:

> I believe that the right to a fair trial is not confined to procedural safeguards but extends also to the final judicial determination itself of the case. Indeed it would have been absurd for the Convention to secure proper procedures for the determination of a right or a criminal charge and at the same time leave the litigant or the accused unprotected as far as the result of such a determination is concerned. Such approach would allow a fair procedure to end up in an evidently unjustified or unfair result.

One could also invoke here the judgment in *Golder v. the United Kingdom*[15] where the Court found that the right to a fair trial implies protection of the right of access to a court. The Court stated that:

> It would be inconceivable that Article 6 § 1 should describe in detail the procedural guarantees afforded to parties in a pending lawsuit and should not first protect that which alone makes it in fact possible to benefit from such guarantees, that is, access to a court. The fair, public and expeditious characteristics of judicial proceedings are of no value at all if there are no judicial proceedings.

It is submitted that it is also inconceivable that "Article 6 § 1 should describe in detail the procedural guarantees afforded to parties in a pending lawsuit" and should not provide protection against unjust judgments. "The fair, public and expeditious characteristics of judicial proceedings are of no value at all" if they result in manifestly unfair results.

As far as I know, the Court has not interfered with any finding of a national court on the ground of unfairness except in one case, that of *Dulaurans v. France*,[16] decided in March 2000, where a finding of the French Court of Cassation, which left undecided one of the claims of

14 Judgment of 2 July 2002, <www.echr.coe.int> (hereafter referred to as Hudoc).

15 *Golder v. the United Kingdom*, Series A no. 18 (1975); 1 *EHRR* 524.

16 33 *EHRR* 1093 (2002). Cf. the case of *Fouquet v. France*, 1996-I 18; 22 *EHRR* 279 (settled before the Court), where the Commission found a breach of the right to a fair trial because the *Cour de Cassation* based itself, errone-

the applicant, was considered as manifestly wrong. This decision is certainly a step in the right direction. Nevertheless the case is exceptional and it was criticised as overstepping the limits of the competence of the Court and as an interference with the judicial competence of national courts. The case does not, I think, establish clearly and unquestionably a general principle to the effect that the judgments of the national courts themselves may amount to a breach of the right to a fair trial.

It is true that in judgments dealing with complaints that decisions of domestic courts infringe the right to a fair trial, reference is made to the lack of "arbitrariness" in respect of these decisions as a factor taken into consideration in arriving at the conclusion that there has been no breach of the right in question. However, it is submitted that, although this is a sign of an attempt for a minimal – albeit superficial – control of the fairness of these decisions, far from being satisfactory, it confirms the practice of avoiding to carry out a substantial review of the fairness of a judicial determination of national courts.

I believe that any manifestly wrong finding or judgment of a national court, even though not "arbitrary", is at the same time an unfair finding which can, for that matter, be reviewed by the Strasbourg Court on the basis of a complaint in respect of a breach of the right to a fair trial. In examining complaints of breaches of other rights under the Convention, such as the prohibition against torture or inhuman and degrading treatment, the Court has repeatedly disagreed with the relevant findings of the national courts. For example in *Ribitch v. Austria*[17] the Court disagreed with the finding of the domestic courts of Austria that the injuries of the applicant while in police custody were caused by a fall against a car door. Contrary to the judgment of the Austrian Superior Court, the Strasbourg Court found that the explanation in question given by the police was unconvincing. The Court adopted the view that the applicant underwent ill treatment, which amounted to both inhuman and degrading treatment. One could give many examples of such situations which in my opinion support the view that the Strasbourg Court does act as a fourth instance court in respect of questions of whether there have been violations of the human rights guaranteed by the Convention. It is submitted that such competence may very well include the possibility of the Strasbourg Court reviewing judgments of national courts in cases

ously, on the finding that the applicants had admitted fault in their pleadings.

17 Series A no. 336 (1995); 21 *EHRR* 573.

where there is a complaint that such judgments amount to a breach of the right to a fair trial because they were themselves manifestly wrong, irrespective of whether the matter in issue concerned any one of the other rights covered by the Convention or not.

3.2 Evidence

The same approach should apply, in my view, to the question whether the right to a "fair hearing" imposes certain standards regarding the admission and assessment of evidence. I believe that the Strasbourg Court must have competence to review the rules of the admissibility of evidence and the way it should be assessed. As already stated, the case-law of the Court adopts the opposite view according to which these are "primarily matters for regulation by national law and national courts". In actual fact, the Court does not interfere with the rules of admissibility of evidence. I disagree with this position and I will illustrate my disagreement by an example.

We know that in the continental legal systems the judge has generally a discretion to allow whatever evidence he considers relevant to the issue before him. There are in fact no strict rules of evidence comparable to those applied in common law systems, like those in England and Wales and in Cyprus. In these two common law systems there have been many discussions and deliberations regarding the revision of their rules of evidence. One of these rules relates to the exclusion of hearsay evidence. The abolition of this rule has become a special issue. The rule has its origin in the late 18th and early 19th centuries. As pointed out by Lord Justice Auld, at that time "the cards at trial were so stacked against defendants that judges felt the need to even the odds".[18] The objective of the rule was to protect the laymen who compose the jury from evidence which might prove to be unreliable because it has not been tested in cross-examination. However, such a rule can lead in many cases to unjust and undesirable results by excluding credible evidence beneficial for the case of private individual litigants, including persons accused of criminal offences.[19]

18 Auld, *Review of the Criminal Courts of England and Wales* (London: Stationery Office, 2001) at 556 (available at <www.criminal-courts-review.org.uk>).

19 Ibid., para. 95.

In a Consultation Paper of the Law Commission for England and Wales,[20] the following examples are given of cases where the hearsay rule excluded evidence which tended to show that the accused did not commit the crime for which he was accused. In the case of *R v. Sparks*,[21] the rule prevented a white man who was accused of assaulting a girl of three, who was not called as a witness, from leading evidence that she had initially described her attacker as "a coloured boy". In *R v. Thomson*[22] the accused was charged with using an instrument to procure an abortion. His defence was that the woman had induced the miscarriage herself, but he was not allowed to adduce evidence that she had told others not only that she intended to do this, but also that she had done so.

I believe that if a defendant was not allowed to use exculpatory evidence as a result of the hearsay rule he should be able to complain successfully that this violates his right to a "fair hearing".[23]

It might be useful to stress here the difference between admissibility of evidence and reliance on it in reaching a conclusion. Article 6 of the Convention does not regulate the admission of any evidence. This is a matter of domestic law. Even the express requirement of Article 6 of the Convention regarding the right of an accused person to examine witnesses against him does not amount to a rule of non-admissibility of evidence. Failure to observe this requirement may amount to an unfair trial and the Court has adopted such a finding in many cases. But

20 Law Commission Consultation Paper No. 138.

21 [1964] AC 964.

22 [1912] 7 Cr. App R 276.

23 It is true that the Commission has held that the rule excluding hearsay evidence is legitimately based on the aim of ensuring the best evidence before the jury, who can evaluate the credibility and demeanour of the witness and avoid reliance on the evidence which cannot be tested by cross-examination: *Blastland v. the United Kingdom*, no. 12045/86, 52 D.R. 273 (1987). The applicant, convicted of buggery and murder, complained of the exclusion of hearsay evidence consisting of statements made by a third party to the police and others implicating another in the commission of the crime. The Commission considered that the exclusion of the evidence was not unfair in the circumstances. However, it seems that the applicant had the possibility to call the third party as defence witness. The applicant also had the right to challenge the hearsay ruling. According to a note on this case in the above mentioned Consultation Paper, *supra* note 20, p. 73: "This consideration weighed heavily with the Commission and if this possibility had not existed it looks as if the answer might have been different."

evidence cannot under the terms of the Convention be excluded on the ground that it does not satisfy the requirements of Article 6.[24] Whether such evidence may be taken into account by the court in the end is another matter. This approach is particularly significant as regards evidence produced by the prosecution which the accused did not have the possibility to put to the test of cross-examination. Particular caution is required in deciding whether and to what extent reliance should finally be placed on such evidence. Although the case-law of the Court on this subject is to a certain degree inconsistent and unclear[25] it appears that in specific circumstances such evidence may exceptionally be taken into account in convicting an accused person. A typical example is the case where statements of prosecution witnesses are produced in evidence and relied on by the court when the absence of the witnesses is due to reasons which the court finds acceptable (for example, the need to protect an informer) and the statements are not the only evidence against the accused.[26]

---

24 Contra Osborne, "Hearsay and the European Court of Human Rights", (1993) *Crim L. R.* 255.

25 *UnterPertinger v. Austria*, Series A no. 110 (1986); 13 *EHRR* 175; *Kostovski v. Netherlands*, Series A no. 166 (1989); 12 *EHRR* 434; *Asch v. Austria*, Series A no. 203 (1991); 15 *EHRR* 597; *Isgro v. Italy*, Series A no. 194-A (1991); *Doorson v. Netherlands*, 1996-II 447; 22 *EHRR* 330.

26 *Asch v. Austria*, supra note 25. However, for the sake of completeness it should be noted that the question of relying on evidence originating from parties who do not themselves testify before the courts in civil or criminal proceedings was dealt by the Court until now only in relation to statements made by persons for the purpose of being used as evidence in proceedings against an accused person. As far as I know, the Court has not dealt in this context with statements of third parties repeated by witnesses in court in cases where such statements were not made by the third parties in order to be used as evidence. In such circumstances it may be argued that the requirement as to the examination of 'witnesses against' the accused is not applicable as regards such third parties because they should not, strictly speaking, be considered as 'witnesses against' the accused, such witnesses being only the persons who give evidence in respect of the relevant proceedings and include as part of their testimony or statement the hearsay evidence in question (but see Osborne, supra. note 24). The examination of these witnesses aiming at testing the accuracy of their version of events and their credibility may also cover this part of their evidence which, although admitted by the court, may in the end be discarded as unreliable

In England and Wales the rule against hearsay has been abolished completely in civil matters and there is now an ongoing effort to abolish it to a great extent in respect of criminal matters. In Cyprus the rule is still in force in both civil and criminal matters.

As indicated by Lord Justice Auld, "(t)he rules of evidence should facilitate rather than obstruct the search for truth ..."[27] Inherent in a search for truth is fairness to an accused person or to private litigants and their protection from wrongful decisions.[28] "The rule can operate unfairly against a defendant as well as the prosecution."[29] That is why the Court in Strasbourg should be able to examine the rules of evidence applied in any particular case before it and also review the assessment of evidence in respect of a complaint of unfair trial.

3.3 Illegally Obtained Evidence

Speaking about evidence I would now like to deal with the question of admissibility of illegally obtained evidence. The matter is dealt with in the textbook of Harris, O'Boyle and Warbrick.[30] On the basis of the existing case-law at the time of the writing of the book, that is in 1995, it is pointed out that the Strasbourg Court found that the use of evidence obtained illegally under national law is not in itself a breach of the right to a fair hearing. In this respect the authors cite as an authority a Swiss case[31] where an illegally obtained tape recording that incriminated the accused was admitted in evidence. According to the same textbook, this approach of the Strasbourg Court was due to the fact that the defence had been able to challenge the use and authenticity of the tape and that there was other evidence supporting the accused's conviction. The authors express the view that "the Court might have reached a different conclusion if the tape were the only or the main incriminating evidence and/or there were doubts as to its authenticity that could have been

or be given little weight. See the proposals for reform of the rule against hearsay by Lord Justice Auld, supra note 18, 560.

27 Lord Justice Auld supra note 18, 559.

28 Ibid.

29 Ibid., at 560.

30 *The Law of the European Convention on Human Rights* (London; Butterworths, 1995), at 210.

31 *Schenk v. Switzerland*, Series A no. 140 (1988); 13 *EHRR* 242.

raised by the defence". From the way the authors have tried to explain this case I discern a certain expectation on their part that the matter of illegally obtained evidence might in the future be approached differently by the Strasbourg Court. I found the same expectation or concern in other writings. For example, in the textbook of Van Dijk and Van Hoof,[32] under the general title "the Right to a Fair Trial", the authors state the following:

> As to the admissibility according to domestic law, the Strasbourg organs are guided in the first place by the opinion of the national court. However, if the latter has taken the position that it may use the evidence, though unlawfully obtained, in forming its opinion, a Strasbourg review of the way in which use is made of this evidence is very urgently needed if the principle of 'fair trial' is not to be frustrated.

Soon after the new Strasbourg Court was established, an English case was brought before it, which in fact gave an opportunity to the Court to deal with the question of admission of evidence obtained contrary to the provisions of the Convention. That was the case of *Khan v. the United Kingdom*[33] in which the complaint was that the applicant was convicted exclusively on the basis of the material which had been obtained through a tape recording device installed on the premises of a friend of the applicant by the police in breach of his right to respect for his private life. The majority of the judges of the Section which decided the case found that although the evidence against the applicant was obtained in breach of his Article 8 right to respect for his private life, its admission leading to the conviction of the applicant did not amount to an infringement of the right to a fair trial. According to the majority, there was no risk of the evidence being unreliable. The majority also took into account the fact that the domestic courts would have excluded the evidence had they found that its admission would have given rise to substantive unfairness.

I disagreed with that decision. In my dissenting opinion I expressed the view that a trial cannot be "fair" if a person's guilt for any offence is established through evidence obtained in breach of the human rights guaranteed by the Convention. Indeed I do not think that one can speak

32 *Theory and Practice of the European Convention on Human Rights*, 3rd edn. (The Hague: Kluwer, 1998), at 436.

33 2000-V 279; 31 *EHRR* 1016.

of a "fair trial" if it is conducted in breach of the law.[34] Furthermore I cannot see how the police can be effectively deterred from repeating their impermissible conduct unless the evidence resulting from such conduct is inadmissible. Breaking the law in order to enforce it is a contradiction in terms and an absurd proposition. Madame Tulkens, the Belgian judge, agreed with this position, in another case.[35] However, the judgment of the majority in the *Khan* case was reiterated in more recent cases. One was against Cyprus.[36] In that case, the applicant's conviction was based on the results of an illegal post mortem examination but the application was dismissed as inadmissible. The other was against the United Kingdom.[37] In the latter case there was evidence against the applicant in the form of recorded conversations through a listening device installed in his home illegally by the police who unlawfully entered the applicant's house for this purpose by copying his key. The Court, relying on the *Khan* judgment, found that there had been no unfair trial. I hope that this line of jurisprudence will be changed.

---

34 See the judgment of the Supreme Court of Cyprus in *Police v. Georgiades* (1983) 2 C.L.R. p. 33. Cf. the position in New Zealand where the criminal courts have adopted a rule of *prima facie* exclusion of evidence obtained in consequence of a breach of the Bill of Rights Act 1990: *Simpson v. A-G* (Baigent's Case) [1994] 3 N.Z.L.R. 667, the rationale of the rule was stated in *R. v. Te Kira* [1993] 3 N.Z.L.R. 257. 276: "The court's duty to uphold the rights affirmed by the Act requires it to make an appropriate response where there has been a breach ... Often the only effective way in which the court can affirm the right is by refusing to recognise or to give effect to what has resulted from it". Cf the Irish case-law on the same subject, for example, *The People (Director of Public Prosecutions) v. Kenn*, [1990] 2 I.L.R.M. 569. A more qualified approach was adopted by the Privy Council in *Allie Muhammed v. State* [1999] 2 W.L.R. 552, where it was stated that "... it would generally not be right to admit a confession where the police have deliberately frustrated a suspect's constitutional rights". Cf. the US "exclusionary rule" and the doctrine of "the fruits of the poisonous tree" aiming at excluding evidence which is the result of breaches of constitutional rights: Antieau, *Modern Constitutional Law* 2nd edn. (St Paul: West, 1997) at § 40.68 et seq.

35 *PG & JH v. the United Kingdom*, 2001-IX.

36 *Parris v. Cyprus*, no. 56354/00, 4 July 2002, Hudoc.

37 *Chalkley v. the United Kingdom*, no. 63681/00, 26 September 2002, Hudoc.

3.4 Reasoning of Judgments

In any event, I must emphasise that the Court has improved in many respects the right to a fair trial by establishing as implied requirements of a "fair hearing" a number of guarantees or conditions which are not expressly mentioned in the Convention. Such a requirement is the obligation of the courts to give reasons for their judgment. In particular they must "indicate with sufficient clarity the grounds on which they base their decision".[38] It is of course difficult to envisage compliance with such an obligation in all those cases of jury trials in various legal systems where juries give no reasoned verdicts. However, until now there is no clear authority dealing with this issue. No direct complaint against such a verdict was ever brought before the Court on the ground of lack of reasoning. I do not know the actual grounds for the unwillingness to raise the issue before the Court but I do not exclude the possibility that this may be due to a belief on the part of the lawyers that if it is raised the relevant jurisprudence will be qualified in order to avoid far reaching consequences for the legal systems of many High Contracting Parties to the Convention.

There was an Austrian case[39] where the jury in a criminal case gave no reasons for their verdict and the complaint of unfairness was only examined by the Commission and not the Court. The Commission found no unfairness since the jury were given by the presiding judge precise questions to answer which formed the framework for the jury's verdict and could be put at the request of the prosecution and the defence. According to the Commission, this specificity made up for the lack of reasons.[40]

---

38 *Hadjianastasiou v. Greece*, Series A no. 252 (1992); 16 *EHRR* 219 para. 33.

39 *Planka v. Austria*, no. 25852/94, 15 May 1996, Hudoc.

40 In *Saric v. Denmark*, no. 31913/96, 2 February 1999, Hudoc, the Court stated the following: "The absence of reasons in the High Court's judgment was due to the fact that the applicant's guilt was determined by a jury, something which cannot *in itself* be considered contrary to the Convention" (see application no. 15957/90, decision of 30 March 1992, DR 72. p. 195; italics added). Bearing in mind the wording of this general statement especially its italicised part and the absence of explicit relevant complaint by the applicant, the statement cannot be considered sufficient to establish authoritatively the principle that the absence of reasoning by juries is compatible with the requirements of fair trial. The decision of the Commission

3.5 Equality of Arms

Another requirement of a "fair hearing" established by the case-law of the Court is the principle of "equality of arms" which implies that "each party must be afforded a reasonable opportunity to present his case under conditions which do not place him at a substantial disadvantage *vis-à-vis* his opponents".[41] Recent case-law emphasises that: "a party to the proceedings must have the possibility to familiarise itself with the evidence before the court, as well as the possibility to comment on its existence, contents and authenticity, in an appropriate form and within an appropriate time, if need be, in a written form and in advance".[42]

Invoking this principle, lawyers argue that there is a duty on the part of the state authorities to provide them, before a criminal trial, with the opportunity to inspect and if necessary examine through their own experts any material intended to be used as evidence against their client.[43]

The Court found that under certain circumstances the principle of "equality of arms" does create a positive obligation on Contracting Parties to give to an accused person the opportunity before his trial to carry out his own expert tests, on equal terms with the prosecution, in connection with objects or other material that may be used as evidence against him.[44] Such an obligation, however, presupposes that the facts of the case are such as to make it physically possible to carry out parallel tests on the same exhibit, and that the results of any test made by the accused may have a bearing on the relevant issues in the case. For instance, it is physically impossible to give the opportunity to an accused person to carry out his own expert tests in respect of traces of blood on a tiny piece of cloth which is liable to be destroyed after a single test. But, to the extent that parallel tests can be carried out, there is an obligation to facilitate that. If this is impossible then arrangements must be

to which reference is made cannot either be considered as an authority for the principle in question due the specific facts of the case (comparable to those of the above-mentioned Austrian case) and the reasoning of the Commission.

41 *Dombo Beheer v. Netherlands*, Series A no. 274 (1993); 18 *EHRR* 213 para. 34.

42 *Krcmár and Others v. Czech Republic*, judgment of 3 March 2000, Hudoc.

43 See, for example, *Korellis v. Cyprus*, judgment of 7 January 2003, Hudoc.

44 Ibid.

made by the prosecution so that the experts of the accused will be enabled to follow effectively the tests carried out by the prosecution experts and make their own observations in respect of them.

4. The Problem of Publicity

I will now say few words about the problem of extensive publicity, which may affect the examination of cases by the national courts.

As far back as 1962 the European Commission of Human Rights had accepted that in some cases a virulent press campaign can adversely affect the fairness of the trial and involve the State's responsibility, particularly when it is sparked off by one of the State's organs.[45] This principle was reiterated by the Commission in later cases, while accepting at the same time that the press "and even the authorities responsible for crime policy, cannot be expected to refrain from all statements, not about the guilt of the accused persons but about their dangerous character where uncontested information is available to them".[46] A press comment on a trial involving a matter of public interest was also considered permissible.[47] Equally permissible must, in my opinion, be any publication or statement regarding actual facts relating to a pending case.

According to the case-law, it is left to the applicants to prove that any hostile publicity has actually contributed to their conviction.[48] This is practically a difficult if not an impossible task.

The Commission went further to accept that professional judges are not easily influenced by the publicity surrounding the proceedings. The approach of the Commission was adopted by the Court in its recent jurisprudence which underlines the fact that "the experience and training of professional judges enables them to disregard any influence outside the proceedings".[49]

The consequence of this case-law is that, while in theory the possibility of a violation on this ground exists, both the Commission and the Court have followed a consistent practice of not accepting that any

45 *X v. Austria*, no. 1476/62, 11 Coll. Decns. 31, at 43 (1963).

46 *Ensslin, Baader, Raspe v. FRG*, 14 DR 64 (1978).

47 *X v. Norway*, no. 3444/67, 13 YBECHR 302 (1970). See also *Sunday Times v. the United Kingdom (No 1)*, Series A no.30 (1979); 2 *EHRR* 245.

48 *X v. Norway*, *supra* note 47.

49 *Craxi v. Italy*, no. 34896/97 judgment of 5 December 2002, Hudoc.

publicity surrounding judicial proceedings amounts to an interference with the right to a "fair hearing" or the presumption of innocence.

Without calling in question the integrity of professional judges, I feel the need to express my doubts as to whether the principle that it is difficult for judges to be influenced by hostile publicity against an accused person is correct. If there is virulent widespread publicity hostile to any litigant of such an extent as to influence the society in which the judges live, I do not believe that they will remain immune to such influence. As rightly observed by the American judge Benjamin Cardozo, "judges are subject to human limitations ... The great tides and currents which engulf the rest of men do not turn aside in their course and pass the judges by".[50] He also rightly pointed out that there has been a certain lack of candour in much of the discussion of this theme, or rather perhaps in the refusal to discuss it, as if judges must lose respect and confidence by the reminder that they are indeed subject to human limitations. Judge Cardozo added that "we shall not help the cause of truth by acting and speaking as if the judges stand aloof on the chill and distant heights".[51]

It may be correct that professional judges are less vulnerable to the influence of mass media than members of juries, but I believe that they are liable to succumb to such an influence if people around them have the same fate. It is not difficult to imagine cases where the mass media have given such extensive hostile publicity to persons suspected of committing crimes, especially abhorrent crimes, that everybody, even before the trial begins, is convinced that the suspects are guilty of what they are accused. I do not suggest that in so acting the mass media are trying to distort the facts. They may be basing themselves on actual facts, which they publish as part of their everyday task of informing the public on matters of public interest or, more precisely, on matters that the public finds interesting. But the fact of the matter remains that in these circumstances judges may, just like many other individuals, be reluctant to go against the general belief of the society where they function.

As I have already pointed out, the Commission and the Court have not until now found any violation of the right to a fair trial because of publicity suggesting or supporting indirectly the guilt of the accused. I can understand the difficulty which the Court may face in coming to a different conclusion but it should be accepted that we must enhance

50 Cardozo, *The Nature of the Judicial Process* (New Haven: Yale University Press, 1968), at 168.

51 Ibid.

the protection of accused persons from the real danger of having an unfair trial as a result of a prior conviction by public opinion. There are no easy solutions to the problem. Change of venue of the trial may be one way to solve it. But this is not effective when the publicity is nationwide. Maybe, in a united Europe, the change of venue can, in extreme cases, be extended to territories outside the European country where the crime was committed. The trial of the Libyans in the Netherlands accused of placing a bomb in a plane in the well-known Lockerbie tragedy may provide food for thought.

5. Access to a Court and Immunities

I now turn to the question of access to a court.

One of the most important decisions of the Strasbourg Court was the one in the *Golder v. the United Kingdom*[52] according to which the right to a fair trial implies a right of access to a court. In that case, a convicted prisoner was refused permission to write to a solicitor with a view to instituting civil proceedings against a prison officer. The Court held that although there was no express mention of the right of access in Article 6, its protection could be inferred from the text.

The right of access to a court is not absolute, but is subject to limitations. However, like all limitations on the rights guaranteed by the Convention, they must not restrict or reduce the relevant right in such a way that its very essence is impaired.[53] Furthermore, such a limitation must pursue a legitimate aim and must be reasonably proportionate to the aim sought to be achieved. Many limitations of a procedural nature such as time bars and prescription periods have been upheld by the Court. Such limitations do not call for any criticism. What has caused certain controversy is the subject of immunities which effectively prevent an action taking place under any circumstances.

The Court in the case of *Osman v. the United Kingdom*,[54] which concerned an immunity from suit in negligence for the police when acting in an investigative capacity, found that the immunity constituted a dis-

52 Supra note 15.

53 *Ashingdane v. the United Kingdom*, Series A no. 93 (1985); 7 *EHRR* 528 para. 57.

54 1998-VIII 3124; 29 *EHRR* 245 paras. 151-154. See now, however, *Z v. the United Kingdom*, 2001-V; 34 *EHRR* 667, in which the Court revised its view in *Osman* of immunity for suit in the English law of negligence.

proportionate restriction on the applicants' right of access to a court. The Court came to this conclusion because of the absolute nature of the immunity, which applied in all cases regardless of the competing interests at stake, thus preventing access to court in deserving cases. The Court stated that it must be open to domestic courts to have regard to the presence of other public interest considerations apart from those justifying the immunity, so as to allow the possibility of the non-automatic application of the immunity in consequence of the weight of considerations which pull in the opposite direction. I fully endorse this approach. I believe that there should be no automatic absolute bar preventing access to court by virtue of any immunity. This is the position that I adopted in three later cases involving State immunity invoked by the defendants in civil actions against them.

The first case is that of *Al-Adsani v. the United Kingdom*.[55] It concerned a civil action against the Government of Kuwait in respect of acts amounting to torture allegedly involving officials of the state of that Government. The second case is that of *McElhinney v. Ireland*.[56] It concerned a civil action for an alleged assault by a British soldier. The third case is that of *Fogarty v. the United Kingdom*.[57] It concerned an action by an ex-employee of the US Embassy in London for the refusal of the Embassy to re-employ her, allegedly as a consequence of her previous successful sex discrimination claim. In actual fact, all three cases concerned claims which amounted at the same time to violations of human rights, the most serious one being torture. The torture case was dismissed by the Court by 9 votes to 8, the majority holding that the immunity claim was supported by international law and was a justified restriction on the applicant's right of access to court. More specifically the majority stated that sovereign immunity is a concept of international law, developed out of the principle *par in parem non habet imperium* by virtue of which one State shall not be subject to the jurisdiction of another State and that the grant of sovereign immunity to a State in civil proceedings pursues the legitimate aim of complying with international law to promote comity and good relations between States through the respect of another State's sovereignty. Furthermore, the majority adopted the view that measures taken by a High Contracting Party which reflect generally

55 ECHR 2001-XI; 34 *EHRR* 273.

56 ECHR 2001-XI; 34 *EHRR* 322.

57 ECHR 2001-XI; 34 *EHRR* 302.

recognised rules of public international law on State immunity cannot in principle be regarded as imposing a disproportionate restriction on the right of access to court as embodied in Article 6(1). Just as the right of access to court is an inherent part of the fair trial guarantee in that Article, so some restrictions on access must likewise be regarded as inherent, an example being those limitations generally accepted by the community of nations as part of the doctrine of State immunity. Similar reasoning was applied in the other two cases. The assault case was dismissed by 12 votes to 5 and the sex discrimination case was dismissed by 16 votes to 1.

In all these three cases I expressed in my dissenting opinions the view that any form of blanket immunity, whether based on international law or national law, which is applied by a court in order to block completely the judicial determination of a civil right without balancing the competing interests, namely those connected with the particular immunity and those relating to the nature of the specific claim which is the subject matter of the relevant proceedings, is a disproportionate limitation on Article 6 of the Convention and for that reason amounts to a violation of that Article. The courts should be in a position to weigh the competing interests in favour of upholding an immunity or allowing a judicial determination of a civil right, after looking into the subject matter of the proceedings.

I have followed a similar approach in a recent case where the majority found that an absolute parliamentary immunity preventing defamation proceedings for any statement made by Members of either House of Parliament (MPs) in the United Kingdom in their places in the House does not amount to a violation of the right to access to Court under Article 6 of the Convention.[58] Such a finding was made even though the majority agreed with the applicant's submissions to the effect that: "the allegations made about her in the MP's speech were extremely serious and clearly unnecessary in the context of a debate about municipal housing policy. The MP's repeated reference to the applicant's name and address was particularly regrettable ... the unfortunate consequences of the MP's comments for the lives of the applicant and her children were entirely foreseeable."[59]

In my dissenting opinion I found that such immunity is a disproportionate restriction on the right of access to the court. I expressed

58 *A v. the United Kingdom*, judgment of 17 December 2002, Hudoc.

59 Para. 88 of the judgment.

the view that there should be a proper balance between freedom of speech in Parliament and protection of the reputation of the individuals through a system which takes account of the individual facts of the particular case on the basis of relevant conditions and exceptions attached to both rights. In that connection I pointed out the following:

> Such balancing entails that neither of the two rights should be allowed to prevail absolutely over the other. There should be a harmonious reconciliation through appropriate qualifications so that the necessary protection is given to both rights. If freedom of speech were to be absolute under any circumstances it would not be difficult to imagine possible abuses which could in effect amount to a licence to defame or, as the US Justice Stevens described "an obvious blueprint for character assassination".[60]

I also believe that in a present day democratic society an absolute immunity from judicial proceedings appears to be an anachronistic doctrine incompatible with the demands of justice and the rule of law.[61] Moreover, I hold the view that when dealing with the application of the provisions of the European Convention on Human Rights, the *lex specialis* is the Convention and because of that one should be reluctant to accept substantial restrictions on Convention rights derived from principles of international or national laws, such as those establishing immunities.

6. Established by Law

One of the express requirements for a fair trial in Article 6(1) is that the competent tribunal "must be established by law". I will now make some comments in respect of this requirement. The case-law of the Court has interpreted a similar requirement in respect of other human rights guaranteed by the Convention as imposing also a certain quality of the relevant law. In *Olsson v. Sweden (no. 1)*[62] the Court stated that "the phrase 'in accordance with the law' does not merely refer back to

60 *Philadelphia Newspapers Inc v. Hepps* 89 L Ed 2d 783 (1986).

61 An encouraging sign of a possible progressive development of the jurisprudence is given by the fact that the First Section of the Court has recently declared admissible a complaint that the applicant was prevented to sue a member of the Parliament for libel because of Parliamentary immunity (appl. no. 40877/99).

62 Series A no. 130; 11 *EHRR* 25, para. 61 (b).

domestic law but also relates to the quality of the law, requiring it to be compatible with the rule of law". Although in that case the Court gave as an example of what it meant the necessity that the law should provide protection against arbitrary interference by public authorities. I believe that one can reasonably assume that the relevant law on the basis of which a court is established must also be a law enacted by a competent institution of a democratic State. This is dictated by the objectives of the Convention as evidenced in its Preamble, which include the furtherance of political democracy and the rule of law.

However, I believe that in the judgment in the inter-state case of *Cyprus v. Turkey,*[63] decided in 2001, the Court overlooked this approach. In that case there was undisputed evidence to the effect that the subordinate illegal administration in the Turkish occupied part of Cyprus has set up courts on the basis of an illegal constitution, contrary to the will of the majority of the people, the relevant treaties concerning the establishment of the Republic of Cyprus, the UN Security Council's resolutions and relevant principles of international law. In respect of a number of complaints for grave violations of human rights of Greek Cypriots in that area, the majority of the Court adopted the position that the requirement to exhaust domestic remedies and the right to access to a court applied to the judicial remedies of the courts in question, regardless of whether they were illegal or not and therefore the inhabitants of that area had to resort to those remedies and to exhaust them before applying to the European Court of Human Rights. In so deciding, the Court invoked a principle of international law established by the Advisory Opinion of the International Court of Justice in the *Namibia Case*[64] to the effect that the illegality of an administration should not prevent the recognition of acts such as for instance the registration of births, deaths and marriages, the effects of which can be ignored only to the detriment of the inhabitants of the territory.

I will not elaborate here why, in my opinion, the decision of the majority on this point was wrong. This has been done by the strong dissenting opinion of six judges. I will simply repeat the view that I have already expressed in an article in a recent issue of the *Leiden Journal of International Law*[65] according to which it is inconceivable for the Con-

63 ECHR 2001-IV; 35 *EHRR* 731.

64 ICJ Rep 1950, 128.

65 "The Judgment of the European Court of Human Rights in the Case of Cyprus v. Turkey", 15 *Leiden Journal of International Law* 225 at 235 (2002).

vention to express respect for the rule of law and at the same time to require individuals to exhaust illegal remedies before resorting to the Convention institutions.[66]

7. Impartiality and Appearances

I now turn to the application of the criterion regarding the required impartiality of a tribunal as an express condition of a fair trial in Article 6(1).

According to the case-law, in order to satisfy this requirement the tribunal must comply with both a subjective and an objective test. In the words of the Court: "The existence of impartiality for the purposes of Article 6 must be determined according to a subjective test, that is on the basis of the personal conviction of a particular judge in a given case, and also according to an objective test, that is ascertaining whether the judge offered guarantees sufficient to exclude any legitimate doubt in this respect".[67]

As regards the subjective test, the question is whether it can be shown that a member of the Court has actually acted with personal bias against the applicant. The presumption is that a judge is impartial until there is proof to the contrary. Under the objective test,[68] it must be determined whether, quite apart from the judge's personal conduct, there are ascertainable facts which may raise doubts as to his impartiality. In this respect even appearances may be of a certain importance. In deciding whether in a given case there is a legitimate reason to fear that a particular judge lacks impartiality, the standpoint of the accused is important but not decisive. What is decisive is whether this fear can be held objectively justified. As rightly observed in the text book of Harris, O'Boyle and Warbrick:[69] the objective test of "impartiality" is comparable to the

66 Cf. the judgment in the *Golder* case, supra note 15 at 17 where the Court pointed out that the demands of the rule of law of must be borne in mind "when interpreting the terms of Article 6 § 1 according to their context and in the light of the object and purpose of the Convention".

67 *Hauschildt v. Denmark*, Series A no. 154 (1989); 12 *EHRR* 266, para. 46.

68 See Van Dijk, "Article 6 § 1 of the Convention and the Concept of 'Objective Impartiality'", in Mahoney et al. (eds.), *Protecting Human Rights: The European Perspective: Studies in Memory of Rolv Ryssdal* (Koln: Heymann, 2000), 1495.

69 Supra note 30, at 235.

English law doctrine that "justice must not only be done: it must also be seen to be done".

Quite honestly, I never liked this maxim. It is, I believe, somewhat anachronistic. I always preferred realities to appearances. And I consider realities as the only criteria that count. In a modern democratic society, conclusions or decisions should not be based on impressions or appearances. They should only be based on actual facts; the more so when we enter the field of the administration of justice. It is, I think, sufficient if justice is really done. Therefore, in deciding whether there exist objectively doubts as to the impartiality of a judge, appearances should play no role. The question should rather be whether in any particular case there exist such facts as to create a real danger of the judge acting in a manner incompatible with the required impartiality.

The case of *Piersack v. Belgium*[70] can be used to illustrate my point. In that case the presiding judge had previously served as a senior deputy to the Brussels *procureur du Roi* (the public prosecutor) and until his judicial appointment he was the head of the section to which the applicant's case was referred. The applicant was pleased to pay tribute to the judge's personal impartiality. There was no evidence that the judge had actual knowledge of the investigation of the applicant's case during his service in the public prosecutor's department. Yet the Court found that there was a breach of the requirement of impartiality because, according to the judgment of the Court, in the circumstance of the case the impartiality of the judge in question "was" on the basis of the objective test "capable of appearing open to doubt". The Court was basically influenced by the fact that the judge held in the past a post in the public prosecutor's department whose nature was such that he might have to deal with a given matter relating to the case under consideration in the course of his duties, even though in actual fact the judge did not play any relevant part in the proceedings.

It is clear that the case was decided on the basis of appearances. The evidence did not establish a real danger of the judge not acting in an impartial way. This is the kind of approach which I personally do not approve.

Going through the case-law I found that another judge of the Court has in the past expressed similar reservations. In the case of *Bulut v. Austria*[71] the Belgian judge De Meyer in his separate opinion observed

70 Series A no. 53 (1982); 5 *EHRR* 169.

71 1996-II 346; 24 *EHRR* 153.

the following: "As regards a tribunal's impartiality, we must firstly, it seems to me, not be obsessed with "appearances", as we too often are in the reasoning of our judgments, but simply take into account the reality of the proceedings, in the light of what common sense tells us". The same judge in his concurring opinion in *Padovani v. Italy*[72] raised the – for him apparently rhetorical – question: "Whether the Court is not sometimes more sensitive to appearances than to reality when considering the independence and impartiality of tribunals".[73]

It is, I think, useful to repeat here the very pertinent statement of the Court in the case *De Jong, Baljet and Van den Brink*, namely, that "one must ... look beyond the appearances ... and concentrate on the realities of the situation".[74]

However, in fairness to the Court's jurisprudence I must add that in most of the cases in respect of which the Court found that a particular judge or a tribunal failed to satisfy the so called objective test, we find that there existed in actual fact on the basis of the relevant circumstances of these cases a real danger of lack of impartiality. The following are examples of such cases:

- Members of a Court who were expected to decide the lawfulness of a regulation had previously pronounced on this question in an advisory capacity.[75]
- A judge, who was expected to try a criminal case against a person in respect of whom he had previously decided the pre-trial detention on the basis that there was "a particularly confirmed suspicion" that the accused committed the offence (explained as meaning that the judge had to be convinced that there was "a very high degree of clarity as to the question of guilt").[76]
- A judge who, prior to the trial of a case by him, had acted as an investigative judge in respect of the same case.[77]
- The House of Representatives that tried the applicant for breach of parliamentary privilege was also found on the basis of the objective test not to be impartial, because two of its members who partici-

72 Series A no. 257-B (1993).

73 Ibid., at 22.

74 Series A no. 77 (1984); 8 *EHRR* 20 para. 48.

75 *Procola v. Luxembourg*, Series A no. 326 (1995); 22 *EHRR* 193.

76 *Hauschildt v. Denmark*, Series A no. 154 (1989); 12 *EHRR* 266.

77 *De Cubber v. Belgium*, Series A no. 86 (1984); 7 *EHRR* 236.

pated in the proceedings were the Members who were criticised in the article that was the subject of the alleged offence.[78]

Consequently one can say that in practice the Court in principle gives more weight to the existence in actual fact of real dangers than to mere appearances.

8. Public Pronouncement of Judgments

I am now coming to the question of the required public nature of the proceedings and more specifically of the public pronouncement of judgments as a necessary condition of a fair trial.

Article 6 of the European Convention states that:

> [E]veryone is entitled to ... a public hearing ... Judgment shall be pronounced publicly but the press and public may be excluded from all or part of the trial in the interests of morals, public order or national security in a democratic society, where the interests of juveniles or the protection of the private life of the parties so require, or to the extent strictly necessary in the opinion of the court in special circumstances where publicity would prejudice the interests of justice.

The basic objective and philosophy of the requirement for public hearings is the protection of litigants against the administration of justice in secret with no public scrutiny and the maintenance of confidence in the courts. As pointed out in *Sutter v. Switzerland*:[79] "By rendering the administration of justice visible, publicity contributes to the achievement of the aim of Article 6, namely a fair trial, the guarantee of which is one of the fundamental principles of any democratic society, within the meaning of the Convention".

From the wording and objective of the relevant provision it is apparent that publicity of the proceedings is the rule and trials in camera are the exception. Such exceptional course has to be decided on the facts of each particular case.

What raises a problem is the provision regarding the public pronouncement of judgments which is expressed in such a way that it does not admit of any exceptions. The Court itself has through its case-law

78 *Demicoli v. Malta*, Series A no. 210 (1991); 14 *EHRR* 647.

79 Series A no. 74 (1984); 6 *EHRR* 272.

made that clear and added that the public pronouncement of judgments is not subject to any implied limitations. The question then arises whether the public pronouncement of a judgment in case of a trial which has been conducted in camera in the interest of any of the objectives set out in Article 6 such as national security does or does not frustrate such objectives. In other words what is the point of having a hearing behind closed doors if the evidence produced in such a hearing will be reflected in a public judgment? In this respect one may compare the provision under consideration with the corresponding provision of the International Covenant on Civil and Political Rights according to which there are exceptions to the rule of publication of judgments at least for some of the cases for which a trial in camera is permissible. Incidentally I am tempted to point out here that, strangely enough, the case where the hearing is not public for reasons of national security is not included in these exceptions.

Be that as it may, when a case came before the Court about a year ago in which this issue arose,[80] I had difficulty escaping from the express wording of the article and together with another judge we delivered a dissenting opinion where we disagreed with the approach of the majority decision. According to the majority, a literal interpretation of the provisions of Article 6 concerning the public pronouncement of the judgment in the case would be "unnecessary for the purposes of public scrutiny and might even frustrate the primary aim of Article 6, which is to secure a fair hearing". The case concerned a rule of law in England according to which hearings of family cases should be in camera. While realising the practical problem of public pronouncement of judgments in respect of such proceedings, I felt that I had to abide by the commands of the relevant provision. As regards the problems that might ensue from such publication, the following approach was adopted in my relevant dissenting opinion, joined by Judge Tulkens:

> [W]hat has taken place in a private hearing is not fully reflected in a publicly pronounced judgment and, certainly, care can be taken so that names and other information which may lead to identification of the parties or, indeed, very much detail about the family's personal life may be avoided in such judgments without affecting the approach and the solution given by the Court to the issues arising in the case which should be made public

80 *B v. the United Kingdom* and *P v. the United Kingdom*, 2001-III; 34 *EHRR* 529.

> in order to achieve the purpose of public scrutiny that constitutes the primary objective of the principle of publicity.

However, I believe that neither the solution given by the majority nor the one given by the minority are satisfactory. This is an area possibly demanding modifications of the Convention.

9. Waiver of the Guarantees

A final question of this article is whether a waiver of the guarantees of a fair trial is possible.

I believe that the correct answer should be in the negative. The reason is that human rights are conferred on the individual in the public interest in order to effectuate a policy of protecting him from the omnipotence of the State and of establishing a certain public order in Europe. They are not private personal rights that can be negotiated, compromised, waived or released by the individual. The individual may choose not to exercise any of the human rights guaranteed by the Convention. But this is a different thing from a waiver. The individual may not, for instance, claim compensation for his property which has been illegally confiscated and destroyed but if he decides to raise such a claim he cannot be met with a legal objection to the effect that through his conduct he has lost his right once and for all. Waiver of a human right, which in my opinion should not be legally possible, must be distinguished from refraining to exercise the right or pursue a remedy for its breach. Moreover, the human rights guaranteed by the Convention impose corresponding duties and standards of behaviour on the part of the States concerned, which constitute the Public Order of Europe. A waiver of any of these rights would amount in effect to a release of the relevant duty of the State. Such a result is incompatible with the maintenance of the Public Order in Europe which was intended to be established by the Convention and which could not, for that matter, depend on individual persons' decisions. It may also be considered as inconsistent with the express terms of the agreement of the High Contracting Parties to the Convention under Article 1 thereof which creates the obligation on the part of such Parties to "secure to everyone within their jurisdiction the rights and freedoms defined ... in the Convention". Therefore in my opinion no waiver could be valid in respect of a fair and public hearing by an independent and impartial tribunal established by law.

However, it seems that the Strasbourg case-law has accepted the possibility of waiving at least certain rights guaranteed by the Convention. In the case of *Albert and Le Compte*[81] the Court stated: "The rule requiring a public hearing, as embodied in Article 6, may also yield in certain circumstances to the will of the person concerned. Admittedly, the nature of some of the rights safeguarded by the Convention is such as to exclude a waiver of the entitlement to exercise them, but the same cannot be said of certain other rights."

There is no clear criterion on the basis of which the Strasbourg case-law determines which rights can be waived and under what circumstances they can be waived. From a review of the case-law it emerges that both the nature and importance of the right and, generally the demands of public interest are taken into account in order to decide whether a particular right can be waived, taking also into account the facts of the particular case in which the question arises.[82] This is illustrated, for instance, by the decision that the right to liberty "is too important in a democratic society" within the meaning of the Convention for a person to lose the benefit of the protection of the Convention for the single reason that he gives himself up to be taken into detention. Detention might violate Article 5 even though the person concerned might have agreed to it.[83]

In another case[84] the Court stated:

> The public character of court hearings constitutes a fundamental principle enshrined in Article 6. Admittedly neither the letter nor the spirit of this provision prevents a person from waiving, of his own free will, either expressly or tacitly, the entitlement to have his case heard in public. However, a waiver must be made in an unequivocal manner and must not run counter to any important public interest.

81 *Albert and Le Compte v. Belgium*, Series A no. 58 (1983); 5 *EHRR* 533.

82 See in this respect Ferguson, "Trial in Absence and Waiver of Human Rights" in (2002) *Crim L R* 554.

83 *De Wilde, Ooms and Versyps cases*, Series A no. 12 (1971); 1 *EHRR* 375 para. 65.

84 *Hakansson and Sturesson v. Sweden* , Series A no. 171-A (1990); 13 *EHRR* 1.

Commenting on this statement Reid rightly observes that this "appears to suggest that in serious cases the appearance of justice will require a public hearing regardless of the applicant's views".[85]

The case-law has left open the possibility of a waiver of the right to an impartial tribunal according to the objective test. In a case against Austria the Court found that the failure to object to two court judges who had been investigating judges and disqualified was not sufficient.[86] A waiver of the right to an impartial tribunal according to the subjective test or of the general right to fair trial is, to my mind, inconceivable even in the light of the flexible approach of the Strasbourg jurisprudence.

I have already expressed my opinion that there can be no waiver of the human rights guaranteed by the Convention. My personal view is that no distinction between rights that can be waived and those that cannot be waived is justified. But even if waiver of any human right is accepted it is obvious that a waiver can never apply to the right to a fair trial.

10. Concluding Comment

I have dealt with some problems in respect of the case-law on the right to a fair trial. I must however emphasise that the work of the Court in interpreting and applying the Convention is not an easy one. The Court has to take into account the practical problems that may follow from its judgments both as regards the effective implementation of the rights guaranteed by the Convention and as regards the deeply rooted institutions of the legal systems of the High Contracting Parties. Sometimes this leads to a compromise between an ideal solution and a realistic or practical approach in the light of the particular facts of the cases under examination. Consistency with the Court's jurisprudence is another consideration in deciding cases. The judgments of the Court are also influenced by the personality of the judges who deal with the particular cases. This factor plays an ever expanding role given the increasing number of judges and the variety of the cultural, social, economic, political and legal characteristics of the countries from which they come. All these judges have also their own specific philosophy of life. Furthermore there are judges who are by nature formalists or conservative and others

85 *A Practitioners Guide to the European Convention of Human Rights* (London: Sweet & Maxwell, 1998), 124.

86 *Pfeiffer and Plankl (no. 1) v. Austria*, Series A no. 227 (1992); 14 *EHRR* 162.

who are more progressive. I personally try to support an idealistic progressive approach regarding the protection of the rights guaranteed by the Convention within the permissible limits allowed by the wording of such rights. And in this respect I bear in mind the case-law of the Court according to which "the right to a fair trial holds so prominent place in a democratic society that there can be no justification for interpreting the [relevant guarantees] restrictively."[87]

87 *Moreira de Azevedo v. Portugal*, Series A no. 189 (1990); 13 *EHRR* 721.

Chapter 12 The Right of Access to a Court and the Doctrine of Political Acts

1. The Issue

Article 6 of the European Convention on Human Rights secures to everyone the right to have a claim relating to his civil rights and obligations brought before a court established by law. In many countries Parties to the Convention, individuals are denied a judicial determination of their claim arising out of acts described as "acts of government" (*actes de gouvernement*) or "political acts".

I will first deal with the doctrine of government acts in terms of national legal systems: its legal basis, meaning its *raison d'être*, its limits and its application in practice; I will then examine the matter in the context of the right of access to a court safeguarded under Article 6 of the Convention.

2. The Doctrine in National Systems[1]

The doctrine under consideration, whether called "*actes de gouvernement*", "political acts" or, in common-law systems, "Crown prerogative" or "acts of state", is not, generally, founded on any express constitutional or statutory provision. It has been developed by the jurisprudence and the legal theory. It originates from the stance that "the exercise of the function of government is not a matter for the control of the court but possibly for the political control of the legislature".[2] It has also historical roots.[3] Legal theory draws a distinction between acts of government as administration and political acts of government.[4] The former, however

1 I am grateful to the Research Division of the European Court of Human Rights for their excellent Report on this subject.

2 Quotation from R. Chapus in the *Dictionnaire Constitutionnel*, O. Duhamel, Y. Meny, 1992, p. 7.

3 V.L. Debbasch and J.-C. Ricci, *Contentieux administratif*, 5 éd., para. 62.

4 H.J. Laferrière, *Traité*, 2e éd., t. 2, p. 32 et seq.

wide the authorities' discretionary powers, are subject to judicial scrutiny whereas the latter are in many cases immune from it.

3. Absence of Definition

There is an obvious difficulty of using the "political" nature of an act emanating from the executive as the criterion for deciding whether the act should escape judicial control. In a sense every act of the executive is political. In actual fact there is no precise and exhaustive definition of the acts covered by this doctrine but these are usually invoked in respect of acts connected with international affairs, foreign policy, diplomatic negotiations and war.

The category of these acts presents certain variations from country to country and acts are included or excluded from this category by decisions of the Court, there being in general no constitutional or even statutory list of such acts. In some countries there is only a provision to the effect that "government acts" are not justiciable without any indication as to the nature of such acts. It is left to the courts to decide on each case whether any claim by the Government falls within the class of government acts. It is true that there is a tendency on the part of the courts to extend their competence over acts claimed to be acts of government. However the fact remains that until today the doctrine of government acts or political acts which cannot be subject to judicial review remains valid and blocks the way to the judicial examination of many cases very often with unjust results. The absence of a clear and strict definition of the acts in question defining precisely the limits of government activity which escapes judicial control gives rise to legitimate criticisms that the doctrine concerning these acts is contrary to the rule of law, the principle of equal protection of the law and amounts to a danger based on the "reason of the state".

4. Control of Legality

The view is propounded that the judges cannot substitute the government or block the political decisions of the latter, in other words, there should be no government by the judges. But the correctness of this plausible approach is based on the premise that judicial control amounts to substitution of the discretion of the government by that of the judiciary. This is wrong: judicial control in the case of acts emanating from the government or the administration is and must be confined to the legality of the acts, i.e. their conformity with the limits regarding competence of the organ concerned and all other legal conditions. It is not the task of the courts to examine questions concerning the expediency or correctness of the particular solution adopted by the government organs. On the other hand, as far as civil courts are concerned they have to do mainly with the question of damages regarding the effects of such solution on the rights of individuals, a question which again does not deal with the correctness or political expediency of the policy decision from which the damage stems.

5. The Doctrine in Various Countries

The concept of the act of government exists in many European countries, including France and Spain. In France, however, over a period from the early 1960s to the late 1970s, the *Conseil d'Etat* was inconsistent, declaring in some cases that it had no jurisdiction while in others it was prepared to consider the substance of applications. Legal theorists criticised this as misleading the litigant into believing that their rights were better secured because the substance of a case was being examined. In Spain, an Act was passed in 1998 empowering the courts to rule on acts of the executive, but the line taken in the case-law has been to accord the Government a very large degree of discretion.

In Belgium, Germany and the Netherlands the theory of acts of government is not applied in domestic law. Nonetheless when cases concerning acts that fall within the French-type act of government are brought before the courts they tend to be unsuccessful. This is because, on the one hand, the national courts require applicants to demonstrate a personal interest and, on the other, because they accord their respective governments a broad measure of discretionary power.

In Poland and Norway judicial review is available where an individual's rights have been infringed. The doctrine of *actes de gouvernement* is not applicable. In the United Kingdom, the concept of a "political" or "government act" comes under the general rubric of Crown prerogative. To quote the classic authority on English constitutional law:

> The prerogative is the name of the remaining portion of the Crown's original authority, and is therefore, as already pointed out, the name for the residue of discretionary power left at any moment in the hands of the Crown ... (Dicey).

6. Tendency to Extend Judicial Review

The landmark judgment on the power of the courts to scrutinise prerogative acts is the *GCHQ* case,[5] decided by the House of Lords in 1985. Prior to this decision, it was settled law that when faced with a prerogative act, the most any court of law could do was to confirm that this was indeed an exercise of prerogative power, that it had been exercised in an appropriate form and that Parliament had not restricted it through legislation. Any other issue, such as legality, procedural propriety or bad faith, was off-limits. To borrow a vivid phrase from a recent Court of Appeal decision, prerogative was a no-go area for the courts.

The *GCHQ* case was a significant development in constitutional law. The prerogative at issue was that of the Government to determine the terms and conditions of employment for civil servants (who were, as a rule, not covered by general employment legislation). A majority of the House of Lords held that the mere fact that, formally, a government act was an exercise of prerogative power was not sufficient to make it immune to judicial scrutiny. Rather, the decisive factor was the subject-matter. There was a spectrum of acts, ranging from the clearly non-justiciable to the clearly cognisable. Lord Roskill gave examples of subject-matters that would by their very nature be non-justiciable: the making of treaties, the defence of the realm, the prerogative of mercy, the grant of honours, the dissolution of Parliament and the appointment of Ministers.

The principle laid down in *GCHQ* opened the way for judicial review of matters previously deemed not to be amenable to the judicial process, including one of the examples given by Lord Roskill: the High Court reviewed the Home Secretary's refusal to grant a posthumous pardon to the last man hanged in the United Kingdom, and found that the decision was tainted with illegality.[6] Similarly, a refusal to issue a passport may be challenged before the courts.[7] The Government's argument that the power to issue passports is part of the broader foreign affairs prerogative found no favour with the High Court. Other prerogatives now

5 *The Civil Service Unions v. The Minister for the Civil Service* [1985] A.C. 374.

6 *R. v. Secretary of State for the Home Department, ex p. Bentley* [1994] Q.B. 349.

7 *R. v. Secretary of State for Foreign and Commonwealth Affairs, ex p. Everett* [1989] Q.B. 811.

subject to judicial review are the discretion of the Crown Prosecution Service to continue or discontinue criminal proceedings,[8] and the making of *ex gratia* payments to persons convicted, imprisoned and then acquitted on appeal (prerogative of bounty).[9]

The tendency to exercise judicial control over acts emanating from government authorities that were considered previously untouchable is supported also by the jurisprudence of other European countries including France.[10] The French *Conseil d'Etat* has also developed the theory of the separable acts (*actes détachables*) which allowed judicial review of acts which although connected with international relations may be separated from them and examined independently.[11]

7. Absolute Immunity

The procedural ground for the exclusion from judicial review of the *actes de gouvernement,* or acts of State or other "political acts" is the fact that they enjoy absolute immunity. The courts are not allowed to examine the relevant claim even if it concerns a right under the domestic law which, but for the fact that it relates to an act of government or act of state, etc., could be the subject of judicial examination of the merits. Halsbury's *Laws of England* makes the following remark: "... the courts have no jurisdiction to question the validity of an act of state, and an individual cannot rely upon an act of state in order to found a cause of action."

This immunity extends both to the judicial review of the validity of the act as well as the actions for compensation as regards the consequences of such acts. For instance the French *Conseil d'Etat* in line with its constant jurisprudence rejected a claim for damages for the immobilisation of a cargo ship by the French navy detained by the latter in order to verify its cargo. According to the *Conseil d'Etat* "(t)he relevant measures

8 *The Chief Constable of Kent, ex p. L. and R. v. Director of Public Prosecutions, ex p. B* [1993] 1 All E.R. 756.

9 *R. v. Secretary of State for the Home Department, ex p. Harrison* [1988] 3 All E.R. 86.

10 Dupuis, G., Guédon M.-J., *Institutions administratives. Droit administratif,* Paris, 1986, p. 464.

11 R. Chapus, *Droit administratif général,* Tome 1. 15th ed., para. 1156.

must be considered as linked with military operations, by their nature are not susceptible to judicial examination."[12]

8. Criticism of the Doctrine

The doctrine which allows the exclusion from judicial control of government acts or their equivalent political acts has been under severe criticism by jurists.

Thus it has been said that

> *L'existence des actes de gouvernement dans le droit administratif est particulièrement regrettable pour l'efficacité de la protection juridictionnelle. Étant donné qu'aucune juridiction n'est compétente pour en connaître, aucun recours n'est possible à leur encontre. La doctrine s'est toujours élevée contre cette vacance du contentieux soit en niant l'existence des actes de gouvernement – et pourtant ils existent – soit en suggérant qu'au moins le recours en indemnité soit possible contre eux.*[13]

> *Cette doctrine est critiquable. Elle est dangereuse, contestable, indéfendable, même, dans les conséquences qu'elle peut avoir parce qu'elle n'impose aucune limite au domaine des actes qui échappent à tout contrôle juridictionnel (raison d'État). C'est contraire à l'État de droit.*[14]

In Belgium *Conseiller d'Etat* Leroy wrote in 1999:

> Nowhere in the case-law is there a single decision offering sound reasons for exempting certain cases from the *Conseil d'Etat's* jurisdiction solely on the grounds that they concern acts of government.

He added:

12 *Société Ignazio Messina et Cie*: AJDA 1966, p. 382; see also Mirtoon-Stemchip and Co.: Dalloz 1958, p. 10: rejection of claim for damages for the requisition of a ship because the requisition was linked with the conduct of war and at the same time with the international relations and therefore escaped judicial control.

13 V.L. Debbasch and J.-C. Ricci, *Contentieux Administratif*, 5th ed.; see also V.L. Favoreu, "L'acte de Gouvernement, acte provisoirement et accidentellement injusticiable" *R.F.D.A.* 1987, p. 544.

14 <http://fr.jurispedia.org/index.php/Acte_de_gouvernement_(fr)>, p. 6.

> Such a theory has no place in a state governed by the rule of law. It is merely another name for *raison d'État*, which is a negation of the rule of law.[15]

I endorse these statements and I consider them very pertinent in balancing the purported public interest which is served by the immunity applying to the acts of government against the public interest of the judicial determination of claims of individuals. Similarly pertinent is the fact that in many domestic legal systems it is now accepted that the doctrine of government act and its equivalents cannot exclude the judicial examination claims for violations of human rights.

In Spain the new Administrative Courts Act of July 13 1998 provides:

> Administrative courts shall have competence in respect of the following matters:
>
> a) judicial protection of basic rights, matters subject to regulation and the determination of appropriate compensation in the context of acts of the Government or of the governments of Autonomous Communities, whatever the nature of the acts [...]

The Supreme Court applied this Act in a ruling on 13 October 2000 and held that it did not preclude judicial scrutiny of acts coming within Article 97 of the Constitution ("political acts"), because these were

15 M. Leroy, "Les actes de gouvernement: Un spectre qui hante la jurisprudence du Conseil d'État belge", *Administration Publique*, Vol. 3/1999, pp. 183-189; see also R. Chapus, *Droit administratif général*, Tome 1, 15th edition, par. 11.52: *"On est en droit, bien entendu, de regretter cette immunité, qui paraît mal s'accorder avec l'idée de l'État de droit – ainsi qu'avec la disposition de la convention européenne des droits de l'homme, selon laquelle (art. 13) toute personne doit disposer d'un 'recours effectif', en cas de violation des droits et libertés que la convention lui garantit (cela, dans l'hypothèse où il apparaîtrait que les actes de gouvernement sont susceptibles, compte tenu de ce qu'ils sont, de méconnaître ces droits et libertés)."*; see also R. Ergec, "Le contrôle juridictionnel de l'administration dans les matières qui se rattachent aux rapports internationaux: actes de gouvernement ou réserve du pouvoir discrétionnaire?", *Revue de Droit international et de droit comparé*, 1986, pp. 72-134 and Cédric Raux, "Acte de gouvernement et Convention européenne des droits de l'homme. Étude à partir de l'arret du Conseil d'État de France", in: *Revue Trimestrielle des Droits de l'Homme*, Vol. 16, No. 64, October 2005, pp. 855-868. Some legal commentators (a minority) do not entirely dismiss the theory of the act of government.

regulated by constitutional law. Even an act of government in the field of international relations would be subject to constitutional and administrative law rather than international law. While the scope of judicial review in this field is more tightly restricted than in other areas, it is nevertheless possible for the Supreme Court to scrutinise those aspects of government acts that are subject to regulation.[16]

It is clear from this case-law that the administrative courts are at present competent to rule on whether an act of government is lawful and constitutional, specifically with regard to protection of fundamental rights.

9. The Ban Becoming Less Absolute

In a report on the legal foundation for foreign policy, published on 19 June 1998, the Venice Commission considered the very specific question of whether or not governments' foreign-policy choices and actions – an area generally regarded as falling within the sovereign powers of the executive – could be subject to judicial review.

The report notes at the outset that it is difficult to subject to judicial review the desirability and necessity of using force in international relations in order to defend the integrity and security of the State, but goes on to describe recent developments in other fields with regard to judicial review of matters relating to foreign policy. It is pointed out, *inter alia*, that:

> ... the ban on judicial review is becoming less absolute in nature. Firstly, it is open to review whether in taking a foreign policy decision a given organ of the State exceeded the powers conferred on it by the constitution ... Secondly, certain constitutional courts have established precedents for reviewing not only whether decision-makers acted within the bounds of their authority, but also the very substance of the decision itself. This is true of preventive review of treaties' conformity with the constitution but also – and above all – of the concept whereby the executive is deprived of its traditional freedom of action whenever fundamental human rights are in issue.

10. Policy Choices

In those cases where the doctrine of *actes de gouvernement* or other political acts are excluded from judicial review the rationale for the ex-

16 Judgment of 14 October 2000, Third Chamber.

clusion focuses on the policy choices and value determinations of the executive branch rather than the consequences thereof on the rights of any individuals affected. Thus the final court of appeal in Amsterdam stated that it was not the role of the ordinary courts to assess different *political options*.[17]

In the US case *Ange v. Bush*,[18] the court found non-justiciable a challenge to the President's deployment orders and activities in the Persian Gulf in the absence of a congressional declaration of war. The court noted that:

> The judicial branch is neither equipped nor empowered to intrude into the realm of foreign affairs where the Constitution grant operational powers only to the two political branches and where decisions are based on political and policy considerations.

In *Aktepe v. the United States*,[19] the court examined the claim of some 300 Turkish Navy sailors for death and personal injury suffered when two missiles fired from a US aircraft carrier struck their vessel during NATO training exercises. It found that the case presented a non-justiciable political question because it would require a court to *interject itself into military decision-making and foreign policy*, areas the Constitution had committed to coordinate branches of government.

11. Consequences of Political Acts

I think that the extension of the immunity from judicial review of political acts not only as regards the policy decisions but also as regards the consequences of such decisions on individual rights – especially on fundamental human rights – is unjustified. In support of the exclusion of political acts from judicial review it is argued that the judicial branch is not equipped and lacks the necessary training to judge political ques-

17 *Hoge Raad*, 29 November 2002, Case No. C01/027HR, <http://www.rechtspraak.nl>; see also C. Höhn, "Zur Rechtmäßigkeit der NATO-Luftangriffe im Kosovo-Konflikt (Anmerkung zum Urteil der Arrondissementsrechtbank 's-Gravenhage vom 7 April 1999)", *Z.a.ö.RV.*, pp. 863-875; on the stationing of nuclear weapons see *Hoge Raad*, 10 November 1989, NJ, 1991, No. 248; on their possible use see *Hoge Raad*, 21 December 2001, NJ, 2002, No. 217.

18 752 F. Supp. 509 (D.D.C. 1990).

19 105 F. 3d 752 F. Supp. 509 (D.D.C. 1990) 1400 (11th Cir 1997).

tions. Leaving aside the irrelevance of the argument (given that judicial review does not mean substitution of the decision of the court to that of the executive but only examination of the legality of the impugned decision) I do not see any relation of the argument in respect of the judicial review of the effects, especially the material ones, of any political decision on individual rights. Judges are very well equipped to examine such effects and compensate the victims in the context of relevant legal principles such as torts and human rights. This approach is illustrated by the following American case.

In *Koohi v. the United States*,[20] the court found that the plaintiffs' action for damages could not be dismissed on the basis of the political question doctrine. In that case, a US warship had erroneously shot down an Iranian civilian aircraft during the Iran-Iraq war following which the heirs of some of the deceased passengers and crew filed a claim against the US for the negligent operation of the warship. The court stated as follows:

> We note, as an initial matter, that governmental operations are a traditional subject of damage actions in the federal courts. Thus the federal courts have previously allowed damage actions alleging the negligent operation of naval vessels. Accordingly, the fact that the plaintiff's lawsuit involves the operation of a United States warship does not render it beyond judicial cognizance.
>
> Nor is the lawsuit rendered judicially unmanageable because the challenged conduct took place as part of an authorized military operation. The Supreme Court has made clear that the federal courts are capable of reviewing military decisions, particularly when those decisions cause injury to civilians. ...
>
> A key element in our conclusion that the plaintiffs' action is justiciable is the fact that the plaintiffs seek only damages for their injuries. Damage actions are particularly judicially manageable ...
>
> In addition, because the plaintiffs seek only damages, the granting of relief will not draw the federal courts into conflict with the executive branch. Damage actions are particularly non-intrusive ...
>
> The Supreme Court's review in The Paquete Habana of the Navy's decision to seize two enemy fishing vessels in the course of a military operation makes it clear that the fact that an action is taken in the ordinary exercise

20 976 F. 2d 1328 (1992).

> of discretion in the conduct of war "does not put it beyond the judicial power".

The court nevertheless found that the claim was barred by the Federal Torts Claims Act which contained an explicit exception for

> any claim arising out of combatant activities [...] during time of war.

The distinction between the military "political" decision and the ability of the Courts to deal with its ensuing harm to the individuals is made out clearly in the above case. But for the exclusion of the cause of action for the relevant tort by express provision in the Act in question there would be no problem for the determination of the relevant claim by the court. The political nature of the decision which was the original source of the harm was no obstacle for such determination. And why should it be?

12. Political Acts and the Right of Access to a Court

I will now examine the impossibility of judicial control of government acts and their equivalent other categories of political acts in the light of the right of access to a court under Article 6 of the Convention.

One of the most important decisions of the Strasbourg Court was the one in the *Golder* case[21] according to which the right to a fair trial implies a right of access to a court for the determination of a particular civil issue. The right of access to the court is not absolute, but is subject to limitations. However, like all limitations on the rights guaranteed by the Convention, they must not restrict or reduce the relevant right in such a way that its very essence is impaired.[22] Furthermore, such a limitation must pursue a legitimate aim and must be reasonably proportionate to the aim sought to be achieved.

The Court in the case of *Osman v. the United Kingdom*,[23] which concerned immunity from suit in negligence for the police when acting in an investigative capacity found that the immunity constituted a disproportionate restriction on the applicants' right of access to a court. The

21 Op. cit.

22 *Ashingdane* case, Series A no. 93, para. 57.

23 *Reports of Judgments and Decisions* 1998-VIII, paras. 151-154.

Court came to this conclusion because of the absolute nature of the immunity, which applied in all cases regardless of the competing interests at stake, thus preventing access to court in deserving cases. The test adopted by the Court was to the effect that it must be open to domestic courts to have regard to the presence of other public interest considerations apart from those justifying the immunity, so as to allow the possibility of the non-automatic application of the immunity in consequence of the weight of considerations which pull in the opposite direction. I believe that this approach should apply to any kind of immunity. In other words there should be no automatic absolute bars preventing access to court by virtue of any immunity.

This is the position that I have adopted in respect of three cases involving State immunity invoked by the defendants in civil actions against them[24] and in another case concerning parliamentary immunity.[25] In respect of the first three cases the majority upheld the immunity on the ground that it reflected generally recognised rules of public international law and could not for that matter be considered as disproportionate limitations on the right of access to a court. The parliamentary immunity was again upheld by the Court as justified by the fundamental importance of free debate in parliament.

It appears that the *Osman* test should still be considered as being good law. It is true that later in the case of *Z. v. the United Kingdom*[26] the Court came to the conclusion that in the *Osman* case it wrongly found that the facts disclosed the application of an immunity. However, the criterion adopted in the *Osman* case regarding the exclusion of automatic application of immunities remained unaffected.

13. The Distinction between Procedural Bar and Delimitation of a Right

Sometimes it can be difficult to decide whether a particular rule of domestic law relates to the non-existence of a right or whether it acts as procedural bar to obtain determination of a right.[27] However, as pointed

---

24 See "Questions of Fair Trial" in this book, footnotes 55, 56, and 57.

25 Ibid., footnote 58.

26 (2002) 34 *EHRR* 97.

27 See K. Reid, *A Practitioner's Guide to the European Convention on Human Rights*, 2nd ed., p. 81, and Jacobs and White, *The European Convention on Human Rights*, 4th ed., p. 171.

out above, I believe that it is evident that the exclusion of judicial review of claims on the ground of *actes de gouvernement* or similar doctrines concerning "political acts" amounts to an immunity – which is a procedural bar – and not to a negation of a substantive right. The tortious or other civil-law liability for any harm or injury caused to an individual as a result of the political act is not suppressed. The effect of the *acte de gouvernement* or the political character of the act from which the harm stems is to prevent the judicial examination of that act and not to deprive it of its tortious or other legally wrongful character. According to the phraseology used by the French *Conseil d'Etat* in such cases, for instance in the case of *Société Ignazio Messina et Cie* referred to above: "*Les mesures ainsi intervenues doivent être regardées comme se rattachant à des opérations militaires; par leur nature elles ne sont pas susceptibles d'être discutées.*"[28] According to Chapus: "*Il fait apparaître que l'immunité des actes de gouvernement résulte de l'incompétence des juridictions administrative et judiciaire.* "[29] Dupuis and Guedon also speak of the *immunity* of these acts: "*Certes, le fait que les actes de gouvernement sont soumis à un régime d'immunité juridictionnelle est de nature à faciliter leur identification dans la jurisprudence (lorsqu'ils ont fait l'objet de décisions de justice) et cette immunité, dans l'état actuel du droit positif, achève de les définir. Mais même si ce régime d'immunité était aboli...*"[30]

The above-cited American case of *Koohi v. the United States* illustrates the survival of the tortious nature of the consequences of government or military acts so that the court in that case had to resort to a

28 See also http://fr.jurispedia.org/index.php/Acte_de_gouvernement_(fr) where it is stated:

> *D'après elle, certains actes pris par des autorités administratives bénéficient d'une immunité absolue. Ces actes ne peuvent être attaqués en annulation par la voie du recours en excès de pouvoir. C'est-à-dire aussi qu'ils ne peuvent donner lieu à indemnisation s'ils causent un préjudice. Cette immunité va loin au-delà de la simple incompétence. C'est en présence de cette jurisprudence qu'a été élaborée la théorie dite de l'acte de gouvernement. On qualifie d'acte de gouvernement les actes auxquels la jurisprudence reconnaît une telle immunité.*

29 R. Chapus, op. cit., para. 1153; at para. 1152 reference is made to "*immunité juridictionnelle*".

30 Op. cit., p. 465.

special law excepting the case of acts *arising out of combatant activities [...] during time of war* from liability for torts.

14. The *Osman* Test in the Case of Political Acts

Applying the *Osman* test to the immunities under consideration it is submitted that the reasonable conclusion should be that the exclusion from judicial review of claims connected with *actes de gouvernement* or other concepts of political acts is in principle incompatible with the right of access to a court safeguarded by Article 6 of the Convention, provided that such review is confined to the control of the legality of the impugned act and the award of compensation for a specific tort or other legally wrongful act based on the domestic law e.g. assault, trespass, wrongful detention, confiscation of property, etc.

Any immunity preventing access to a court is automatically a restriction to the right in question. Does this restriction in the case of the immunity under consideration pursue a legitimate aim? The answer is doubtful. The rationale of the relevant doctrine is that the judicial branch is not equipped and lacks the necessary training to judge political questions. An additional argument is that political acts belong to the executive and the courts cannot, by virtue of the principle of separation of power, interfere with the competence of the executive. An answer to both arguments is the fact that a judicial review of the legality of the political acts (competence, compatibility with the relevant constitutional and other legal requirements) or the award of compensation for any civil wrong does not deal with the propriety, expediency or wisdom of the political policy choices. Like *Conseiller d'Etat*, Leroy, quoted above, I find it difficult to accept that there are any "sound reasons for exempting certain cases from the *Conseil d'Etat's* jurisdiction solely on the grounds that they concern acts of government".

But even assuming that the restriction pursues a legitimate aim such as the principle of separation of powers, the next question is that of proportionality. I believe that the answer should be in the negative, taking into account the following:

a) The immunity is absolute and allows of no judicial discretion or balancing of competing interests in each particular case.
b) The immunity is too general and extends beyond the purported protection of the policy decisions of the government.
c) The doctrine is anachronistic and incompatible with the rule of law, the principle of equal protection of the law and amounts to

a danger of the "reason of the state"; in fact it is unnecessary in a modern democratic society.

d) There is no precise definition or even a clear criterion of the *actes de gouvernement* or other equivalent concepts and in most countries this immunity is not prescribed by law.

e) There is now a judicial tendency to restrict the application of this immunity because of the demands of the rule of law.

15. The Case of *Marković v. Italy*

The European Court of Human rights recently had the opportunity to deal with a case where the judicial determination of the applicants' claim was rejected because it was connected with acts of war. The case was that of *Marković v. Italy*[31] the facts of which relate to the same events as those considered by the Court in its decision in the case of *Banković and Others v. Belgium and 16 Other Contracting States.*[32] The facts may be summarised as follows:

> After all efforts to achieve a negotiated political solution to the Kosovo crisis had failed, the North Atlantic Council (NAC) decided on, and on 23 March 1999 the Secretary General of NATO announced, the beginning of air strikes against the FRY. The air strikes lasted from 24 March to 8 June 1999. Three television channels and four radio stations operated from the RTS facilities in Belgrade. The main production facilities were housed in three buildings at Takovska Street. The master control room was housed on the first floor of one of the buildings and was staffed mainly by technical staff.
>
> On 23 April 1999, just after 2 a.m. approximately, one of the RTS buildings at Takovska Street was hit by a missile launched from a NATO forces aircraft. Two of the four floors of the building collapsed and the master control room was destroyed. [...] Twenty-four targets were hit in the FRY that night, including three in Belgrade.

The partial collapse of the RTS building caused the death of sixteen people, including the five relatives of the applicants.

The applicants brought an action in damages in the Rome District Court under Article 2043 of the Italian Civil Code which provides:

---

31 Application no. 1398/03 Grand Chamber.

32 (dec) [GC] no. 52207/99, ECHR 2001-XII).

> Any unlawful act which causes damage to another will render the perpetrator liable in damages under the civil law.

The Court of Cassation found that the Italian courts had no jurisdiction. It relied *inter alia* on the doctrine of acts of government or political acts as follows:

> The claim seeks to impute liability to the Italian State on the basis of an act of war, in particular the conduct of hostilities through aerial warfare. The choice of the means that will be used to conduct hostilities is an act of government. These are acts through which political functions are performed and the Constitution provides for them to be assigned to a constitutional body. The nature of such functions precludes any claim to a protected interest in relation thereto, so that the acts by which they are carried out may or may not have a specific content. With respect to acts of this type, no court has the power to review the manner in which the function was performed.

15.1 The Submissions of the Parties

The applicants filed an application before the European Court of Human Rights ("the Court"). Relying on Article 6 of the Convention, combined with Article 1, the applicants complained of the Court of Cassation's ruling that the Italian courts had no jurisdiction. As regards the doctrine of government acts the applicants argued that even if this limitation could still be said to exist in the Italian system after the entry into force of the Constitution it could not prevent the judicial determination of their claim which concerned a right to compensation for damage caused by the acts of a public authority, even though those acts stemmed from a political decision.

The respondent Government's position was that the dispute was not of a type that could be brought before the courts. In deciding that it was a "political act" that escaped the scrutiny of the courts, the Court of Cassation had not set a limit on the right of access to a court but had defined the scope of the substantive right claimed by the applicants. In the respondent Government's submission, the political-act doctrine did not create a procedural bar that removed or restricted the right to refer complaints to the courts, it precluded an action against the State *in limine*. In any event the Government argued that there are other acts asserting "State authority" at the highest level: these were acts of international policy and, through them, acts of war. The rule that acts implementing a State's fundamental political decisions were legitimately excluded from the realm of judicial competence stemmed from the principle of the separation of powers and the need to avoid involving the judiciary – which by definition had no democratic legitimacy – in the task of identifying the objectives that served the general interest or of choosing the means used to achieve such objectives. In sum, the judiciary could not be involved, even after the event, in the task of deciding national policy.

In the respondent Government's submission, there was thus in any event a legitimate purpose to the limitation imposed on access to the courts when the impugned act had a political objective. Nor was there any doubt that the aim pursued by the political-act doctrine could be achieved only by ousting the jurisdiction of the courts.

15.2 The Finding of the Court

The Court found by a majority of 10 to 7 that there had been no violation of Article 6 of the Convention. As regards the political acts issue the Court noted that the Court of Cassation had already ruled in an earlier case that the Italian courts had no jurisdiction over the authorities for acts of a political nature and that such acts did not give rise to a cause of action against the State because they did not damage personal legal interests, which were the only interests capable of affording a right to compensation under the domestic case-law... In determining the limits of its jurisdiction, the Court of Cassation marked out the bounds of the law of tort (para. 113)... The Court then stated:

> The Court considers that the Court of Cassation's ruling in the present case does not amount to recognition of an immunity but is merely indicative of the extent of the courts' powers of review of acts of foreign policy such as acts of war. It comes to the conclusion that the applicants' inability to sue the State was the result not of immunity but of the principles governing the substantive right of action in domestic law. At the relevant time, the position under the domestic case-law was such as to exclude in this type of case any possibility of the State being held liable... (para. 116)... It follows that the applicants cannot argue that they were deprived of any right to a determination of the merits of their claims. Their claims were fairly examined in the light of the domestic legal principles applicable to the law of tort. (para. 117)

15.3 Criticism of the Judgment

It is submitted that the above approach adopted by the majority in the *Marković* case is wrong. The Court of Cassation clearly closed the door to the judicial examination of the claim of the applicants by invoking the political nature (act of government) of the acts on which the claim was based. The Court of Cassation did not address or refer to the question of the legal liability of the State in respect of the claims in question in terms of the domestic civil law. Therefore the dismissal of the applicants' case cannot be considered to be the result of the application of "legal principles applicable to the law of tort" but a procedural bar preventing the bringing of potential claims to court. The act of government approach amounted to an exclusion of a judicial examination of (to use the language of the Court of Cassation) "any claim to a protected interest in relation thereto". According to the same Court "(w)ith respect to acts of this type, *no court has the power to review...*" (Emphasis added).

If we proceed on the premise that the exclusion of a judicial examination of the applicant's claim was due to what I believe was an absolute immunity it is not difficult to find that such course taken by the Italian Court of Cassation was legally unjustified, because the immunity in question is incompatible with Article 6 of the Convention for the reasons explained above. The facts of the *Marković* case and the reasons given in the dissenting opinion of the Italian Judge Zagrebelsky joined by Judges Zupančič, Jungwiert, Tsatsa-Nikolovska, Ugrekhelidze, Kovler and Thór Björgvinsson strengthen these reasons. In the dissenting opinion we read the following:

> In reaching its conclusion, the Court of Cassation chose to disregard the nature of the court proceedings instituted by the applicants: these proceedings did not directly concern Italy's participation in the armed conflict as a member of NATO and their purpose was not to have an act of government set aside. Their aim was simply to obtain compensation for the remote consequences of the political act concerned, consequences that were purely potential and unrelated to the purpose of the acts. Despite the general nature of the right set out in Article 2043 of the Italian Civil Code, the Court of Cassation ultimately refused to accept that any Italian court had jurisdiction to hear the applicants' claims under domestic law, solely because the decision to participate in the aforementioned military operations was political in nature. The Court of Cassation thus went beyond any

legitimate aim the political-act doctrine may be recognised as furthering and far beyond the bounds of proportionality.

16. Concluding Remarks of General Application in the Light of the *Marković* Case

I believe that the judgment in the *Marković* case was governed by the same considerations as those which led to the judgment in the *Banković* case. The result is another set back in the effort to achieve an effective promotion of and respect of human rights by the High Contracting Parties to the Convention in relation to the exercise of any political activity within or outside their country. It is an erroneous approach influenced by the facts and the surrounding circumstances of the case. I want to believe that this "jurisprudence" will change. In this context, I would repeat the words of Judge Cardozo:[33]

> The work of a judge is in one sense enduring and in another sense ephemeral. What is good in it endures. What is erroneous is pretty sure to perish. The good remains the foundation on which new structures will be built. The bad will be rejected and cast off in the laboratory of the years.

I would like to conclude by setting out the following passages from the dissenting opinion in *Marković* case which I fully endorse:

> In his address to the Parliamentary Assembly on 19 August 1949 presenting the proposal to institute the European Court of Human Rights, P.H. Teitgen said: "Three things still threaten our freedom. The first threat is the eternal reason of State. Behind the State, whatever its form, were it even democratic, there ever lurks as a permanent temptation, this reason of State. ... Even in our democratic countries we must be on guard against this temptation of succumbing to reason of State".[34] Is there any reason to suppose that this warning addressed to the 14 member States of which the Assembly of the Council of Europe was composed at the time is of any less relevance to our present-day Europe of 46 nations? ...

---

33 *The Nature of the Judicial Process*, New Haven and London Yale University Press, p. 178.

34 Collected edition of the *Travaux Préparatoires*, Vol. I, p. 41, Martinus Nijhoff, The Hague, 1975.

"Reason of state" has little time for law, still less for the "rule of law", which one can scarcely conceive of without there being a possibility of having access to the courts ...

... It is a matter of great concern that neither the Court of Cassation nor the Court provided any definition of what might qualify as an "act of government" or "political act" ... or of what the limitations on such acts might be. Any act by a public authority will, directly or indirectly, be the result of a political decision, whether it is general or specific in content ...

Chapter 13 The Right of Return

1. Introduction

In this chapter I will deal with the legal developments and the principles which have been incorporated in the international and human rights law in relation to the right of refugees and internally displaced persons to return to their homes and properties after their forcible displacement. The issues arising from this topic appear at first sight quite simple and the responses indisputable, yet many efforts, debates and interpretations were necessary in order to set up a corpus of rules which would regulate all the aspects of the subject. We must bear in mind that the relevant problems arise as a rule in conflict situations, when abnormal conditions prevail and generally the eviction of persons from their homes constitutes the aim of the State which is responsible for the displacements: either to change the ethnological composition of the population, or more particularly for purposes of ethnic cleansing,[1] or in order to consolidate its military and political power by expelling all those who are considered or suspected to be opponents of the new regime. Moreover, the displaced persons as a rule number in the thousands or even in the millions. Consequently, in the development and adoption of the principles which recognise and regulate the right of return, many political forces failed to cooperate. At the same time the formulation of these principles faced the following two problems: firstly, the usually long duration of the displacement which created certain *faits accomplis*, and secondly, how to solve the humanitarian problems of the persons who in the meantime occupied the homes of the displaced persons. The

---

1 For the problem of ethnic cleansing in conjunction with the right of return of those displaced in Bosnia and Herzegovina and for the difficulties of implementing this right, see Marcus Cox, "The Right to Return Home. International Intervention and Ethnic Cleansing in Bosnia and Herzegovina" in the *International and Comparative Law Quarterly*, Vol. 47, 1998, p. 599 et seq.

greatest problem, of course, has been the implementation of the relevant principles.[2]

2. International Law and the UN Security Council

For a long time the right of return was not regulated clearly by any rules of international law. In the beginning the Hague Regulations of 1907 were invoked on account of their provisions, which referred to the obligations of the occupying forces towards the civilian population and in particular the obligation to preserve the social and legal *status quo* of the occupying territory and allow the population to remain in the occupied territory.[3] Thereafter, the 1949 Geneva Convention relative to the protection of civilians in times of war was invoked.[4] There had been a problem as regards the right of displaced groups of persons in contrast with small numbers of individuals.[5] In a British case, where the question of admission to Britain of Asians who had been expelled from Uganda arose, Lord Denning stated: "Mass expulsions have never hitherto come within the cognisance of international law." And he based his reasoning on the impracticality of requiring a State to accept persons numbering in the thousands.[6] However, finally the view has prevailed that the right of return also applies to members of groups displaced *en masse* regardless of their numbers. This view has also been confirmed by the organs of the United Nations. For instance, there have been resolutions of the Security Council and the General Assembly calling upon States who

2 Ibid.; see also Bret Thiele, "Housing and Property Restitution in the Context of the Return of Refugees and Internally Displaced Persons: Developments at the United Nations", *Netherlands Quarterly of Human Rights*, Vol. 18/2, pp. 283-288, 2000.

3 For this subject and generally for the different sources and the relevant rules of international law, see John Quigley, "Mass Displacement and the Individual Right of Return", *The British Yearbook of International Law* 1997, p. 65 *et seq.*

4 Ibid., p. 70.

5 Ibid., p. 75-88.

6 *R v. Secretary of State for the Home Department, ex parte Thakrar*, [1974] I QB 684, 702. Lord Denning said "Is it to be said that by international law every one of them has a right if expelled to come into these small islands? Surely not. This country would not have room for them. It is not as if it was only one or two coming. They come not in single files 'but in battalions'."

were responsible for the displacements of thousands and even millions of persons, to allow the return of this population. These States include Bosnia and Herzegovina,[7] Croatia,[8] South Africa[9] and Turkey.[10] The displacement in the case of Turkey was the result of the invasion and occupation of the northern part of Cyprus and the forcing out of the Greek Cypriot population of the occupied area in order to promote a policy of ethnic cleansing.

3. Pretexts for Impediments to the Return of the Displaced

Countries which refuse to repatriate and generally allow the return of displaced persons invoke a variety of reasons either for the delay or for the refusal to carry out their obligation. These reasons are the following: firstly, the unstable and abnormal conditions in the territory to which the return must take place. This ground was rejected by a resolution of the Security Council in the case of the refusal of the Abkhaz authorities to repatriate large numbers of Georgians on the ground of bad economic conditions.[11] The President of the Security Council had already stated that he was "deeply concerned at the continued obstruction of the return of the refugees and displaced persons by the Abkhaz authorities" and described the obstruction as "totally unacceptable".[12] Secondly, it was the fact that no final peace settlement had been reached which would have solved the dispute that had led to the displacement. The

7 Resolution of the Security Council, 779, doc. UN/RES 779 (1992).

8 Resolution of the Security Council, SC 1009, doc. UN/RES 1009 (1995). See also Resolution nr 1019, according to which the Security Council demanded that Croatia "respect fully the rights of the local Serb population including their right to remain or return in safety" and called on Croatia "to lift any time limits placed upon the return of refugees to Croatia to reclaim their property".

9 Resolution of the Security Council, 385, doc. UN/S/INF/32 (1977).

10 Resolution of the Security Council, 365, doc. UN/S/INF/30 (1975) which endorsed the Resolution of the General Assembly 3312 which stated in para. 6 "that all the [Cypriot] refugees should return to their homes in safety", and called upon the parties concerned "to take urgent measures to that end".

11 SC Res. 1036, SCOR 51st Session, UN Doc. S/RES/1036 (1996).

12 Statement of Security Council President Juan Somavia, UN Doc. S/PRST/1996/20.

return of displaced persons has, at times, been handled in the context of an overall settlement.[13] For instance Turkey has left the matter of repatriation of any displaced Greek Cypriots to be dealt with as part of an overall settlement of the question of Cyprus. However, United Nations organs have demanded repatriation before any disputes are settled. This was the case in South Africa[14] and Israel.[15] It is interesting to note here that the United States opposed an amendment proposed by Guatemala, which accepted Israel's view that repatriation prior to peace agreements would lead to "constant friction between Arabs and Jews". In opposing the amendment the United States argued that "[t]he unfortunate people should not be made pawns in the negotiations for a final settlement".[16] The proposed amendment by Guatemala was thoroughly defeated.[17] Another reason invoked by the countries which refuse the return of displaced persons is the fact that the relevant hostilities which led to the displacement continue. This excuse was rejected by the United Nations in the case of Bosnia[18] and also in the case of Afghanistan.[19]

Other reasons for the denial of the right to return, such as the threat to State security, the continuation of conflict in States in which those persons have sought refuge, and the use of the denial as a countermeasure, have been rejected by academic commentators as being incompatible with international law and human rights.[20]

4. Exchange of Populations

In some cases, in the first fifty years of the twentieth century, treaties were made between countries which provided for an exchange of populations. Examples of these treaties are those between Greece and Bul-

13 Quigley, op. cit. p. 112.

14 SC Res. 385, para. 11 (d), SCOR, 31st Session, Resolutions and Decisions, p. 8 UN Doc. S/INF/32 (1977).

15 Quigley, op. cit. pp. 112-113.

16 GAOR, 3rd Session, Part I, C.1, Summary Records of Meetings 21 September – 8 December 1948, p. 909, UN Doc. A/C.I/SR.226 (1948) (Mr Rusk, USA).

17 Quigley, op. cit. p. 113.

18 SC Res. 779, SCOR, 47th Session, UN Doc. S/RES/779 (1992).

19 GA Res. 48/152, preamular para. 15, 85th plenary meeting, UN Doc. A/RES/48/152 (1993).

20 Quigley, op. cit. pp. 116-122.

garia of 1919 and between Greece and Turkey of 1923. Moreover, after the Second World War there were agreements between those States that won the war for the expulsion of millions of Germans from the countries they were living in.[21]

After the establishment of human rights law in the second half of the twentieth century, resulting in persons acquiring personal subjective rights, the treaties for the exchange of populations could no longer be based on the rights and duties of the contracting States in disregard of the will of the affected individuals as used to be the case in the past when there were no individual rights.[22] Consequently, the International Law Commission's Working Group, referring to human rights law, has found population exchanges unlawful.[23] Accordingly it is submitted that population exchange treaties which are contrary to the will of the individuals concerned can no longer be considered as legally valid.[24]

5. The European Convention on Human Rights

5.1 *The Case of* Cyprus v. Turkey

The European Convention on Human Rights of the Council of Europe (the European Convention) which entered into force in 1953 has contributed to the development and establishment of the legal principles relating to the right of return.

In 1974, on the pretext of restoring the constitutional order of the Republic of Cyprus after a *coup d' état* against the President of Cyprus by the Greek *junta*, Turkey invaded the island and occupied its northern part.[25] The mass human rights violations committed by Turkey in the occupied area included the forcible displacement of about two hundred thousand Greek Cypriots from their homes. These internally displaced persons were forced to flee their homes and find refuge in the Government-controlled area in the southern part of Cyprus. Turkey has con-

21 Alfred de Zayas, *Nemesis at Potsdam*, Routledge, 1979.

22 Quigley, op. cit., p. 124.

23 Report of the International Law Commission on the work of its Forty-Seventh Session, GAOR, 50th Session, Supplement no. 10, p. 271, at p. 276.

24 Art. 53 of the Vienna Convention on the Law of Treaties.

25 See the Report of the European Commission of Human Rights (the Commission) in the case of *Cyprus v. Turkey*, applications nos. 6780/74 and 6950/75, adopted on 10 July 1976, paras. 6-15.

tinued to occupy the northern part of Cyprus ever since, and has continued to refuse to allow the displaced persons to return to their homes and properties. The Republic of Cyprus has filed four interstate applications against Turkey for violations of the European Convention. The first three applications[26] were examined by the European Commission of Human Rights, and led to two reports of the Commission according to which Turkey was found responsible for the refusal to allow

> the return of more than 170,000 Greek-Cypriots refugees to their homes in the north of Cyprus [and consequently] Turkey violated and was continuing to violate Art. 8 of the Convention in all these cases.

The Commission also found it:

> established that there has been deprivation [by Turkey] of possessions of Greek Cypriots on a large scale, the exact extent of which could not be determined.[27]

In its Report of 4 October 1983, in respect of application no. 8007/77, the Commission found that:

> by her continued refusal to allow over 170,000 Greek Cypriots to return to their homes in the north of Cyprus, Turkey continues to violate Art. 8 in all these cases.

Turkey did not recognise the jurisdiction of the European Court of Human Rights (ECHR) until January 1990. In a fourth interstate case, *Cyprus v. Turkey*,[28] the problem of the denial of Turkey to allow the refugees to return to their homes was brought before the Court to the jurisdiction of which Turkey was by that time accountable. The Court found

---

26 Applications nos 6780/74 , 6950/75 and 8007/77.

27 Report of the Commission in respect of applications nos. 6780/74 and 6950/75 adopted on 10 July 1976. These two applications were joined and examined together by the Commission.

28 Application no. 25781/94 (*Reports of Judgments and Decisions* 2001-IV).

> that there has been a continuing violation of Article 8 of the Convention by reason of the refusal to allow the return of any Greek-Cypriot displaced persons to their homes in northern Cyprus[29]

and that

> there has been a continuing violation of Article 1 of Protocol No. 1 by virtue of the fact that Greek-Cypriot owners of property in northern Cyprus are being denied access to and control, use and enjoyment of their property as well as any compensation for the interference with their property rights.[30]

The Court rejected the argument of the Turkish government according to which the fact that property rights were the subject of inter-communal talks involving both communities in Cyprus provided a justification for this situation under the Convention.[31]

The judgment of the Court was legally binding. It was delivered in 2001, and ever since it has been pending before the Committee of Ministers of the Council of Europe, which has the competence to monitor the execution of the judgments of the Court. Unfortunately, no steps at all have been taken until now for compliance with the obligation to allow the Greek-Cypriot displaced persons to return to their homes and properties. It is evident that the political interests and expediencies of the majority of the countries which participate in the Committee have been responsible for the negative attitude taken by it.

5.2 *The Case of* Doğan and Others v. Turkey

Recently, in a case against Turkey,[32] the Third Section of the ECHR had to deal with the complaint of several villagers living in Turkey who were either evicted or forced to flee from their homes and leave their villages as a result of violent confrontations between the Turkish Security Forces and members of the PKK; they had also been denied access to their

29 Ibid., p. 49, para. 175 and p. 100.

30 Ibid., p. 52, para. 189 and p. 101.

31 Ibid., p. 52, para. 188 and *Loizidou v. Turkey* (merits), judgment of 18 December 1996, *Reports of Judgments and Decisions* 1996-VI, para. 64.

32 *Doğan and Others* v. *Turkey* (just satisfaction), 13 July 2006; see also judgment of 29 June 2004, ECHR 2004-VI.

possessions since 1994. The Court found a violation of their right of respect to their homes under Article 8 of the Convention and a breach of their right to the peaceful enjoyment of their possessions under Article 1 of Protocol No. 1 to the Convention. As regards the displacement of the applicants, the Court stated:

> ... the authorities have the primary duty and responsibility to establish conditions, as well as provide the means, which allow the applicants to return voluntarily, in safety and with dignity, to their homes or places of habitual residence, or to resettle voluntarily in another part of the country (see in this respect Principles 18 and 28 of the United Nations Guiding Principles on Internal Displacement, E/CN.4/1998/53/Add.2, dated 11 February 1998).

The Court also rejected the "Government's argument that the applicants should be required at this stage of the proceedings to apply to the competent compensation commissions in order to seek reparation for their damages". It pointed out that the parties failed to reach an agreement on the issue of just satisfaction and the proceedings have already lasted a very long time.

5.3 *The* Xenides-Arestis v. Turkey *Case*

5.3.1 The judgment

According to Article 43 of the Hague Regulations: "The authority of the legitimate power having in fact passed into the hands of the occupant, the latter shall take all the measures in his power to restore, and ensure, as far as possible, public order and safety, while respecting, unless absolutely prevented, the laws in force in the country." That entails that the occupant does not have a right to legislate or establish courts or other organs in occupied areas in order to replace the domestic legal order or to adjust it to its own policies and objectives. Moreover, this regulation (as well as Article 46 of the same Regulations which stipulates that "[f]amily honour and rights, the lives of persons and private property ... must be respected") prohibits the confiscation and the illegal possession of properties in the same area and the prevention of people from returning to the properties belonging to them under the domestic law.[33]

33 See Chapter 8, "The Protection of the Right to Property in Occupied Territories" in this book.

I make this point because of the erroneous approach taken in the recent judgment of the Third Section of the ECHR in the case of *Xenides-Arestis v. Turkey*[34] which concerned a complaint about the seizure of the applicant's house in the territory occupied by Turkey[35] and the refusal of Turkey to allow her to return therein. Contrary to what it stated in the *Doğan and Others* case, the Court not only avoided saying anything regarding the duty of Turkey to allow and facilitate the return of the applicant, but it also gave recognition to the illegal "Compensation Commission" established by Turkey in the occupied part of Cyprus through a "law" enacted by the illegal Turkish subsidiary local administration.[36]

Before citing the relevant parts of the judgment it is, I think, necessary for a better understanding of its negative aspects to refer to the previous judgment in the same case, because the two judgments must be read together.

In the previous judgment (dated 22 December 2005) the Third Section of the Court held that there had been a continuing violation of the applicant's rights guaranteed by Article 8 of the Convention and Article 1 of Protocol No.1 by reason of the complete denial of the rights of the applicant with respect to her home and the peaceful enjoyment of her property in northern Cyprus. However instead of awarding compensation to the applicant in line with its previous case law (see *Loizidou*, cited above) and express the same directions to the respondent government for the return of the applicant to her home and properties (as in the *Doğan and Others* case), it decided:

34 Application no. 46347/99, judgment delivered on 7 December 2006, see also the previous judgment in the same case of 22.12.05.

35 In the town of Famagusta, which is occupied and kept empty of its inhabitants by Turkey.

36 The Court in *Cyprus v. Turkey* (op. cit.) found that the court remedies provided to the enclaved Greek Cypriots living in the occupied area satisfied the requirements of Article 13 of the Convention. I believe this finding is wrong for the reasons set out by the dissenters in respect of this issue (see also the article "The judgment of the ECHR in the case of *Cyprus v. Turkey*" in this book). In any case this finding is distinguishable from the position that remedies such as the one referred to in the *Xenides-Arestis* case are acceptable for the displaced persons living outside the occupied area.

> ... that the respondent State must introduce a remedy which secures the effective protection of the rights laid down in Article 8 of the Convention and Article 1 of Protocol No. 1 in relation to the present applicant as well as in respect of all similar applications pending before the Court. Such a remedy should be available within three months from the date on which the present judgment is delivered and redress should be afforded three months thereafter ...

This was decided at a time when Turkey was, to the knowledge of the judges of the Third Section, in the process of "enacting" in the occupied area the "law" for the establishment of the "Compensation Commission" in question.

There followed the judgment of 7 December 2006 by which the Third Section of the ECHR, instead of finding that the respondent Government had failed to "secure the effective protection of the rights laid down in Article 8 of the Convention and Article 1 of Protocol No. 1" and "afford redress" in respect thereof in accordance with the previous judgment, and without even examining the question of the illegality and ineffectiveness of the "remedy" provided by the "law" enacted in the occupied area, stated that it

> ... welcomes the steps taken by the Government [the establishment by 'law' of a 'Compensation Commission' in the occupied area] in an effort to provide redress for the violations of the applicant's Convention rights as well in respect of all similar applications pending before it.

The Court went on as follows:

> The Court notes that the new compensation and restitution mechanism, in principle[37], has taken care of the requirements of the decision of the Court on admissibility of 14 March 2005 and the judgment on the merits of 22 December 2005. The Court points out that the parties failed to reach an agreement on the issue of just satisfaction where, like in the case of *Broniowski v. Poland* ... it would have been possible for the Court to address all the relevant issues of the effectiveness of this remedy in detail. The Court cannot accept the Government's argument that the applicant should now be required at this stage of the proceedings ... to apply to the

37 As regards fundamentals: *The Concise Oxford Dictionary.*

> new Commission in order to seek reparation for her damages (*Doğan and Others v. Turkey*).
>
> Having regard to the above considerations, and in the absence of an agreement between the parties, the Court, making its assessment on an equitable basis and formally in accordance with the Commission's proposal [the Turkish Commission in the occupied area], awards the applicant EUR 800,000 under this head. (Emphasis added.)

5.3.2 Legal deviation

This judgment deviated from the right legal course and ran counter to the requirements of international law applicable in occupied territories and the rule of law as already mentioned above. At the same time it constitutes a setback to the relevant case-law of the Court. In paragraph 168 of the judgment in the *Cyprus v. Turkey* case the Court referred to the position of the European Commission of Human Rights in the same case, according to which:

> The refusal of the 'TRNC' authorities to allow the displaced persons to return to their homes reflected an acknowledged official policy and, accordingly, an administrative practice. In these circumstances there was no Convention requirement to exhaust domestic remedies.

The Court went on to state:

> ... that in the proceedings before the Commission the respondent Government did not dispute the applicant Government's assertion that it was not possible for displaced Greek Cypriots to return to their homes in the north. It was their contention that this situation would remain unchanged pending agreement on an overall political solution to the Cypriot question. In these circumstances the Court, like the Commission, considers that the issue of whether the aggrieved persons could have been expected to avail themselves of domestic remedies in the 'TRNC' does not arise.[38]

Furthermore the Court observed:

> ... that the essence of the applicant Government's complaints is not that there has been a formal and unlawful expropriation of the property of the displaced persons but that these persons, because of the continuing denial

38 *Cyprus v. Turkey*, op. cit., para. 171, p. 48.

> of access to their property, have lost all control over, as well as possibilities to enjoy, their land. As the Court has noted previously ..., the physical exclusion of Greek-Cypriot persons from the territory of northern Cyprus is enforced as a matter of 'TRNC' policy or practice. The exhaustion requirement does not accordingly apply in these circumstances.[39]

5.3.3 Serious obstruction to the right of return

As the situation described in the judgment of the Court in *Cyprus v. Turkey* remains the same[40], it is difficult to comprehend how a mechanism such as the "Compensation Commission" in the occupied area could possibly provide an effective remedy for the return of the displaced Greek Cypriots to their homes and properties. The decisions of this "Commission" already confirm this view given that in the *Xenides-Arestis* case the decision as regards restitution was, according to the "law" in question, to the effect that restitution of the immovable property of the applicant could only be considered "after the settlement of the Cyprus problem"(!). Moreover, as already pointed out, the "remedy" in question was an illegal product of the occupying country implementing, as expected, its own policies. Evidently it is difficult on a practical level for the victims of displacement to seek redress from such an illegal organ, also bearing in mind that it functions in the part of their country still under occupation.

Consequently, the effect of the judgment is to obstruct seriously the possibility of a remedy or at least of a legitimate pressure for the achievement of an effective exercise of the right of return in respect of all affected persons.

I dealt with this case at some length because of its importance in respect of the right to return. The case did not only refer to one particular individual, but as expressly stated in the preceding judgment in the same case of 22 December 2005, the "remedy" expected from Turkey – and later on found to be in principle in line with such an expectation – should have secured the effective protection of all similar applications

39 Op. cit, para. 185, p. 51.

40 The only change that has taken place in the meantime has been the making of the occupied area accessible, under restrictions, for the limited purpose of travelling in non-military parts, thus enabling the victims of displacement to simply view, like tourists, their homes and properties. Greek Cypriots are not allowed to reside in the occupied area or use their homes and properties.

pending before the Court, which are estimated to be about 1,500 and concerned thousands of displaced persons who were not even given the opportunity to plead their case. It is obvious that the Third Section of the ECHR was reluctant to proceed with these cases and preferred to send them to a kind of procedure offered readily (for the sake of her own objectives and interests) by Turkey without even an elementary examination of the question of its legality and effectiveness. But this approach was unfair and legally wrong. It is only to be hoped that this case-law will be reversed.

5.4 Radanović v. Croatia[41]

In the more recent case of *Radanović v. Croatia*, the applicant was deprived of her flat for a long time because it was given by the State to a temporary displaced occupant. The applicant complained of a breach of her right to her property under Article 1 of Protocol No. 1 to the European Convention. The Court found in favour of the applicant on the basis of the following reasoning:

> The Court recognises that the Croatian authorities faced an exceptionally difficult task in having to balance the rights of owners against those of temporary occupants in the context of the return of refugees and displaced persons, as this involved dealing with socially sensitive issues. Those authorities had, on the one hand, to secure the protection of the property rights of the former and, on the other, to respect the social rights of the latter, both of them often being socially vulnerable individuals. The Court therefore accepts that a wide margin of appreciation should be accorded to the respondent State. However, the exercise of the State's discretion cannot entail consequences which are at variance with Convention standards ... In this connection the Court reiterates that a situation [such] as the one in the present case calls for a fair distribution of the social and financial burden involved. This burden cannot be placed on a particular social group or a private individual alone, irrespective of how important the interests of the other group or the community as a whole may be ... However, in the instant case the applicant was forced to bear a burden – which should have been borne by the State – of providing the temporary occupant with a place to stay, a weight she eventually had to carry for more than six years.

41 Application no. 9056/02, 21 December 2006.

Notwithstanding the State's margin of appreciation, and in the absence of adequate compensation ..., the Court considers that the Croatian authorities failed to strike the requisite fair balance between the general interest of the community and the protection of the applicant's right to property. As a result thereof the applicant had to bear an excessive individual burden; therefore the interference with her right to property cannot be considered proportionate to the legitimate aim pursued."[42]

6. Increase in the Efforts for an Effective Protection of Displaced Persons

From the point of view of regional legal developments we now have the relevant jurisprudence of the ECHR based on Articles 8 of the Convention and Article 1 of Protocol No 1 to the Convention. Protocol No. 12 to the Convention, which came into force on 1 April 2005 and which prohibits discrimination on any ground by the authorities of the States bound by the Protocol, is an additional weapon in the armoury of those seeking the protection of the right to return. In the meantime, the international community has shown a serious interest and determination to protect the rights of displaced persons.

In a speech delivered on 8 October 2005, Mrs Mayra Gomez of the Centre on Housing Rights and Evictions highlighted the need for efforts to increase the protection of the displaced persons as follows

> Today, there are approximately 12.4 million refugees worldwide, and an additional 25 million Internally Displaced Persons (IDPs). For them, returning home in safety and dignity is often seen as the most desired, sustainable and dignified solution to their displacement. The loss of land, housing and property, however, is an all too common reality for persons caught up in situations of displacement and forced migration, and often presents itself as an obstacle to return. Not only are housing and property restitution programmes a pressing concern in light of the sheer numbers of displaced people, but we should also recall the vital role of these programmes in promoting regional stability, peace and security. In reality, the observance of these rights is central to the process of peace-building and

42 Paras. 49-50.

> conflict resolution, thereby fostering an environment of security in which the promise of peace can be realised.[43]

In August 2002 the UN Sub-Commission on the Promotion and Protection of Human Rights appointed Mr Paulo Sérgio Pinheiro, a well known international law jurist, to act as a Special Rapporteur for the preparation of a report setting out the principles on housing and property restitution for refugees and internally displaced persons. Mr Pinheiro submitted his final report in June 2005[44], and as a consequence we now have a report which covers fully and fairly the principles on all aspects of the right of return and of restitution of the properties of the refugees and other displaced persons. It is expressly stated in paragraph 8 of the Report that these principles reflect widely accepted principles of international human rights, refugee and humanitarian law and related standards.[45] They also reflect the Guiding Principles on Internal Displacement which had already been adopted in 1998 by the UN High Commissioner on Human rights.[46]

The Principles on housing and property restitution for refugees and displaced persons apply equally to all refugees, internally displaced persons and to other similarly situated displaced persons who fled across national borders but who may not meet the legal definition of refugee (hereinafter "refugees and displaced persons") who were arbitrarily or unlawfully deprived of their former homes, lands, properties or plac-

43 Mayra Gomez, "Housing and Property Restitution for Refugees and Displaced Persons": *The Cyprus Yearbook of International Relations* 2006, p. 95.

44 E/CN.4/ Sub.2/2005/17.

45 As pointed out by Mayra Gomez (op. cit., p. 98) "The Principles draw upon existing international human rights and humanitarian law in order to develop a universal approach to housing and property restitution policy at both the national and international level. It is important to note that the Principles do not seek to articulate or advance new rights. Rather, they rely on existing rights (as confirmed and developed in practice) recognised by the international community, and apply them to the specific question of housing and property restitution, as a form of restorative justice. These underlying international human rights and humanitarian standards are integrated into the principles themselves."

46 Document E/CN.4 1998/53/ Add.2, dated 11 February 1998; see Catherine Phuong, *The International Protection of Internally Displaced Persons*, Cambridge University Press, p. 39 et seq.

es of habitual residence, regardless of the nature or circumstances by which displacement originally occurred.[47]

7. The Pinheiro Principles

7.1 The Protection of Displaced Persons

The main principles set out in the Report are the following:

> All refugees and displaced persons have the right to return voluntarily to their former homes, lands or places of habitual residence, in safety and dignity. Voluntary return in safety and dignity must be based on a free, informed, individual choice. Refugees and displaced persons should be provided with complete, objective, up-to-date, and accurate information including on physical, material and legal safety issues in countries or places of origin. (§10.1)
>
> The right to return cannot be abridged nor can it be subject to arbitrary or unlawful time limitations. [§10.2] Refugees and displaced persons shall not be forced, or otherwise coerced, either directly or indirectly, to return to their former homes, lands or places of habitual residence. Refugees and displaced persons should be able to effectively pursue durable solutions to displacement other than return, if they so wish, without prejudicing their right to the restitution of their housing, land and property. (§10.3)
>
> All refugees and displaced persons have the right to have restored to them any housing, land and/or property of which they were arbitrarily or unlawfully deprived, or to be compensated for any housing, land and/or property that is factually impossible to restore as determined by an independent, impartial tribunal. (§2.1)
>
> Restitution is only deemed factually impossible in exceptional circumstances, namely when housing, land and/or property is destroyed or when it no longer exists, as determined by an independent, impartial tribunal Even under such circumstances the holder of the housing, land and/or property right should have the option to repair or rebuild whenever possible. (§21.2)

47 §1.2 of the Report.

States shall demonstrably prioritize the right to restitution as the preferred remedy for displacement and as a key element of restorative justice. The right to restitution exists as a distinct right, and is prejudiced neither by the actual return nor non-return of refugees and displaced persons entitled to housing, land and property restitution. (§2.2)

Everyone has the right to be protected against being arbitrarily displaced from his or her home, land or place of habitual residence. (§5.1)

States shall prohibit forced eviction, demolition of houses and destruction of agricultural areas and the arbitrary confiscation or expropriation of land as a punitive measure or as a means or method of war. [§5.3]

States shall take steps to ensure that no one is subjected to displacement by either State or non-State actors. States shall also ensure that individuals, corporations, and other entities within their legal jurisdiction or effective control refrain from carrying out or otherwise participating in displacement. (§5.4)

States should adopt positive measures aimed at alleviating the situation of refugees and displaced persons living in inadequate housing. (§8.2)

Everyone has the right to freedom of movement and the right to choose his or her residence. No one shall be arbitrarily or unlawfully forced to remain within a certain territory, area or region. Similarly, no one shall be arbitrarily or unlawfully forced to leave a certain territory, area or region. (§9.1)

States shall not recognize as valid any housing, land and/or property transaction, including any transfer that was made under duress, or which was otherwise coerced or forced, either directly or indirectly, or which was carried out contrary to international human rights standards. (§15.8)

States should ensure that the rights of tenants, social-occupancy rights holders and other legitimate occupants or users of housing, land and property are recognized within restitution programmes. To the maximum extent possible, States should ensure that such persons are able to return to and repossess and use their housing, land and property in a similar manner to those possessing formal ownership rights. (§16.1)

7.2 Secondary Occupants

States should ensure that secondary occupants [48] are protected against arbitrary or unlawful forced eviction. States shall ensure, in cases where evictions of such occupants are deemed justifiable and unavoidable for the purposes of housing, land and property restitution, that evictions are carried out in a manner that is compatible with international human rights law and standards, such that secondary occupants are afforded safeguards of due process, including an opportunity for genuine consultation, adequate and reasonable notice, and the provision of legal remedies, including opportunities for legal redress. [§17.1]

States should ensure that the safeguards of due process extended to secondary occupants do not prejudice the rights of legitimate owners, tenants and other rights holders to repossess the housing, land and property in question in a just and timely manner. [§17.2]

In cases where evictions of secondary occupants are justifiable and unavoidable, States should take positive measures to protect those who do not have the means to access any other adequate housing other than that which they are currently occupying from homelessness and other violations of their right to adequate housing. States should undertake to identify and provide alternative housing and/or land for such occupants, including on a temporary basis, as a means of facilitating the timely restitution of refugee and displaced persons' housing, land and property. Lack of such alternatives, however, should not unnecessarily delay the implementation and enforcement of decisions by relevant bodies regarding housing, land and property restitution. [§17.3]

In cases where housing, land and property has been sold by secondary occupants to third parties acting in good faith, States may consider establishing mechanisms to provide compensation to injured third parties. The egregiousness of the underlying displacement, however, may arguably give rise to constructive notice of the illegality of purchasing abandoned prop-

48 "'Secondary occupants' are persons who take up residence in a home after the home's rightful occupants have fled due to, *inter alia*, forced displacement, forced eviction, violence or threat of violence, or natural or human-made disasters." Document E/CN.4/Sub.2/2005/17/Add.1, 11 July 2005, § 63.

erty, pre-empting the formation of bona fide property interests in such cases. [§17.4]

7.3 The Legal Status of the Principles

These are the main substantive principles adopted by the report of Mr Pinheiro, which are the result of intensive consultations and deep study of the problem of refugees and other displaced persons in conjunction with the relevant principles of human rights and international humanitarian law.

The principles are generally acceptable and they are invoked in various international legal and political fora. In any event,

> ... the right of refugees and displaced persons to return to their homes is recognized by the international community as a free-standing, autonomous right in and of itself. In 1980, the General Assembly, in its resolution 35/124 on international intervention to avert new flows of refugees, reaffirmed 'the right of refugees to return to their homes in their homelands'. Many later resolutions of a number of bodies, including the Security Council, have reaffirmed that principle. [49]

> There are also examples referring to specific cases of displacement. For example, the Security Council, in its resolution 820 (1993) concerning Bosnia and Herzegovina, adopted on 17 April 1993, reaffirmed that 'all displaced persons have the right to return in peace to their former homes and should be assisted to do so'. Similar language by the Security Council reaffirming the right to return to one's home can be found in resolutions addressing displacement in numerous countries and regions [some of which have been referred to above]. [50]

> Likewise, the [UN] Sub-Commission [of Human Rights] reaffirmed 'the right of all refugees ... and internally displaced persons to return to their homes and places of habitual residence in their country and/or place of origin, should they so wish' with the adoption, without a vote, of resolution

49 Ibid., § 42; see also *Internally displaced people: a global survey* /Global IDP Project and Norwegian Refugee Council., 2d ed. 2002, p. 135.

50 Ibid., § 43 and footnotes 7-10 supra.

1998/26, entitled 'Housing and property restitution in the context of the return of refugees and internally displaced persons'.[51]

Furthermore, the rights which are set out in the Pinheiro Report emerge from specific provisions of relevant treaties or general rules of international law which have an autonomous existence. As already stated, such provisions are found in European Convention (Articles 3, 8 and 1) and in areas under occupation, in the Hague Regulations and the Geneva Convention of 1949 safeguarding the right of return of civilian populations. The provisions of the last two instruments are now part of the customary law.

8. Does the Passage of Time Destroy the Right?

A question which usually arises in relation to the right of return of displaced persons is whether, after the passage of a long time, forty or eighty years, for example, it is possible for the new occupants of the properties of the displaced persons to acquire such rights so as to prevent the restoration of the rights of the displaced persons, including the right to repossess their property. To this question I give the following answer. The change of factual conditions must inevitably be taken into account but, in a situation where a choice must be made between two hardships, the one that accords more the rule of law and justice must be remedied at the expense of the other. This is generally the objective of the law whenever a solution must be found in respect of conflicting claims, interests or situations. And although it is correct to admit that *faits accomplis* through the passage of time may establish situations that may become materially impossible to be reversed, the law should retain as much and as long as possible its constructive role as an instrument to deter or avert the prevalence of force over justice. This must be so if the rule that the fruits of aggression must not be recognised is to have any meaning. *Ex injuria jus non oritur* is an inescapable principle of law.[52]

51 Ibid., § 45.

52 See Loukis G. Loucaides, *Essays on the Developing Law of Human Rights*, 1995.

9. Conclusion

In conclusion, I should sum up by saying that the right of return of displaced persons is the best durable solution to cases of mass displacement.[53] As Mayra Gómez pointed out: "As many experts agree, there can be no prospect of workable peace agreement until the return and property restitution question is properly addressed."[54]

Many former Communist countries of Europe, such as the Czech Republic, Slovakia, Slovenia, Croatia, Romania and Bulgaria, have enacted laws on the basis of which the houses and properties confiscated forty, fifty or sixty years ago by totalitarian regimes should be returned to their lawful owners, and at the same time giving compensation or offering alternative housing to those occupying those properties even for many years after the confiscation. This proves that the right of return and restoration of properties of displaced persons can in practice be implemented as long as the States concerned respect human rights and the rule of law.

The international community has been unable or unwilling to implement the right of return effectively in many cases, but it should be realised that "no peace can be sustained against the background of unfulfilled desires for return: they will remain destabilising factors for generations to come. We cannot betray the right to return to homes of origin".[55]

53 For an examination of durable solutions to refugee and IDP crises, see UNHCR Issues: Durable Solutions, <http://www.unhcr.ch/issus/durable/durable.htm>.

54 Op. cit., p. 97.

55 Cf. Cox op. cit., pp. 628-629.

Permissions

The following chapters are reproduced with kind permission from the publishers:

Chapter 2, "The Concept of 'Continuing' Violations of Human Rights", first published in *Protecting Human Rights: The European Perspective, Studies in Memory of Rolv Ryssdal,* Carl Heymanns Verlag KG, Köln, Bonn, München, 2000.

Chapter 5, "Determining the Extra-territorial Effect of the European Convention: Facts, Jurisprudence and the *Banković* Case", first published in *European Human Rights Law Review,* Issue 4, 2006.

Chapter 7, "The Judgement of the European Court of Human Rights in the Case of *Cyprus* v. *Turkey*", first published in 15 *Leiden Journal of International Law* 2002.

Chapter 8, "The Protection of the Right to Property in Occupied Territories", first published in *International and Comparative Law Quarterly,* Volume 53, July 2004, pp. 677-690.

Chapter 9, "Freedom of Expression and the Right to Reputation", first published in "Mélanges offerts à Silvio Marcus Helmons", Bruylant, Bruxelles, 2003.

Chapter 10, "Environmental Protection through the Jurisprudence of the European Convention on Human Rights", first published in *The British Yearbook of International Law,* 2004, Seventy-Fifth Year Issue, Oxford University Press, Oxford.

Chapter 11, "Questions of Fair Trial under the European Convention on Human Rights", first published in *Human Rights Law Review,* Volume 3, No.1, Spring 2003, Nottingham University Press.

Index

Nijhoff Law Specials

60. S. Skaale (ed.): *The Right to National Self-Determination: The Faroe Islands and Greenland*. 2004 ISBN 90 04 14207 X

61. E. McWhinney: *The September 11 Terrorist Attacks and the Invasion of Iraq in Contemporary International Law: Opinions on the Emerging New World Order System*. 2004 ISBN 90 04 14143 X

62. B.G. Ramcharan, *The Protection Role of National Human Rights Institutions*. 2005. ISBN 90 04 14526 5

63. C. de Cooker, *Accountability, Investigation and Due Process in International Organizations*. 2005. ISBN 90 04 14793 4

64. P. S. Jones & K. Stokke, *Democratising Development: The Politics of Socio-Economic Rights in South Africa*. 2005. ISBN 90 04 14821 3

65. R. S. Lee (ed.): *Swords Into Plowshares: Building Peace Through the United Nations*. 2005. ISBN 90 04 15001 3

66. J.A. Bovenberg, *Property Rights in Blood, Genes & Data: Naturally Yours?* 2006 ISBN 90 04 15053 6

67. F. Hoffmeister: *Legal Aspects of the Cyprus Problem*. 2006 ISBN 978 9004152 23 6

68. R. Bredel: *The Ethical Economy of Conflict Prevention and Development*. 2006 ISBN 978 9004153 05 9

69. P. Nedergaard: *European Union Administration: Legitimacy and Efficiency*. 2007 ISBN 978 9004155 73 2

70. L.G. Loucaides: *The European Convention on Human Rights*. 2007 ISBN 978 90 04 15883 2

71. F. Falcón y Tella: *Challenges for Human Rights*. 2007 ISBN 978 9004 16022 4

For more titles in this series, consult our web site: **http://www.brill.nl**

MARTINUS NIJHOFF PUBLISHERS – LEIDEN • BOSTON

www.ingramcontent.com/pod-product-compliance
Lightning Source LLC
Chambersburg PA
CBHW061203240926
51846CB00006B/1100
* 9 7 8 9 0 0 4 1 5 8 8 3 2 *